Chronicle of Alfonso X

Translated by
Shelby Thacker
and José Escobar

With an Introduction
by Joseph F. O'Callaghan

THE UNIVERSITY PRESS OF KENTUCKY

Publication of this volume was made possible in part
by grants from the Program for Cultural Cooperation
between Spain's Ministry of Education, Culture, and Sports
and United States Universities, Asbury College, the College
of Charleston, and the National Endowment for the Humanities.

Scholarly publisher for the Commonwealth,
serving Bellarmine University, Berea College, Centre
College of Kentucky, Eastern Kentucky University,
The Filson Club Historical Society, Georgetown College,
Kentucky Historical Society, Kentucky State University,
Morehead State University, Murray State University,
Northern Kentucky University, Transylvania University,
University of Kentucky, University of Louisville,
and Western Kentucky University.

Editorial and Sales Offices: The University Press of Kentucky
663 South Limestone Street, Lexington, Kentucky 40508–4008

02 03 04 05 06   5 4 3 2 1

Frontispiece: Cantiga 192. "How St. Mary saved from death
by drowning one of the King's men"

Endpaper map and family tree from *The Learned King:
The Reign of Alfonso X of Castile,* courtesy of Joseph F. O'Callaghan.

Library of Congress Cataloging-in-Publication Data

Crónica de Alfonso X. English
Chronicle of Alfonso X / translated by Shelby Thacker and
José Escobar ; with an introduction by Joseph F. O'Callaghan.
p.   cm. — (Studies in Romance languages ; 47)
Often attributed to Fernán Sánchez de Valladolid.
Includes bibliographical references and index.
ISBN 0-8131-2218-X (cloth : alk. paper)
1. Castile (Spain)—History—Alfonso X, 1252–1284. 2. Alfonso X,
King of Castile and Leon, 1221–1284. I. Sánchez de Valladolid, Fernán,
fl. 1325–1348? II. Thacker, Shelby, 1956– III. Escobar, José.
IV. O'Callaghan, Joseph F. V. Title. VI. Studies in
Romance languages (Lexington, KY.); 47.
DP140.3 .C76   2002
946'.03—dc21   2001007150

Contents

Preface

For decades scholars, students, and the general educated public have relied upon the edition of the *Crónica de Alfonso X* prepared by Cayetano Rosell for the *Biblioteca de Autores Españoles* (hereafter *BAE*) published in 1875. With minor corrections it was published again in 1953. We believe that Rosell chose for his edition the manuscript we know as *Biblioteca Nacional 826* (hereafter *BN 826*) because it was penned in such a clear manuscript hand. We know that thirty-four manuscripts are extant, but Rosell could not have realized there were so many.

Today various scholars consider *BN 826* to be defective, and this, of course, means that they regard Rosell's edition as defective. A great many of the defects in the edition are due to the requirements of the *BAE,* a series designed to enable readers to understand medieval texts. Therefore, Rosell altered orthography; for example, he changed *auja* (*avia*) to *había;* he inserted accent marks not in existence in the fourteenth century; he failed to correct certain chronological and factual errors; he erroneously transcribed a few geographical names, as well as the proper names of some Moorish individuals; when *BN 826* abbreviated some sequences, so did Rosell; and what critics regard as his worst defect is that he did not examine other manuscripts, even though he must have known that the archives of El Escorial contained at least two he could have seen. Rosell studied the earliest printed edition (1793) and corrected some of its errors. A complete list of defects in *BN 826* was made known by Paula K. Rodgers in her doctoral dissertation, *Prolegomena to a Critical Edition of the Crónica de Alfonso X* (University of California at Davis, 1983). We had expected a critical edition by her, but it has not yet appeared.

The occurrence of so many defects was troubling to José Escobar and Shelby Thacker when they planned their translation. Since they are not specialists in the transcription of medieval manuscripts, they believed that their best source for a translation was Rosell's edition. Of course, they were cognizant of the edition of *BN 826* prepared by Nancy Joe Dyer for the Madison Texts transcribed in the format of that series. Since she edited *BN 826*, she also must have included the various defects. Thacker and Escobar saw the problem of the defects solved when Joseph F. O'Callaghan wrote his scholarly introduction to their translation, together with nearly two hundred detailed notes. Manuel González Jiménez, in the introduction to his forthcoming edition, which I believe we may regard as definitive, parallels much of the thinking and corrections of O'Callaghan.

Readers of the *Chronicle of Alfonso X*, with the explanations and corrections of O'Callaghan along with his copious notes, can now read in English much of what can be learned about the reign of the Learned King. The serious errors and defects of Part I have been resolved, as have the much fewer and less serious mistakes in the latter parts of the *Crónica*. Alfonso's last fifteen years were fraught with terrible problems: the revolt of the nobles, the incursions of the Benimerines Moors, the critical problems of the royal succession, and the attempts to take the royal power away from the maddened and dying monarch.

In my opinion, the author of the *Crónica*—believed by most scholars to be Fernán Sánchez de Valladolid, commissioned to write the history of the reign of Alfonso X, of Alfonso's son Sancho IV, and of Fernando IV—wrote what he had found in various documents and from hearsay from people whose forebears had given them information about the reign of Alfonso X. He knew that Alfonso had gone mad, that he had committed some incredible atrocities, such as having his brother Fadrique strangled without a trial and Fadrique's friend (lover?) burned at the stake, also with no trial; and he related some of Sancho's savage deeds as he removed his own enemies. If he leaned toward favoring Sancho over Alfonso, I cannot detect indications in the *Crónica*.

In decades of experience in transcribing and translating medieval Spanish manuscripts, I have never encountered prose as turgid or cumbersome, convoluted syntax as difficult to follow, nor sentences that run as long as those of this author. Escobar and Thacker's work was onerous, and they are to be congratulated for translating the *Crónica*. Perhaps Sánchez's peculiar writing was due to his professions: he was counselor of King Alfonso XI, he was a legist, an ambassador, and a diplomat.

Let us regard *The Chronicle of Alfonso X* as the first, and probably the only, translation of the reign of Spain's most significant monarch, who was so vigorous in the pursuit of knowledge and culture. It is proper that the distinguished historiographer Robert I. Burns, S.J., called Alfonso X the Emperor of Culture.

John Esten Keller

Acknowledgments

The translators would like to express their gratitude to Dr. John E. Keller for his encouragement and invaluable assistance throughout their work on the *Chronicle of Alfonso X*. Dr. Escobar expresses his gratitude to the Division of Languages at the College of Charleston and to its head, Dr. Rick Rickerson, for the financial support of this publication. Dr. Thacker wishes to thank the Provost of Asbury College, Dr. Raymond Whiteman, and the Faculty Development Committee for their generous financial support of the translation of this important medieval chronicle.

Introduction

The Reign of Alfonso X

Chronicle of Alfonso X concerns one of the great monarchs of medieval Europe, namely, Alfonso X, King of Castile-León (1252–1284), known to history as *El Sabio,* the Wise, or the Learned.[1] A brief sketch of the king's reign will help the reader to understand the *Chronicle.* Alfonso X ascended the throne at the age of thirty-one, just a few years after his father, Fernando III (1230–1252), had conquered the great cities of Andalusia: Córdoba (1236), Jaén (1246), and Seville (1248). Islamic Spain had been reduced to the kingdoms of Granada and Murcia, whose rulers acknowledged Fernando III as their overlord and paid an annual tribute to him as a sign of their dependence.[2]

Alfonso X's immediate tasks after his accession were twofold. First, he had to assure the Christian hold on the kingdom of Seville by the distribution of property there to those who had collaborated in the conquest. Partly on that account, he quarreled with his brother Infante Enrique, who went into exile in 1255, first entering the service of the emir of Tunis and later involving himself in the struggle between the Hohenstaufen and Angevin families in southern Italy. For a time, Enrique's brother Infante Fadrique joined him.

King Alfonso's second task was to secure control of the ports on both sides of the Strait of Gibraltar, which had long enabled invaders from Morocco to enter the peninsula. The raid on Salé on the Atlantic coast of Morocco in 1260 resulted from those ef-

forts. With the same intention, the king took possession of the citadel of Jerez on the Guadalquivir River to the south of Seville, began the development of the ports of Cádiz and Puerto de Santa
María on the Atlantic Ocean, and seized Niebla near the Portuguese frontier in 1262. His demand for the surrender of Gibraltar
and Tarifa frightened Ibn al-Ahmar, the King of Granada (1232–
1273), a vassal who paid an annual tribute to Castile. In 1264, Ibn
al-Ahmar stirred up the revolt of the Mudéjars, the Muslims living
under Christian rule in Andalusia and Murcia. Alfonso X appealed
to his father-in-law, King Jaime I of Aragón (1213–1276), for help
in subduing the Mudéjar uprising in Murcia, a task that Jaime I
completed by early 1266. Meanwhile, King Alfonso concentrated
on the suppression of the revolt in Andalusia. Ibn al-Ahmar was
compelled to renew his vassalage to Castile and to resume the payment of annual tribute in 1267, thereby bringing the revolt of the
Mudéjars to an end. As a counterweight to the King of Granada,
Alfonso X encouraged the *arraeces,* or governors, of Málaga and
Guadix—who were members of the Banû Ashqîlûlâ, one of the
principal Granadan families—to challenge Ibn al-Ahmar.

In the meantime, Alfonso X disputed with Afonso III of Portugal (1248–1279) concerning possession of the Algarve, the south-
ernmost portion of modern Portugal, while simultaneously
pursuing the crown of the Holy Roman Empire. As a result of the
double election in 1257, neither King Alfonso nor his rival Richard of Cornwall, a brother of Henry III of England, was ever able
to secure unanimous acceptance. Alfonso X's preoccupation with
the empire influenced every other aspect of his activities and
strained his financial resources.

During these years, jurists acting under his direction compiled
the *Siete Partidas* and the *Fuero Real,* the former a code of law to be
used in the royal court and the latter a code of law intended for
the towns of Castile and Extremadura. At the same time, King
Alfonso's men were actively engaged in translating Arabic books
on astronomy and astrology, while also producing a history of Spain
and a world history (discussed below).[3] Among the most notable
literary works composed under the king's aegis was the *Cantigas de
Santa María,* a collection of more than four hundred poems exalt-
ing the Virgin Mary. Many of the *cantigas* relate events that transpired during the king's reign.[4]

Alfonso X's innovations in taxation and law aroused discontent and provoked the nobility, who protested that they were denied the right to be judged by their peers in accordance with custom. Under the leadership of his brother Infante Felipe, the nobles conspired against the king at Lerma in 1271. The magnates whose names occur again and again in the *Chronicle* represented the principal families of Castile and León: Nuño González de Lara, Lope Díaz de Haro, Esteban Fernández de Castro, Fernán Ruiz de Castro, Simón Ruiz de los Cameros, Álvar Díaz de Asturias, Fernán González de Saldaña, Fernán Ruiz, Gil Gómez de Roa, Lope de Mendoza, Juan García de Villamayor, and others. When Richard of Cornwall died in April 1272, Alfonso X hoped that he might now be able to secure uncontested recognition as Holy Roman Emperor. With that goal in mind, he planned to join the Ghibellines, his supporters in Lombardy, but he had first to come to terms with the magnates and persuade them to accompany him. For that reason, he convened the Cortes of Burgos in September 1272. After acrimonious debate, the nobles repudiated their allegiance and decided to enter the service of the King of Granada. During the fall of 1272 and early 1273, Alfonso X asked his wife, Queen Violante (the daughter of Jaime I of Aragón), and his son and heir Infante Fernando de la Cerda to negotiate with the rebels. A compromise was reached at Almagro in March 1273, and they soon renewed their allegiance to Alfonso X.

Then, after leaving Fernando de la Cerda as regent, King Alfonso set out on his "*ida al emperio,*" or "journey to the empire." While he was attempting to secure recognition as the sole emperor from Pope Gregory X at Beaucaire in southern France, the Benimerines, or Marinids, a new Moroccan dynasty, led by their sultan, Abû Yûsuf Ya'qûb, invaded the peninsula in the summer of 1275. Fernando de la Cerda set out for the frontier to halt the invasion but died suddenly at Villarreal on July 24, leaving his widow Blanche, the daughter of Louis IX of France (1226–1270), and two small children known to history as the Infantes de la Cerda. To compound that tragedy, Nuño González de Lara, the *adelantado mayor de la frontera* entrusted with responsibility for the defense of the Andalusian frontier, was killed at Écija on September 7. A month later, on October 20, Archbishop Sancho II of Toledo fell in a similar attempt. The king's second son, Infante Sancho, now assumed command of the Castilian forces and was able to hold off the enemy and contain the damage. Alfonso X, whose return home had been slowed because of illness, finally regained his kingdom at the end of the year and signed a truce with the Benimerines.

King Alfonso was now faced by the grave problem of determining the succession to the throne. Should he acknowledge his grandson—the five-year-old Alfonso, the oldest son of the deceased Fernando de la Cerda—or his second son, Sancho, who had just successfully halted the advance of the Benimerines? The king opted to recognize Sancho, then seventeen years of age, and convened the Cortes of Burgos in 1276 to secure the acquiescence of his people. However, Juan Núñez de Lara and his brother Nuño, sons of the dead Nuño González de Lara, protested and gave their allegiance to Philip III of France (1270–1285), the uncle of Alfonso de la Cerda.

From this time on, King Alfonso displayed an increasingly erratic and irascible temperament that eventually turned his people and the closest members of his family against him. There seems reason to believe that the king developed a cancerous growth just below the eyes that caused intense pain and brought him close to death's door on several occasions. In March 1277, he horrified his subjects by summarily executing, without trial and for reasons that are not certain, his brother Infante Fadrique and the nobleman Simón Ruiz de los Cameros. Then in January 1278, Queen Violante, whom the king had mistreated, took refuge in the neighboring kingdom of Aragón, ruled by her brother King Pedro III (1276–1285). Violante was accompanied by her daughter-in-law Blanche and Blanche's two sons, the Infantes de la Cerda, who were placed under the protective custody of the Aragonese king.

Following a second invasion by the Benimerines in 1277, Alfonso X determined to besiege Algeciras, a port opposite Gibraltar, whose possession would protect him against further incursions from Morocco; but the siege ended in failure in the summer of 1279. After making peace with the Benimerines, King Alfonso then turned against his vassal, Muhammad II, King of Granada (1273–1302), who had tried to play the Moroccans against the Castilians. In the meantime, Philip III of France increased his pressure on Alfonso X, demanding that he grant a portion of his kingdom to Alfonso de la Cerda. During the Cortes of Seville in the fall of 1281, while also proposing to debase the coinage so as to have additional funds for war against Granada, Alfonso X quarreled with his son and designated heir, Infante Sancho, who objected to any division of the Crown of Castile.

Angered by his father's plans for just such a division, Sancho proceeded to Valladolid, where in April 1282 he summoned an assembly of the estates of the realm: bishops, nobles, and townspeople. Queen Violante (who had returned home in July 1279), Infante Manuel (the king's youngest brother and favorite), and Infantes Pedro, Juan, and Jaime (the king's younger sons) all attended and threw their support to Sancho. After declaring Alfonso X unfit to rule, the assembly deprived him of the essential powers of monarchy, namely, justice, taxation, and custody of royal fortresses, though he was left with the empty title of "King." Sancho in effect became a regent for a monarch who could no longer rule. The demotion only served to divide the kingdom further. Alfonso X, who had remained in Seville, retained the allegiance of most of Andalusia and Murcia, while the rest of the kingdom generally stood by Sancho. In order to regain control, the king sought the help of his erstwhile enemy Abû Yûsuf Ya'qûb, the emir of the Benimerines, who invaded the kingdom again in the summer of 1282. The two monarchs made an alliance on October 24, but their joint attempt to dislodge Sancho from Córdoba was unsuccessful and the Benimerines soon withdrew to Morocco.

Returning to his ever-faithful Seville, Alfonso X bitterly denounced his son and disinherited him entirely on November 8–9. At the king's urging, Pope Martin IV excommunicated Sancho and placed an interdict on the kingdom on August 9, 1283. As a stalemate ensued, Alfonso X denounced Sancho again in his final will of January 22, 1284. Nevertheless, some attempt at reconciliation was undertaken by the king's illegitimate daughter Beatriz, the widow of Afonso III of Portugal, and Infante Sancho's wife, María de Molina. Though the king and his son never met again, Alfonso X's heart seems to have softened, because he wrote to Martin IV on March 23, declaring that he had pardoned Sancho and asking the pope to lift the censures imposed on him. Just a few days later, on April 4, 1284, King Alfonso died at Seville. Whether Sancho knew that his father had pardoned him is uncertain.

The events summarily described above form the substance of

the *Chronicle of Alfonso X,* but before turning our attention to that text, some consideration of the peninsular historiographical tradition will help to put the *Chronicle* in perspective.

The Historiographical Tradition

Although the number of histories written in the Iberian peninsula by Christian authors in the early Middle Ages is rather jejune in comparison with other European kingdoms, there was nevertheless a continuing historiographical tradition developed under royal patronage. From the earliest times, the Christian kings of Asturias-León-Castile encouraged historical writing. The first historical accounts written in Christian Spain after the Muslim invasion of 711, the *Chronicle of Alfonso III* and the *Chronicle of Albelda,* purported to continue the *Gothic History* of Saint Isidore of Seville (d. 634). Written in Latin during the late ninth century, these *Chronicles* linked the kings of Asturias with the Visigoths, who had ruled the peninsula prior to the Muslim invasion. The eleventh- and twelfth-century *Chronicles* of Bishop Sampiro of Astorga (d. 1041), Bishop Pelayo of Oviedo (d. 1129), the Monk of Silos, and the *Chronicle of Nájera* followed this early model. With the *Chronica Adefonsi Imperatoris,* or *Chronicle of Alfonso the Emperor,* we have a fairly substantial narrative of the reign of Alfonso VII of Castile-León (1126–1157). Apart from this series of royal chronicles, the *Historia Compostelana,* written in the early twelfth century, exalted the bishops of Santiago de Compostela while also illuminating the reigns of Alfonso VI (1065–1109) and his daughter Urraca (1109–1126). A few annals containing bare-bones entries of facts and events complete the historiographical picture in the kingdoms of León and Castile from the ninth through the twelfth centuries.[5]

In the first half of the thirteenth century, prior to the accession of Alfonso X, three Latin chronicles of some substance were written. The *Chronicon Mundi,* or *World Chronicle,* of Bishop Lucas of Tuy (d. 1249)—written at the behest of Berenguela, the mother of Fernando III (1217–1252) and grandmother of Alfonso X—recounts the history of Spain from the earliest times to the capture of Córdoba by her son in 1236. Lucas loved a good story and larded his account with marvelous and miraculous occurrences.[6] More precise and to the point is the anonymous *Chronica latina,* or *Latin*

Chronicle, of the Kings of Castile, which extends from the tenth-century counts of Castile to the fall of Córdoba. The likely author of this *Chronicle,* according to Derek Lomax, was Bishop Juan of Osma (d. 1240), Fernando III's chancellor.[7] The third of these narratives, and the most renowned, is the *Historia de rebus Hispaniae,* or *History of the Affairs of Spain,* by Rodrigo Jiménez de Rada, Archbishop of Toledo (d. 1247), who undertook his task at the urging of Fernando III. Rodrigo's history is the most elegantly written of them all, but it too ends with the fall of Córdoba.[8]

Thus, by the time Alfonso X ascended the throne, there was a historiographical tradition associated with the royal house of Castile-León. In general, the histories cited above provided a unified account of the development of the Christian kingdoms of Spain from the Muslim invasion in 711 to the capture of Córdoba 525 years later. The kings of Asturias-León-Castile, construed as the heirs of the Visigothic monarchs, were the focus of all these works. The affairs of Catalonia, Aragón, Navarre, and Portugal were recorded but clearly were not regarded as having equal importance with the rise of León and Castile.[9]

The great innovation of Alfonso X in the writing of history was the use of the vernacular language, Castilian. The *Estoria de Espanna,* or *History of Spain*—an account of the history of Spain from its initial legendary peopling to the death of the king's father, Fernando III, in 1252—drew on all the historical literature then available, utilizing especially the work of Archbishop Rodrigo. It also made use of literary materials and legends such as those concerning the great Castilian hero known as the Cid. The *Estoria de Espanna,* which Menéndez Pidal christened the *Primera Crónica General,* or *First General Chronicle,* greatly influenced the nature and scope of peninsular historical literature thereafter.[10] Before completing the *Estoria de Espanna,* King Alfonso decided to broaden his historical approach and set his scholars to work on the *General Estoria,* or *General History,* a book intended to encompass the entire history of the world and all its peoples. Given the breadth of that enterprise, the king's men were scarcely able to bring their account to the birth of Christ.[11]

Chronicle of Alfonso X

Given King Alfonso's interest in historical writing and the production of the *Estoria de Espanna* and the *General Estoria* under his direction, it is ironic that the *Chronicle of Alfonso X* is the only extended narrative history of his reign.[12] The energy that Alfonso X and his collaborators expended on his other historical works probably did not allow the time needed to write a history of his own times, though as we shall see, there is reason to believe that some parts of the *Chronicle of Alfonso X* were written to establish a continuous narrative of the crisis of 1272–1274. Fortunately, an abundance of documentation and a few other shorter narratives enable us to develop a fuller and more precise picture of his reign.[13]

The *Chronicle of Alfonso X* as we have it today was not a contemporary history, but rather dates from the early fourteenth century, from the time of his great-grandson Alfonso XI (1312–1350). Taken together with the *Chronicle of Sancho IV (1284–1295)* and the *Chronicle of Fernando IV (1295–1312)*, it forms part of a trilogy called the *Tres Crónicas*, or *Three Chronicles*.[14] The prologue that precedes the edited text of the *Chronicle of Alfonso X* was intended to introduce all three *Chronicles* and bears some similarity to the prologue of the *Estoria de Espanna*.[15] The prologue's author tells us that Alfonso XI discovered the gap in the written history of the royal house of Castile-León extending from the death of Fernando III in 1252 to his own day. Although the prologue does not say so, that earlier history was recorded in the *Estoria de Espanna*. Alfonso XI commanded therefore that the history of the three kings who preceded him should be written. The *Three Chronicles*, the similarity in style of which suggests a single author, were intended to remedy that deficiency.

The author of the *Three Chronicles*, and hence of the *Chronicle of Alfonso X*, is not mentioned in the text, so there has been much discussion of the writer's identity. Evelyn Procter judged that the issue would never be resolved satisfactorily and concluded that it was best simply to accept the author's anonymity.[16] Taking up the suggestion of some older scholars, Salvador de Moxó and Diego Catalán have concluded that the author was Fernán Sánchez de Valladolid, an important figure in the court of Alfonso XI.[17] Moxó described him as a jurist, administrator, humanist, and man of general culture. After an apprenticeship in the court of Fernando IV, Sánchez de Valladolid soon emerged as one of the most influential collaborators of Alfonso XI, as a member of the Royal Council

(*Consejo real*), chancellor of the privy seal (*canciller del sello de la poridad*), and chief notary (*notario mayor*) of the kingdom of Castile. In the latter post, which he held at least from 1334 to 1348, he was responsible for the dispatch of royal documents and their archival preservation.[18] When the king reached his majority in 1325, he dispatched Fernán Sánchez, "who had labored for a long time in his service, and had good understanding and was well spoken," to inform the king's regents, Infante Felipe, Juan Manuel, and Juan *el tuerto*, or "the one-eyed," that their services were no longer needed.[19] A few years later, in 1330, the king sent Fernán Sánchez to persuade the turbulent noble Juan Manuel to return to royal service.[20] In 1327 and again in 1338 he was one of the royal ambassadors sent to the papal court at Avignon to ask Popes John XXII and Benedict XII to grant certain graces—probably a crusading indulgence and financial aid—for the war against the Moors.[21] As chief notary of Castile, Fernán Sánchez also formed part of the embassy sent to the French court in 1334 to seek an alliance with King Philip VI.

Two years later, identified this time as chief notary of Castile, chancellor of the privy seal, and member of the Royal Council, "whom the king had previously entrusted with many missions and great affairs," Fernán Sánchez returned to France to conclude a treaty of friendship.[22] In the following year, he was sent to secure the alliance of King Pedro IV of Aragón (1336–1387) against the Muslims of Granada and Morocco.[23] Finally, in 1346, he was one of three royal procurators appointed to conclude a pact arranging the future marriage of the heir to the throne, Infante Pedro, and Joanna, the daughter of King Edward III of England.[24] "In return for the many good services that [he had] done and [did] every day," Alfonso XI in 1345 appointed Fernán Sánchez, "our chief notary in Castile and our chancellor of the privy seal," the lordship of Cubillas de Cerrato.[25] He was also admitted to the Order of the Scarf (*Orden de la Banda*), a new Order of Chivalry created by Alfonso XI.[26] Thus rewarded for his long and loyal service to the king as jurist, administrator, and diplomat, Fernán Sánchez de Valladolid was elevated to the ranks of the minor nobility.[27]

In addition to the *Three Chronicles*, there is little doubt that Fernán Sánchez was also the author of the *Chronicle of Alfonso XI*, a detailed account of the reign until 1344, with a few other chapters bringing the story to the king's death in 1350.[28] All four chronicles taken together fill 392 pages, printed in double columns and with small type in the edition in the *Biblioteca de Autores Españoles (BAE)*. It is a significant achievement, especially for an author who carried on an active career in the public service of the king.

The date of composition of the *Chronicle of Alfonso X* cannot be determined exactly, nor do we know when Alfonso XI decided that the history of his three predecessors should be written. Certainly that decision was made after he reached his majority in 1325; as he was then just thirteen years of age, he more than likely did not commission the writing of the *Three Chronicles* until some years after, when he had reached a more mature age. The details concerning names of persons and places given in the early chapters of the *Chronicle of Alfonso XI* suggest that the author had begun to write the history of that reign almost as it unfolded. That being the case, one might assume that the *Chronicle of Alfonso XI* was anterior to the writing of the *Three Chronicles,* but that sequence has yet to be proven. The prologue to the *Three Chronicles* may be dated between March 1344, when Algeciras was taken, and March 1350, when the king died, because it describes Alfonso XI as the conqueror (*el conqueridor*) and includes Algeciras in the list of his dominions.[29] Work on the *Three Chronicles* may have begun before that time, and the prologue may have been written after much of the work was done. There is some evidence (which will be discussed below) that the author relied on an earlier written text for at least a portion of the *Chronicle of Alfonso X*. In any case, the *Chronicle* as we now have it was composed about ninety-two to ninety-eight years after the death of Fernando III and about sixty to sixty-six years after the death of Alfonso X.

The *Chronicle of Alfonso X* was written in the Castilian language and was edited by Miguel de Herrera and published by Sebastián Martínez in 1554.[30] In 1875, Cayetano Rosell, noting the many errors in the earlier edition, reedited the text, using a codex in the Biblioteca Nacional in Madrid as the basis of his work. He tells us that he collated that text with the most sumptuous of four codices in El Escorial and another codex belonging to the Duke of Osuna but neglected to identify them more exactly.[31] A few years ago, Paula Kelley Rodgers studied thirty-four manuscripts of the *Chronicle of Alfonso X* as preparatory to a critical edition that has not yet been published.[32] In fourteen of the manuscripts, the *Chronicle of Alfonso X* is accompanied by the other two *Chronicles*. She pointed out that the Herrera edition was based primarily on the sixteenth-century MS 1575 in the Biblioteca Nacional in Madrid and that the language was made to conform to sixteenth-century standards.[33] She concluded that Rosell's edition was based on Biblioteca Nacional MS 829 and that his transcription was "capricious" and "extremely defective."[34] Although Rosell's edition in the *BAE* is easily accessible, the one most used by scholars, and serves as the basis for this translation of the *Chronicle of Alfonso X*, it cannot be regarded as definitive.

The text of the *Chronicle of Alfonso X*, consisting of seventy-seven chapters of varying length, follows the prologue to the *Three Chronicles*. Influenced by the practice adopted by Alfonso X and his collaborators for the *Estoria de Espanna*, the author of the *Chronicle* made a deliberate effort to adhere to an annalistic form. The first chapter begins with the death of Fernando III in Seville on May 31, 1252 (which the *Chronicle* wrongly dates as May 29), and the accession of his son Alfonso X, not yet thirty-one years of age.[35] An elaborate chronological scheme follows, as the king's accession is dated according to the eras of Adam; the Hebrews from the Flood; Nebuchadnezzar, the ruler of Babylon; King Philip of Macedon; Alexander the Great; Julius Caesar; the birth of Jesus Christ; the Egyptians; and the Persians. From then on, each chapter—with some interruptions—records the regnal years of Alfonso X, counting from his accession, according to the eras of Caesar and Jesus Christ. Until the latter part of the fourteenth century, it was customary in the kingdom of Castile-León to date events according to the era of Caesar, which is thirty-eight years in advance of the Christian era. Thus, the *Chronicle* dates the king's accession in 1252 according to the Christian era but in 1289 plus 150 days, according to the era of Caesar. Ordinarily one would say A.D. 1252 and 1290 era of Caesar. However, this practice is very deceptive, because it can be shown that the *Chronicle*'s dates are frequently incorrect. The reader should be cautioned that the chronology of the *Chronicle of Alfonso X* is uncertain and erratic, at least in the early chapters.

Evelyn Procter described the *Chronicle* as "an unsatisfactory source," noting that it was not "a unified whole." She proposed to divide it into three sections of unequal length and unequal historical value.[36] Further review of these divisions will illustrate the basis for her judgment.

Part I of the Chronicle

In the first part, which extends through chapter 19, the events of the first seventeen years of the reign are described, that is, from 1252 to 1269 or 1270. Each chapter in Part I, from chapter 2 through chapter 19, is dedicated to a particular year in the king's reign; no year is given for chapter 13, but in the sequence of chapters it would be the eleventh year.

This is the most unsatisfactory and confusing part of the *Chronicle,* because it appears to be based entirely on oral tradition recorded perhaps a generation or so after the events described. With only a few exceptions, no sources are mentioned and very few personages are identified by name. Given the problems of dating and identification of personages, it has seemed best to resolve them in the notes to each chapter. The sequence of events is so jumbled that one cannot accept the *Chronicle*'s evidence without first comparing it to documentary and other sources.[37] Indeed, it is best to ignore the chronology given in this section of the *Chronicle* and read the text as a topical discussion of various events. The *Estoria de Espanna* is mentioned, though not by name, in chapters 2 and 10. Chapter 13 cites a written text— *"segund lo que se fallo en escripto"*— as its source for the Mudéjar revolt. It is quite possible that some written account of the uprising was kept at the royal court. Rodgers commented on the "somniferous style" of this first part of the *Chronicle.*[38]

Part II of the Chronicle

The middle section of the *Chronicle,* from chapters 20 to 58, deals with the revolt of the nobility from its beginnings in 1271, the Cortes of Burgos in 1272, and the eventual resolution of the conflict at Almagro in 1273. This is a much more detailed section of the *Chronicle,* occupying nearly half of the entire text, but it only relates the events occurring over a period of about four years. Whereas chapter 18, for example, purports to deal with the king's eighteenth year, chapters 21 to 37 are all related to the nineteenth year, chapters 38 through 49 to the twentieth, chapters 50 to 57, the twenty-first, and chapter 58, the twenty-second.

More than likely, Fernán Sánchez de Valladolid had before him a thirteenth-century text written either about the same time as the events recorded or within a few years thereof. The specific identification of nobles, the names and titles of officials in the king's court, and even of royal messengers carrying dispatches between the king and the nobles, attest to the contemporaneity of this section. Many of these persons appear in documents of the period.[39] The nobles whose names are repeated so often—Nuño González de Lara, Lope Díaz de Haro, Esteban Fernández de Castro, Fernán Ruiz de Castro, Simón Ruiz de los Cameros, Álvar Díaz de Asturias, Gil Gómez de Roa, and Rodrigo Froilaz—all appear as confirmants to royal privileges. The chronology here is usually correct, though the dating of events is sometimes off by a year or so. Procter suggested that these errors were likely the result of the compiler's attempts to fit events into his chronological scheme. The compilier's thirteenth-century source probably was left incomplete before bringing the story of the king's struggle with the nobility to an end, because it omits any reference to events such as the Assembly of Zamora in 1274.[40]

The incorporation of complete documents or summaries of documents into the middle section of the *Chronicle* suggests that the author had access to the royal chancery and was likely serving there. One wonders whether Alfonso X decided to keep a record of developments to use against the nobles as necessary.

The first group of documents includes several letters of Abû Yûsuf Ya'qûb, the emir of Morocco, and his son 'Abd al-Wâhid, addressed to the rebellious Castilian magnates (chapter 22). According to the *Chronicle*, Fernán Gudiel de Toledo intercepted these letters written in Arabic from Lorencio Rodríguez, a squire in the service of Nuño González de Lara, one of the leaders of the conspiracy against the king. Alfonso Pérez de Toledo and Vasco Gómez translated the letters into Castilian. The authenticity of these documents seems guaranteed by the identification of such secondary figures as Fernán Gudiel, who as *alguacil* of Toledo had received a grant from the king on October 16, 1263,[41] and Alfonso Pérez and Vasco (or Velasco), Gómez, who acted as scribes in several royal charters.[42] The first letter, after an invocation (*"En el nombre de Dios piadoso e mercedoso"*—"In the name of God, the pious and merciful"), identified the author as King Abû Yûsuf, "the old man of the Moroccans and king of Morocco"— *"viejo de los marroquis e rey de*

Marruecos." After greeting Infante Felipe, the body of the letter follows, concluding by wishing the recipient health and the mercy of God. The letter, whose style is reminiscent of that of the formal letters issued by the Moroccan chancery, seems to be recorded in full, although it lacks a date.[43] The salutation is missing from a similar letter sent by the emir's son 'Abd al-Wâhid, which is likely excerpted. Abû Yûsuf's letter to Nuño also omits the salutation given in the letter to Infante Felipe, but otherwise it is probably rendered in full, except for the date. A very brief summary of a letter from 'Abd al-Wâhid (Abdiluait or Aldulián in the *Chronicle*) to Nuño follows. Abû Yûsuf's letter to Lope Díaz de Haro is probably excerpted and is followed by a summary of 'Abd al-Wâhid's letter to Lope. Next come summaries of letters from Abû Yûsuf and 'Abd al-Wâhid to Simón Ruiz de los Cameros, and summaries of Abû Yûsuf's letters to Esteban Fernández de Castro and Gil Gómez de Roa. Finally, there is a letter to Simón Ruiz and Esteban Fernández from the trader or interpreter 'Abd al-Haqq al-Turjumân (Abdolhat Trigrama in the *Chronicle*), who probably acted as a go-between in these negotiations.

A second group of documents consists of Alfonso X's warnings to the rebellious nobles gathered at Atienza under the leadership of his brother Infante Felipe (chapters 28–37). These warnings were not royal letters but rather dispatches that the king's messengers or heralds (*mandaderos*) were commanded to convey to the nobles. The heralds, Gonzalo Ruiz de Atienza and Sancho Pérez, carried royal letters of credence (*cartas de creencia*) identifying them.[44] Their task was to proclaim aloud the text of the royal messages.[45] The first message was directed to Infante Felipe and all the magnates and knights in his company (chapter 28). Following that proclamation are individual messages addressing the king's personal relationships to Infante Felipe (chapter 29), Nuño González de Lara (chapter 30), Lope Díaz de Haro (chapter 31), Fernán Ruiz de Castro (chapter 32), Esteban Fernández de Castro (chapter 33), Juan Núñez de Lara (chapter 34), and Álvar Díaz de Asturias (chapter 35). There is a final message for the nobles of secondary rank (*infanzones* and *caballeros fijosdalgo*) (chapter 36). The nobles then took counsel among themselves and made their reply to the king, the text of which is included in chapter 37.

After that exchange, the *Chronicle* includes a document (*escripto*) sealed with the royal seal, beginning *"Estas son las cosas"*—"These are the things that the queen [Violante] and the archbishop [Sancho II of Toledo] and the bishops asked the king as a favor to Infante Felipe" (chapter 39). This was read to the nobles at Sabiote as they were making their way toward the frontier of the kingdom of Granada.[46] After the magnates presented a written list of their demands, the king responded in a brief letter addressed to Infante Felipe and the others and in separate letters to Lope Díaz de Haro and to Infante Fernando de la Cerda, the king's son and heir. The chapter concludes with a letter from Queen Violante, Archbishop Sancho II of Toledo, and the king's brothers Infantes Fadrique and Manuel (chapter 40), followed by another letter in the next (chapter 41). The most extensive of all the royal missives is Alfonso X's letter written from Ávila, probably in late May or early June 1273, to his son Infante Fernando de la Cerda, advising him as to the best way to deal with the nobles (chapter 52).[47]

One other document is of particular importance. It is the text of an alliance between Ibn al-Ahmar, King of Granada, and Infante Felipe and the nobles, concluded before the rebels entered the kingdom of Granada, probably in December 1272 or the very beginning of 1273 (chapter 43). This document was drawn up in typical form with the notification (*"sepan cuantos esta carta vieren"*—"let all who see this charter know*"), the intitulation (*"Nos Alamir Abboadille Mahomad Avenyuzaf Abenasar, rey de Granada, e Amir Amus Lemin, e nuestro fijo e nuestro e heredero Alamir Abboadille"*—"We the emir Abû 'Abd Allâh Muhammad Ibn Yûsuf Ibn Nasr, King of Granada and emir of the Muslims, and our son and heir the emir Abû 'Abd Allâh"), followed by the substance of the agreement. The King of Granada subscribed his name to the document and the nobles affixed their seals. Unfortunately there is no date, or if there was one, the chronicler has omitted it.

As already noted, Alfonso X's messages to the nobles (chapters 22–37) were not royal letters but admonitions to be proclaimed publicly to the recipients by the king's heralds. We do have the king's letters in chapter 40, but these (as well as those of Queen Violante and her colleagues in chapters 40–41) are not couched in the usual formulae of the royal chancery.[48] The author of this part of the *Chronicle* seems to have omitted the royal intitulation and any salutation. Instead, the letters begin immediately by addressing Infante Felipe and his colleagues. Nor do the letters bear a date, and there is no reference to the royal seal. These are not, then, solemn privileges or letters patently conforming to the established chancery style. Rather one might describe them as mandates or writs, brief informal documents conveying the king's commands.[49] Rodgers is no doubt correct in suggesting that the king's messages to the nobles (chapters 28–37) and his letters (chapter 40) were not drawn up by the chancery but rather by the notary of King Alfonso's private chamber, where they were preserved. The royal chamber, with its complement of scribes and notaries, accompanied the king on his travels and was prepared to handle private or secret affairs more rapidly and with less fuss than the chancery. The office of chancellor of the privy seal (*canciller de la poridad*) appears in the fourteenth century and, as Procter suggested, likely evolved from the post of *escribano mayor de la camara del rey*, or *notario de la camara* (chief scribe, or notary of the king's chamber), held by Sancho Pérez in the reign of Alfonso X.[50] Rodgers notes that Fernán Sánchez de Valladolid was chancellor of the privy seal and as such would likely have had access to these documents.[51] I suspect, however, that the documents were included in a contemporary account of this period in the king's reign, written probably by someone attached to the royal chamber who may indeed have been entrusted with the writing or the preservation of the documents in question. Perhaps that person was Sancho Pérez, or Master Jofré de Loaysa, the royal notary, sent as envoy to England in 1279.[52]

Part III of the Chronicle

The third and final part of the *Chronicle*, extending from chapters 59 to 77 and covering the ten years from 1274 to 1284, is not as detailed as the preceding section, but on the whole it is more reliable than the first section. As in Part II, several chapters are assigned to a given year. For example, chapters 59 to 66 concern the twenty-third year; chapters 67–68, the twenty-fourth; chapter 69, the twenty-fifth; and chapters 70–73, the twenty-sixth. A specific chapter is not allotted to the twenty-seventh year, but chapters 74–77 are each devoted to a specific year from the twenty-eighth through the thirty-first.

No documents are included in this section, but Fernán Sánchez de Valladolid mentions a written text that he had on hand. With reference, for example, to the reasons for the battle of Écija in 1275, he remarks: *"E desto dicen algunos que fue ansi dicho, mas non se falla en escripto si fue la pelea por esto o non"*—"Some say that this was so, but one does not find it written whether the battle was for this reason or not" (chapter 62). Later, speaking of the debate concerning the succession to the throne, he declared: *"E en el escripto que se falla desde aquel tiempo, non dicen que en aquel consejo fuesen dichas mas palabras que estas"*—"In the written text from that time, it does not say that more words than these were spoken in that council" (chapter 67). Finally, speaking of the siege of Algeciras in 1279, the author cites *"la estoria de lo que se fallo en escripto de este fecho"*—"the history of this affair found in writing" (chapter 72). Procter thinks this section of the *Chronicle* is "a fairly reliable source" from about 1275 onward, though it appears to be biased in favor of Infante Sancho, whose relationship with his father steadily deteriorated and culminated in his rebellion in 1282.[53] Pointing out that Fernán Sánchez de Valladolid experienced the consequences of the disputed succession to the throne, Rodgers commented that his "engaging, if not snappy, style reflects that involvement."[54]

The *Chronicle of Alfonso X* is the fullest account of the reign of the Learned King. Despite the inadequacies of Part I, the remaining text of the *Chronicle* provides a reasonably clear and detailed guide to the important events of the final decade and a half of his reign: the revolt of the nobility, the invasion of the Benimerines, the crisis of the succession, and the attempt to deprive the king of his royal powers. Keeping in mind the caveats mentioned above, scholars can learn much about Alfonso X, his family, and his people by reading the *Chronicle*.

Joseph F. O'Callaghan
Fordham University

Notes

1. On the reign of Alfonso X, see Joseph F. O'Callaghan, *The Learned King: The Reign of Alfonso X of Castile* (Philadelphia: Univ. of Pennsylvania Press, 1993); Manuel González Jiménez, *Alfonso X, 1252–1284* (Palencia, Spain:

Diputación Provincial de Palencia, 1993); Antonio Ballesteros y Beretta, *Alfonso X* (Barcelona, 1963; reprint, Barcelona: El Albir, 1984).

2. Julio González, *Reinado y Diplomas de Fernando III*, 3 vols. (Córdoba: Monte de Piedad y Caja de Ahorros de Córdoba, 1980–1986), 1:278–394.

3. See Evelyn Procter, *Alfonso X of Castile, Patron of Literature and Learning* (Oxford: Clarendon, 1951); John E. Keller, *Alfonso X, el Sabio* (New York: Twayne, 1967)

4. See my book, *Alfonso X and the* Cantigas de Santa María: *A Poetic Biography*, Leiden, The Netherlands: E.J. Brill, 1998.

5. For a general overview, see Benito Sánchez Alonso, *Historia de la historiografía española* (Madrid: Consejo Superior de Investigaciones Científicas, 1947); also see Joseph F. O'Callaghan, *A History of Medieval Spain* (Ithaca, N.Y.: Cornell Univ. Press, 1975), 85–88, 189–90, 314–15.

6. Lucas of Tuy, *Chronicon Mundi*, ed. Andreas Schott, *Hispania Illustrata*, 4 vols. (Frankfort: Claudius Marnius et Heredes Joannis Aubrii, 1603–1608), 4:1–116.

7. *Crónica latina de los reyes de Castilla*, ed. Luis Charlo Brea (Cádiz, Spain: Universidad de Cádiz, 1984); Derek W. Lomax, "The Authorship of the *Chronique latine des rois de Castille*," *Bulletin of Hispanic Studies* 40 (1963): 205–11.

8. Rodrigo Jiménez de Rada, *De rebus Hispaniae*, in *Opera*, ed. Francisco de Lorenzana (Madrid, 1793; reprint, Valencia: Anubar, 1968).

9. The deeds of the counts of Barcelona are the focus of the *Gesta comitum Barchinonensium*, while *Crónica de San Juan de la Penya* summarized the history of the kings of Aragón.

10. *Primera Crónica General*, ed Ramón Menéndez Pidal, 2 vols. (Madrid: Gredos, 1955).

11. *General Estoria. Primera Parte*, ed. Antonio G. Solalinde (Madrid: Molina, 1930); *General Estoria. Segunda Parte*, 2 vols., ed. Lloyd Kasten and Victor Oelschlager (Madrid: Consejo Superior de Investigaciones Científicas, 1957–1961). Also see Diego Catalán, *La Estoria de España de Alfonso X: Creación y Evolución* (Madrid: Universidad Autónoma de Madrid, 1992); Francisco Rico, *Alfonso el Sabio y la "General Estoria"* (Madrid: Ariel, 1984); Inés Fernández-Ordóñez, *Las Estorias de Alfonso el Sabio* (Madrid: Istmo, 1992); Francisco Márquez Villanueva, *El concepto cultural alfonsí* (Madrid: Mapfre, 1995), 135–52; Charles F. Fraker, *The Scope of History: Studies in the Historiography of Alfonso el Sabio* (Ann Arbor: Univ. of Michigan Press, 1996); Peter Linehan, "From Chronicle to History: Concerning the *Estoria de España* and Its Principal Sources," in Alan Deyermond, *Historical Literature in Medieval Iberia* (London: Queen Mary and Westfield College, Dept. of Hispanic Studies, 1996), 7–34; O'Callaghan, *The Learned King*, 138–40.

12. There is a brief biographical note of Alfonso X by Fray Juan Gil de Zamora, tutor to the king's son Infante Sancho. Fidel Fita, "Biografías de San

Fernando y de Alfonso el Sabio por Gil de Zamora," *Boletín de la Real Academia de la Historia* 5 (1885): 308–28.

13. On the other sources available, see the bibliography in O'Callaghan, *The Learned King*, 349–59.

14. The *Tres Crónicas* were edited by Cayetano Rosell in *Crónicas de los Reyes de Castilla desde don Alfonso el Sabio hasta los Católicos Don Fernando y Doña Isabel*, 3 vols. in *Biblioteca de Autores Españoles (BAE)*, vol. 66 (Madrid, 1875; reprint, Madrid: Real Academia Española, 1953). See also Casto María del Rivero, "Índice de las personas, lugares y cosas notables que se mencionan en las tres Crónicas de los Reyes de Castilla: Alfonso X, Sancho IV y Fernando IV," *Hispania* 2 (1942): 163–235, 323–406, 557–618.

15. Paula Kelley Rogers, *Prolegomena to a Critical Edition of the Crónica de Alfonso X*, 2 vols. (Ph.D. dissertation, Davis: Univ. of California, 1983), 2: 299–310. For a different view, see Gerald L. Gingras, "Sánchez's *Tres Corónicas*: An Alfonsine Legacy?" *Romance Quarterly* 33 (1986): 289–94.

16. Evelyn Procter, "Materials for the Reign of Alfonso X of Castile, 1252–1284," *Transactions of the Royal Historical Society, 4th Series*, 14 (1931): 52.

17. He should not be confused with Fernán Sánchez de Tovar, a different person altogether as demonstrated in Julio Puyol, "El presunto cronista Fernán Sánchez de Valladolid," *Boletín de la Real Academia de la Historia* 77 (1920): 507–33; Salvador de Moxó, "La promoción política y social de los 'letrados' en la corte de Alfonso XI," *Hispania* 35 (1975): 13–18; Catalán, *La Estoria de España de Alfonso X*, 13, 252; and *Gran Crónica de Alfonso XI*, 2 vols. (Madrid: Editorial Gredos, 1977), 1:15, note 3.

18. He appears as such in charters from March 21, 1337, to March 15, 1348.

19. *Crónica de Alfonso XI*, in *BAE* 66 (1953): 194, ch. 31: "*que avia trabajado en su servicio desde luengo tiempo et avia buen entendimiento et era bien razonado.*"

20. *Crónica de Alfonso XI*, 233, ch. 99: "*que era su Chanciller et del su Consejo.*"

21. *Crónica de Alfonso XI*, 204, ch. 49, and 294, ch. 188.

22. *Crónica de Alfonso XI*, 271, ch. 150, and 285, ch. 174: "*de quien el Rey avia fiado ante desto otras muchas mandaderias et de grandes fechos.*"

23. Gerónimo Zurita, *Anales de la Corona de Aragón*, 9 vols., ed. Ángel Canellas López (Zaragoza, Spain: Consejo Superior de Investigaciones Científicas, 1970–1985), 3:471–72.

24. In 1344, Edward III contacted him seeking his favor in the Castilian court. Thomas Rymer, *Foedera, conventiones, litterae et cuiuscunque acta publica inter reges Angliae et alios quovis imperatores, reges, pontifices, principes*, 3d ed., 10 vols. (The Hague: Joannes Neaulme, 1739–1745), 2.1:167, 195, and 3.1:16.

25. Esther González Crespo, *Colección documental de Alfonso XI: Diplomas reales conservados en el Archivo Histórico Nacional, Sección de Clero. Pergaminos* (Madrid: Universidad Complutense, 1985), 506, no. 303 (March 20, 1345); another charter of August 15, 1345, refers to the king's grant of Nebleda to Fernán Sánchez; ibid., 517, no. 309.

26. *Ordenamiento de la Banda,* El Escorial, Y.II.13, fols. 11–12.

27. Salvador de Moxó, "El patrimonio dominical de un consejero de Alfonso XI: Los señoríos de Fernán Sánchez de Valladolid," *Revista de la Universidad Complutense de Madrid* 22 (1973): 123–62.

28. Diego Catalán, *Un prosista anónima del siglo XIV* (La Laguna, 1955), 124, and "La historiografía en verso y en prosa de Alfonso XI a la luz de nuevos textos," *Anuario de Estudios Medievales* 2 (1965): 291.

29. Procter, "Materials," 52–53, noted that the *Chronicle of Alfonso X,* 12, ch. 17, identified Louis IX of France as Saint Louis (he was canonized in 1297).

30. Miguel de Herrera, *Chronica del muy esclarecido principe y rey don Alfonso: el qual fue par de Emperador e hizo el libro de las siete partidas y ansimismo al fin deste libro va encorporada la Chronica del rey Don Sancho el Brauo, hijo de este rey don Alfonso el Sabio* (Valladolid, Spain: Sebastián Martínez, 1554).

31. See note 14 above for the full citation and Rosell's introduction to his edition of the *Crónicas de los Reyes de Castilla,* vi.

32. Rodgers, *Prolegomena,* 1:1–2. The *Bibliography of Old Spanish Texts,* 3d. ed. (Madison: Hispanic Seminary, 1984), lists the thirty-four manuscripts of the *Crónica de Alfonso X.* Professor Manuel González Jiménez of the University of Seville is preparing a critical edition of the *Chronicle.*

33. See the description of Herrera's edition in Rodgers, *Prolegomena,* 1:256–85.

34. See the description of Rosell's edition in Rodgers, *Prolegomena,* 1:229–55, summarized on 249. She identified the manuscript belonging to the Duke of Osuna as MS 10195, and the sumptuous manuscript of El Escorial as MS M.II.2.

35. Alfonso X was born on the feast of St. Clement, November 23, 1221, so he would celebrate his thirty-first birthday on November 23, 1252.

36. Procter, "Materials," 53.

37. Procter, "Materials," 53–54.

38. Paula K. Rodgers, "Alfonso X Writes to His Son: Reflections on the *Crónica de Alfonso X,*" *Exemplaria Hispánica* 1 (1991–1992): 59.

39. The earlier chapters of the *Chronicle* refer to Pedro III as King of Aragón, whereas in the middle section he is correctly identified as Infante Don Pedro, because he did not become king until 1276. The identification of Juan González, Master of Calatrava; Master Gonzalo, Archdeacon of Toledo, Notary of Castile; and Pedro Lorenzo, Bishop of Cuenca, is correct. Procter, "Materials," 55.

40. Procter, "Materials," 55–56.

41. Ballesteros, *Alfonso X,* 918.

42. For Alfonso Pérez, see Manuel González Jiménez, *Diplomatario Andaluz de Alfonso X* (Seville: El Monte. Caja de Huelva y Sevilla, 1991), 418, 461, 516, 520, nos. 396 (June 27, 1272), 438 (April 24, 1278), 486 (Dec. 1, 1281), 488

(Feb. 10, 1282). For Velasco Gómez, see ibid., 331, 365, 500, nos. 306 (Sept. 23, 1265), 336 (Nov. 23, 1267), 475 (Nov. 4, 1280).

43. One might compare it with Abû Yûsuf's letter to Alfonso X on October 24, 1282, in Louis Mas Latrie, *Traités de paix et de commerce et documents divers concernant les relations des chrétiens avec les arabes de l'Afrique septentrionale au moyen âge*, 2 vols. (Paris: 1866; reprint, Philadelphia: Burt Franklin, 1963), 96–97, no. 6.

44. *Chronicle of Alfonso X,* 24, 29, 30, 36, 38, ch. 27, 37, 38, 49, 51. Gonzalo Ruiz de Atienza had received houses in Seville during the distribution. Julio González, *Repartimiento de Sevilla,* 2 vols. (Madrid: Consejo Superior de Investigaciones Científicas, 1951), 2:103, 156, 176, 247, 263, 265–66, 313; González Jiménez, *Diplomatario Andaluz de Alfonso X,* 63, no. 66 (Sept. 24, 1253). Sancho Pérez, served as *escribano de la cámara del rey* from 1262 to 1264, and as notary of the chamber from 1272 to 1277. He was also treasurer of the cathedral of Jaén and Archdeacon of Baeza. Evelyn Procter, *Curia and Cortes in León and Castile, 1072–1295* (Cambridge, U.K.: Cambridge Univ. Press, 1980), 228.

45. That the king's heralds verbally proclaimed the king's messages is clear from such phrases as *"dijeronles su mandaderia de parte del Rey"* (ch. 27); *"E pues que avemos dicho esta mandaderia a todos los otros, agora diremos a cada uno lo que nos es mandado de parte de nuestro señor el Rey"* (ch. 28); *"el rey vos envia decir"* (ch. 31–32); *"el rey vos dice"* (ch. 33); *"a esto vos decimos"* (ch. 34); and *"decimos vos de parte del rey"* (ch. 36).

46. Gonzalo Ruiz de Atienza again was one of the king's agents.

47. Rodgers, "Alfonso X Writes to His Son," 60–68; on 69–79 she edited the text of the letter by collating seven manuscripts of the *Crónica de Alfonso X.*

48. See Evelyn Procter, "The Castilian Chancery During the Reign of Alfonso X, 1252–1284," *Oxford Essays in Medieval History presented to Herbert E. Salter* (Oxford, U.K.: Clarendon, 1934), 104–21.

49. Unlike the *cartas plomadas* or *cartas abiertas* issued by the royal chancery, Rodgers, "Alfonso X Writes to His Son," 60, noted that the letters do not open with the typical statement, *"sepan cuantos esta carta vieren"*—"Let all those know who see this charter"—nor is there a greeting, a date, or a subscription. Nor are there lists of confirming witnesses as is typical of solemn privileges.

50. Procter, "The Castilian Chancery," 117–18.

51. Rodgers, "Alfonso X Writes to His Son," 59–60.

52. Procter, "The Castilian Chancery," 118, cites "Maestre Joffre nostro notario" Rymer, *Foedera,* I.2. 570.

53. Procter, "Materials," 56–57.

54. Rodgers, "Alfonso X Writes to His Son," 59.

Chronicle of Alfonso X

Prologue

By many ways and means, the sages who lived in times past desired that things that were discovered and events that took place be made known. Thus, by their own nobility, serving as an example by themselves to future generations, they had them written down, understanding that in this fashion those who came after them might be able to understand better and that these deeds would be protected and preserved for the ages. This is how knowledge of the art of astrology and the other sciences were discovered. Likewise, men learned how the patriarchs and prophets came, and of the advent of Jesus Christ, and the other things pertaining to the worship of God.

It is fitting that the deeds of kings, who hold God's place on earth, be found in writing, particularly those of the kings of Castile and León, who through the law of God and the increase of the Catholic Faith took up many tasks and exposed themselves to grave dangers in battles with the Moors, driving them out of Spain. Therefore, the most high and honorable and blessed Alfonso, by the grace of God, King of Castile, León, Toledo, Galicia, Seville, Córdoba, Murcia, Jaén, the Algarbe, and Algeciras, and Lord of Molina, desiring that the feats of the kings who were before him be found in writing, ordered the old histories and chronicles inspected.[1] He found written in the chronicles in the books of his royal chamber the deeds of the kings who were in times past: Visigothic kings up to King Rodrigo,[2] and from the reign of King Pelayo, who was the first King of León,[3] until the death of King Fernando, who conquered Seville and Córdoba, and the towns of the Bishopric of Jaén, and the kingdom of Murcia.[4] Many things happened in the time of the kings who lived after that King Fernando that were not recorded in chronicles; therefore, King Alfonso, called the Conqueror, realizing that these deeds were forgotten, in order to make known all the things that happened in the days of his great grandfather, King Alfonso X, and during the time of his son King Sancho IV, the Valiant, and of his father, King Fernando III, ordered them written in this book so that those yet to come may know how things happened in the days of the aforesaid kings.[5]

Notes

1. Alfonso XI (1312–1350).
2. Rodrigo, the last King of the Visigoths (710–711).
3. Pelayo, the first King of Asturias (718–737).
4. Fernando III, King of Castile-León (1217–1252).
5. Alfonso X (1252–1284), Sancho IV (1284–1295), and Fernando IV (1295–1312).

Chapter 1

❖

How King Alfonso Ruled, and of the Currency
That Circulated at This Time

History tells that after King Fernando died, his son Alfonso was made king of Castile and León in the very noble city of Seville. Don Alfonso began to rule on the twenty-ninth day of the month of May.[1] In the era of Adam, it was the year five thousand twenty-one. In the era of the Hebrews, it was four thousand three hundred and fifty-three Roman years since the Deluge, with one hundred and five more days. In the era of Nebuchadnezzar, it was one thousand nine hundred and ninety-eight years, with ninety more Roman days. In the era of Philip the Great, King of Greece, it was one thousand one hundred and twenty-three Roman years, with twenty-two more days. In the era of Alexander the Great of Macedonia, it was one thousand five hundred and sixty-two Roman years, with two hundred and forty-four more days. In the era of Caesar, it was one thousand two hundred and eighty-nine Roman years, with one hundred and fifty more days. In the era of the birth of Jesus Christ, it was the year one thousand two hundred and fifty-two. In the era of the Galatian Egyptians, it was the year eight hundred and sixty-two. In the era of the Arabs, it was the year six hundred and twenty-nine. In the era of Saint Aespersian, according to the era of the Persians, it was the year six hundred and twenty. King Alfonso was thirty-one years old and was the tenth King of Castile and León to be called by that name.

This King Alfonso, at the beginning of his reign, reasserted for a fixed term the policies and agreements that his father, King Fernando, had made with the King of Granada to deliver the tribute monies, because they did not pay them as faithfully as they did to his father, King Fernando. For in the days of King Fernando, the King of Granada would give half of all his income, which was appraised at six hundred thousand *maravedís* in the currency of Castile. This coin was so thick and worth so many *dineros* to the *maravedí* that it attained the same value as a gold *maravedí*. In King Fernando's day, *pepiones* circulated as the coinage in Castile and in the kingdom of León. One hundred and eighty *pepiones* were worth one *maravedí*. Small purchases were made with the less valuable *metal*. Eighteen *pepiones* made a *metal*, and there were ten *metales* to the *maravedí*. The income of the kingdom of Granada was valued at six hundred thousand *maravedís*, and they would give King Fernando half of that income. Although the King of Granada gave these tributes to King Fernando so that he would let him live in peace, he gave them more as compensation because Fernando provided the King of Granada and other regions of the kingdom with troops to defend against a Moorish clan called the Soysemela, who were very powerful rivals. This King of Granada was called Aben Alhamar I,[2] and Fernando always helped him throughout his life so that the Moors of that kingdom could never rebel against him. For these reasons, King Fernando received such great amounts of tribute from the Moors.[3] His son King Alfonso, at the beginning of his reign, ordered the *pepiones* melted down and minted the coins called *burgaleses*, of which ninety equaled one *maravedí*. Minor purchases were made with *sueldos*. Six *burgaleses* were worth a *sueldo*, and fifteen *sueldos* made one *maravedí*. The King of Granada had to give Alfonso two hundred and fifty thousand *maravedís* each year.[4] During this time, because of the changes in currencies, all things increased in price in the kingdoms of Castile and León and went up a great deal.[5] In that first year, the king engaged in doing things he thought were of benefit to his kingdoms, and he stocked and provisioned the towns, villages, and castles that were on the Moorish frontier. He did the same for the towns and villages of the kingdom of Murcia, which were inhabited by Moors, and that he had won as a prince during his father's time.

Notwithstanding that the high nobility and *infanzones* [those of secondary rank], knights, and lesser nobles of his kingdom lived in peace and harmony with him, he, with greatness of heart and to assure their prompt service when he needed them, largely increased their portions over what they had during the time of his father,

King Fernando. From his holdings, he also gave some of them additional lands and bestowed property upon others who until then had none. Because the chronicle accounts for the years of this king from January on, the aforementioned events were placed in the first seven months of the year 1290 [i.e. 1252 of the Christian Era].

Notes

1. Fernando III died on May 31, 1252 (not on May 29) and was buried on June 1, the date of Alfonso X's accession. O'Callaghan, *The Learned King*, 5–6.

2. Ibn al-Ahmar or Muhammad I, King of Granada (1232–1273), whom the *Chronicle* calls Aben Alhamar.

3. The Soysemela were the Banû Ashqîlûlâ, one of the principal noble families of the kingdom of Granada.

4. See note 2.

5. More than ten years elapsed before Alfonso X altered the coinage; he certainly did not do so in the first years of his reign. O'Callaghan, *The Learned King*, 124–26.

Chapter 2

*How King Alfonso Took Tejada
and Other Moorish Towns
and Made Them Outposts of Seville*

The first year of Alfonso's reign, Era 1291, was the year A.D. 1253. Likewise, before his father's death this King Alfonso married doña Violante, daughter of King Jaime of Aragón and sister of King Pedro. He had no son by her, and he became very unhappy; seeing that this was due to a lack on her part, he therefore sent his envoys to the King of Norway to entreat the king to send his daughter in marriage.[1]

Since very little time had passed since King Fernando had won Seville, and it was newly conquered territory, many neighboring Moors lived near the city. For while the chronicle of King Fernando, Alfonso's father, states that Fernando took Jerez, it was not so. Though he sometimes raided it from Seville, the town remained in Moorish hands. At that time, the Moors held Niebla, Tejada, and the Algarbe as well. Therefore, the city of Seville was much embattled and not secure. Its inhabitants often came under heavy attack by the Moors and suffered great harm.

In order to push back some of the Moors, Alfonso moved against Tejada. The town was held by a Moor called Hamete, who styled himself a king. After a brief siege, this Moor, seeing how little power he had and that he could not defend himself from the king, promised to surrender and asked Alfonso to let him and all of the town's inhabitants leave safely. The king considered it good, and Hamete came to Alfonso and delivered the town.[2] Then the king ordered all the Moors in that place set free; this Moor [Hamete] went overseas. Having won Tejada, Alfonso went to other nearby places held by the Moors and seized them. Upon his return to Seville, he made the town of Tejada and the others that he had taken outposts of Seville. Afterward, he departed and came to Toledo.

Having related how King Alfonso made this conquest, we will now tell how the daughter of the King of Norway was brought to him, and how he married her to Prince Felipe, his brother, for Queen Violante, his wife, was with child.

Notes

1. Alfonso X married Violante, the daughter of Jaime I of Aragón (1213–1276) and the sister of Pedro III (1276–1285), on January 29, 1249. The story that he intended to divorce her because she was barren and marry a princess of Norway is regarded as a fabrication. Violante died in 1300. O'Callaghan, *The Learned King*, 8, 202.

2. Tejada surendered after a short siege in late 1252 or early 1253. O'Callaghan, *The Learned King*, 165.

Chapter 3

How the King of Granada Came to Toledo
to Make Peace with King Alfonso,
and of the Things That Happened

In the second year of King Alfonso's reign, 1292 Era, A.D. 1254, the King of Granada, in order to increase Alfonso's good will and friendship, came to him in Toledo.[1] Alfonso was very pleased with this visit and did him much honor. The King of Granada stayed at King Alfonso's estate near Toledo, and they renewed treaties and agreements they had formerly held. While the two kings were doing this, the messengers Alfonso had sent to the King of Norway returned, bringing his daughter, named doña Cristina,[2] for marriage to King Alfonso. But when the messengers arrived in Castile with the Princess of Norway, Queen Violante was pregnant with a daughter whom they named Princess Berenguela, who later became the Lady of Guadalajara. Thus, at the beginning of the year, a few days after doña Cristina arrived, the queen gave birth to Princess Berenguela.[3] On that account, the king was very ashamed that he had sent for doña Cristina.

Prince Felipe, the king's brother, who was Archbishop-Elect of Seville and was the Abbot of Valladolid and of Cuevas Rubias, had repeatedly told the king that he wished to leave the clergy. Notwithstanding that the king, far from praising his intentions, had hindered him from doing so, when Prince Felipe asked for the king's blessing to marry this princess, the king agreed to it because he saw it as good, holding the wedding immediately.[4] Then the king bestowed upon Prince Felipe part of his income: the tax payable on St. Martin of Ávila's Day, gate tolls, the Jewish quarter, and all other taxes that the king collected in Ávila and its surroundings. The king also gave Prince Felipe each year all the tithes of the

Archbishopric of Toledo and of the Bishoprics of Ávila and Segovia, along with some of his income from other areas as well. As hereditary properties, he gave him Val de Corneja and Valponcheva. Although the Moors held Valponcheva and paid the king its rents each year, all of this Prince Felipe kept through his marriage.

The King of Granada ceded to King Alfonso what he had come there for and returned to his land well pleased. Then, some ten months after the birth of Princess Berenguela, Queen Violante bore another child, named Prince Fernando, the first son and heir of King Alfonso.[5] Later, the king had more children by this queen: Prince Sancho,[6] Prince Pedro,[7] Prince Juan,[8] Prince Jaime,[9] another daughter named Isabel,[10] and another named Leonor,[11] who married the Marquis of Murcia. He also had by the queen another daughter, whom they named Violante, and by a mistress a son named Alfonso the Child.[12] From another mistress, doña Mayor Guillén, daughter of don Pedro Guzmán, he had a daughter named Beatriz,[13] who married King Afonso of Portugal, as will be related later in this chronicle.

Next we shall tell how this King Alfonso captured the town of Jerez.

Notes

1. Ibn al-Ahmar, the King of Granada, visited Toledo during the Cortes held there in the spring of 1254. O'Callaghan, *The Learned King*, 166–67.

2. An embassy from King Haakon IV of Norway came to Castile in late 1255, and a Castilian embassy went to Norway in 1256. Princess Kristin (Cristina) arrived in Castile in December 1257 and married Infante Felipe on March 31, 1258. She died childless in 1262. O'Callaghan, *The Learned King*, 202–4.

3. Princess Berenguela, the king's daughter, was born in 1253 and was recognized as heir to the throne in the Cortes of Toledo in March 1254. See chapter 2, note 1. O'Callaghan, *The Learned King*, 8.

4. Infante Felipe, Alfonso X's third brother, was intended for an ecclesiastical career and was elected, but never consecrated, as Archbishop of Seville. He was assigned royal tributes in Ávila including *martiniega*, a tax due at Martinmas (November 11), tolls (*portazgo*) levied at the gates, and the tribute from the Jewish community, as well as the third of the tithe (*tercias*) of the Archbishopric of Toledo. O'Callaghan, *The Learned King*, 8.

5. Infante Fernando de la Cerda, the king's oldest son, was born on October 23, 1255, and died suddenly at Villarreal on July 24, 1275. By his marriage on November 30, 1269, to Blanche, the daughter of Louis IX of France,

he had two sons, Alfonso and Fernando, usually called the Infantes de la Cerda.

6. Infante Sancho, the king's second son, born in 1258, succeeded to the throne as Sancho IV (1284–1295).

7. Infante Pedro (1261–1283) married Marguerite of Narbonne.

8. Infante Juan (1264–1319) married Joanna of Montferrat and played an active role in the minorities of his nephew, Fernando IV, and his grand-nephew, Alfonso XI.

9. Infante Jaime (1267–1284).

10. Besides Isabel (1265?–?), Violante (1266?–1308?), who married Diego López de Haro in 1282, and the other daughters mentioned in the *Chronicle*, the king had an additional daughter—Constanza (1259?–?).

11. Leonor (1256?–1275) did not marry the Marquis of Montferrat in Murcia. Her older sister, Beatriz (1254–1280), married the marquis in 1271.

12. Alfonso Fernández, el Niño, an illegitimate son of Alfonso X, had an important role in the later military and naval campaigns against the Benimerines. He died in 1281.

13. Beatriz, the king's illegitimate daughter by Mayor Guillén, the daughter of Pedro Guzmán, married Afonso III of Portugal (1248–1279) in 1253, by whom she had a son, King Dinis (Deonis in the *Chronicle*) of Portugal (1279–1325). She died in 1303.

Chapter 4

◼

How King Alfonso Took Jerez, and Arcos,
and Lebrija, and of Other Things
That Happened During This Year

In the third year of his reign (1293 Era, A.D. 1255), King Alfonso, wishing to serve God by doing harm to the Moors, thought it well to seize their lands, especially those near the city of Seville. Since Aben Mafot,[1] King of Niebla and of the Algarbe, and another Moor named Aben Abit, who was Lord of Jerez, were very close to this city, the king held council concerning which of these conquests should come first. Having decided it best to go first and capture the town of Jerez, he led forth his hosts and held it under siege for a month.

The Moors of the town, in order to prevent King Alfonso's army from destroying their olive groves and gardens, planned to remain in the town and on their properties, thinking that at some later time they might deliver themselves from the pressure and power of the Christians. Moreover, because they were ill pleased with their own lord, before King Alfonso might order his men to arms or damage their properties and other goods, they sent word to him that they thought it well to leave them their houses and all of their properties, as they would deliver the town and would give him each year the tribute that they customarily gave to their lord.

Seeing that the capture of this town could take a long time, and furthermore that the town was so large that there would not be enough Christians to populate it afterward (for the city of Seville was not well-populated yet), the king saw their request as a good thing and granted it. After the Moors of the town saw this carried out, they told their Moorish lord, who was in the fortress, to either come to terms with King Alfonso or accept safe conduct and leave.

For this reason, that Moor, Aben Abit, made an agreement with King Alfonso that allowed him to surrender the fortress and leave safely with all of his belongings.

With the *alcázar* under his control, the king supplied it with food and weapons and gave it to don Nuño de Lara to hold for him.[2] Don Nuño, in turn, entrusted it to a knight named Garcí Gómez Carrillo. The king allowed all the Moors in town to stay in their homes and retain all of their possessions.

While he had this town under siege, Alfonso ordered his brother Prince Enrique to go and besiege the town of Arcos, which along with Lebrija was controlled by a Moorish woman. The Moors of these places, when they learned that the king had retaken Jerez, turned them over to Prince Enrique under the condition that they could remain and retain their estates. Thus, they delivered the fortress of Arcos to Prince Enrique in Alfonso's name; Lebrija had no fortress.[3] With these conquests completed, the king departed thence and came to Seville to attend to some matters related to the governance of his realm.

Other things, just as they happened during the time of this king, we will relate henceforth.

Notes

1. Ibn Mahfût (1234–1262) (Aben Mafot in the *Chronicle*) was the King of Niebla and the Algarbe.

2. When the Muslims of Jerez agreed to receive a Castilian garrison in the citadel, or *alcázar*, in late spring or summer 1261, the king entrusted it to Nuño González de Lara. O'Callaghan, *The Learned King*, 174–75.

3. Arcos and Lebrija submitted to Infante Enrique in 1253. O'Callaghan, *The Learned King*, 165.

Chapter 5

How King Alfonso Ordered a Fixed Price Set on All Merchandise

In the fourth year of the reign of this King Alfonso (1294 Era, A.D. 1256), many complaints came before him from all over his realms to the effect that prices had increased so much that people could not afford anything. Because of this, the king instituted the *cotos*, which set a price on all things, what amount each one should cost.[1] If people had trouble affording goods before this, they had it much worse afterward, since the merchants and other people who had things to sell hoarded them and refused to display them for sale. Therefore, everyone was in dire straits; in response, the king had to remove the *cotos* and order that things be sold freely at whatever prices the parties might agree upon. And in this year, nothing else is found that deserves to be related by the *History*.

Note

1. Alfonso X fixed wages and prices in the Cortes of Seville in 1252, repeating those regulations in the Cortes of Valladolid in 1258 and Seville in 1261. A further regulation of wages and prices was undertaken in the Assembly of Jerez in 1268. O'Callaghan, *The Learned King*, 120–21.

Chapter 6

▦

*How King Alfonso Besieged Niebla and Won It
by Following the Advice of Two Friars,
and How He Took the Algarbe*

In the fifth year of the reign of this King Alfonso (1295 Era, and
the year 1257 after the birth of Jesus Christ), after he had pacified
some troubles of which the *History* has told, the king sought a way
to exercise himself in God's service and to exalt the Catholic Faith
by broadening his realms. Because all of the Algarbe was contained
by the Moors, and the capital was Niebla, of which a Moor named
Aben Mafot was then lord, Alfonso had the men of his kingdom
mustered, along with all of the nobles and councilmen. And he
gathered an army and went to lay siege to the town of Niebla.[1]

As soon as he arrived there, he ordered the royal camp pitched
and set up many siege engines, because the town was heavily fortified and surrounded by a good wall and towers, all of stonework.
Likewise, King Aben Mafot was there, who had the town well provisioned with a great deal of good food and many worthy men-at-
arms. Due to all of this, King Alfonso had to maintain the siege for
a very long time, pressing the enemy hard with the machines and
in the many encounters his men had with them.[2]

It so happened that while the king was at the siege, such a great
swarm of flies came upon the men of the Christian encampment
that none of the men in the army could keep down anything they
ate. This brought on diarrhea, and many died of this illness. The
king and all the men of his army agreed to withdraw from that
siege, because they had been there for seven months.

At that time, there were two friars in the army—one named
Andrés and the other Pedro—who came to the king and told him

that they would do wrong to leave there at the moment when they had the town nearly won; for the Moors would resupply it and build up what the king's army had torn down with the siege engines so that when they tried at another time to take the city, they would not be able to bring it to such a state again. The king replied that he did not know what to do, since the plague that was in the camp was great and men were dying from it. The friars replied that they could provide a solution for that. Then they ordered it proclaimed throughout the army that anyone who brought a measure of flies to the tent of the friars would receive two silver *torneses* for each measure. The men in the ranks took vengeance on the flies to earn the silver *torneses* and brought many of them, so that in this way they filled two old underground granaries that existed there from another time. And so the swarm diminished, curing the malady from which the men were dying and allowing the Christians to carry out everything needed to take the town. Aben Mafot, King of Niebla, was brought to the extreme of not having food for himself or for the men who were with him. Seeing how the king and the army persevered and did not wish to leave without taking the town, even after nine and one-half months of siege, King Aben Mafot sent to beseech King Alfonso to let him and those who were with him leave safely with all of their belongings and to grant him level farmlands from which he could support himself for the rest of his life. In exchange, he would surrender the town of Niebla and the lands of the Algarbe. King Alfonso considered this request satisfactory, and the town of Niebla was handed over to him in this fashion. Alfonso gave to King Aben Mafot land on which to live for the rest of his life, and this property was in the part of the Algarbe that is near Seville. With it came all the rights that the king had there and the tithe of the olive oil from the region. Alfonso also gave Aben Mafot the farmland of Seville and assured quantities of *maravedís* from the Jewish quarter of the city of Seville and other things from which this King Aben Mafot maintained himself honorably for the rest of his life.

Some of the places that King Alfonso won at that time he left inhabited by Moors. After King Alfonso had taken Niebla, he won with it all of the Algarbe, which is the town of Niebla with its outlying districts of Gibraleón and Huelva, Serpia and Mora, Alcatín and Castro Marín, Tavira and Faro, and Loulé.

Notes

1. The siege of Niebla began sometime after June 1261; the town surrendered in February 1262. O'Callaghan, *The Learned King,* 174–78.

2. Sancho II (1223–1248) and Afonso III (1248–1279) of Portugal had occupied Mora, Serpa, Castro Marín, Tavira, Loulé and Faro by 1249. O'Callaghan, *The Learned King,* 157.

Chapter 7

How the King of Portugal was Disinherited and of How the King of Castile Kept Him Honorably in His Realm

In the sixth year of this reign of King Alfonso, which was in the Era of 1296, and the year 1258 after the birth of Jesus Christ, he left Seville and came to Toledo. He found out that the King of Portugal, named Sancho Capiello, had arrived and was there. Sancho told Alfonso how his brother Afonso had rebelled against his rule and that some of the people had taken Afonso as their king; Sancho asked King Alfonso to help him so that he might regain his kingdom.[1] King Afonso, upon learning of this discussion, sent to request that King Alfonso see fit not to interfere in that affair nor oppose him, and that he would marry Alfonso's daughter doña Beatriz, who was wealthy and a granddaughter of don Pedro Guzmán and daughter of doña Mayor Guillén. King Alfonso, out of the great favor in which he held his daughter, and seeing that it was a great honor to marry her to that king, granted what King Afonso requested and the marriage took place.[2] Along with his daughter, the King of Castile gave him the Algarbe lands taken from the Moors, which are those from the Guadiana River to Portugal, named Tavira and Faro, and Loulé and Castro Marín, and Alcatín. So throughout those lands, that King Afonso and those who came after him were called Kings of Portugal and of the Algarbe. King Alfonso of Castile honorably supported King Sancho for the rest of his life, and when King Sancho died, King Alfonso ordered him buried in the great church of Toledo, where he lies buried in the Kings' chapel.

In this year, Alfonso ordered the currency of the *dineros prietos* minted and the currency of the *burgaleses* destroyed. Of these *dineros prietos*,[3] fifteen made a *maravedí*.

Notes

1. Sancho II of Portugal, ousted from power by his brother Afonso III, accompanied his ally Infante Alfonso, the future Alfonso X, to Toledo in 1247; he died there on January 4, 1248. O'Callaghan, *The Learned King*, 156–57.

2. The marriage of Afonso III and Beatriz, the illegitimate daughter of Alfonso X, took place in 1253. Alfonso X was allowed to retain the Algarbe for life, but on February 16, 1267, he yielded all claims there to Afonso III. O'Callaghan, *The Learned King*, 156–62.

3. The *dineros prietos* were issued in 1269. O'Callaghan, *The Learned King*, 124–26.

Chapter 8

※

How King Alfonso Tried to Imprison
Don Enrique, and of the Things That
Happened to This Prince Enrique

In the seventh year of the reign of this King Alfonso, which was in
the Era of 1297, and the year 1259 after the birth of Jesus Christ,
King Alfonso was in Seville and Prince Enrique was in Lebrija, and
the king was told that Prince Enrique had been conspiring with
some noblemen and knights of the realm to his disservice. On this
account, the king ordered don Nuño to go and arrest the prince.[1]

So don Nuño left Seville, and as he was approaching Lebrija,
don Enrique learned that don Nuño was going to seize him and
sallied forth. They fought and it happened that they wounded each
other. Don Nuño was wounded on the face and was nearly at the
point of defeat—for don Enrique and his men fought very fiercely—
when don Nuño was reinforced by a large army that the king sent
him. Then don Enrique and his men had to leave the battlefield
and return to Lebrija.

That night don Enrique left and went to Puerto de Santa María.
Despite the fact that the region was not yet settled, some ships were
there, one of which he boarded and sailed to Cáliz. There he found
a ship that was going to Valencia, and in it he traveled to the kingdom of Aragón, even though King Jaime, father-in-law of King
Alfonso, was alive at this time. King Jaime did not want to act contrary to Alfonso's will and ordered the prince to leave the realm.
Therefore, Prince Enrique asked him for ships in which to travel
so that he might go overseas, and King Jaime agreed.

From Barcelona, Prince Enrique went to Tunis, and the King
of Tunis welcomed him warmly and bestowed wealth upon him,
because he knew that he was a king's son. Prince Enrique lived

there with him for four years and served very well in the battles and conflicts that this King of Tunis had with his Moorish neighbors, acquiring great fame for his prowess and knightly honor throughout the land. The Moors of the kingdom of Tunis spoke with the king and told him that the prince was truly winning the hearts of the people of the land, and that those who opposed him feared him greatly. They said he had brought many Christians among them, and that from such things could come very great harm and very great disservice to the king. They also said it was necessary to order him out of the kingdom, because the king and his men could protect and defend their land without him, as they had done before.

Though he was saddened to hear what they told him about the prince, the King of Tunis could not help but believe his own people, and so they looked for a way to cast the prince out of the kingdom. They feared that if the king should tell him or send someone to tell him, he would create an uprising in the kingdom or go over to their enemies with the men he had there, and it was therefore appropriate to find some way to kill him. As they could find no easy means to do it, for fear of his men, who were very powerful knights, they agreed to have the king call Prince Enrique to a parley in a courtyard in which they might put with him two lions, which were in a separate place, so that these beasts would kill him. Having adopted this plan, they set it in motion, and later the king had don Enrique called to the meeting. Enrique went inside the courtyard where he was advised to enter. All the men of his bodyguard remained in other buildings where they were lodging, at some distance from that place. While Prince Enrique was with the King of Tunis, the king told him to wait for him there, that he would return right away. The king went out that side of the courtyard, and from the other side came in the two lions, confident of killing the prince. Don Enrique unsheathed the sword he had with him, which he was never without, and turned to face them. But the lions did not go after him, and don Enrique went to the door and got out of the courtyard. While he was doing this, the Moors seized all of Enrique's men.

After Enrique escaped from the courtyard, the king refused to let his men kill him, nor did the king wish to see him, and sent orders that he leave the kingdom. Don Enrique asked the king to let his men go free. The king ordered a very few of them set free, only those who had come over with him; of the Christians who were there first and who had served him, not one was released. Don Enrique set out for Rome, to the war the Romans were having against the King of Apulia and of Calabria and the Count of Provence. Now the *History* ends the story of don Enrique and will tell of the deeds of King Alfonso of Castile.[2]

Notes

1. Soon after his accession, King Alfonso quarreled with his brother Infante Enrique and in 1255 sent Nuño González de Lara to take possession of Lebrija. Enrique went into exile, allying himself first with Jaime I of Aragón against Castile, but left the peninsula for France and England in 1256. He served the emir of Tunis from about 1260 to 1264, when he went to Italy, where he was elected senator of Rome in 1267.

2. With papal support, Charles of Anjou, Count of Provence, overthrew the Hohenstaufen rulers of the kingdom of Naples and Sicily and captured Infante Enrique in 1268. He was imprisoned until 1293, when he returned to Castile and became one of the regents for Fernando IV; he died in 1303. O'Callaghan, *The Learned King*, 73–75, 209–10.

Chapter 9

❄

*How King Alfonso Made the Legal Code, and of
the Messengers Who Came to Him from Egypt*

In the eighth year of his reign, which was in the Era of 1298 and
the year 1260 after the birth of Jesus Christ, this King Alfonso ordered everything translated from Latin to Castilian Spanish so that
he might have knowledge of all writings. He ordered the legal statutes to be composed in this tongue, wherein he summarized very
briefly many laws governing rights and privileges. He gave it as a
legal code to the city of Burgos and to other cities and towns of the
kingdom of Castile, since in the kingdom of León they had the
Fuero Juzgo, which the Visigoths had made in Toledo.[1] The towns of
Extremadura also had different, separate statutes, and because not
all disputes could be resolved by these statutes, and because King
Fernando, his father, had begun to prepare the books of the
Partidas, King Alfonso had them finished.[2] He ordered that all men
of his kingdom consider them as the law and statutes and that judges
settle disputes by them. Likewise, he ordered the Bible translated
into Castilian,[3] as well as all the history of the church and the ecclesiastical hierarchy and the art of astrological divination.[4]

Also, King Alfonso had commemorated each year the anniversary of his father King Fernando's death, in this fashion: A great
many men would come from all over Andalusia to do Fernando
honor, and they brought with them all the banners and standards
of each place, and with each banner they brought many wax candles.
They would put all of the banners they brought in the great church
and would light the candles very early in the morning; they burned
all day, since the candles were very large. King Aben Alhamar of

Granada,[5] for this honor, and while they were carrying it out, sent King Alfonso important men of his court and with them one hundred foot soldiers; each one of them carried a lighted candle of white wax, and these hundred candles they would place around the tomb where King Fernando lay buried. This, Aben Alhamar did in honor of the king. King Alfonso always celebrated this festival every year as long as he had the kingdoms under his rule; and it was a custom that on the day of the anniversary and the day before it no shops would open, nor did workmen perform any labor.

While King Alfonso was in Seville and all the men with him during this honor that they did for his father, messengers came to him from Alvandexáver, King of Egypt.[6] They brought presents to King Alfonso of many precious cloths of different kinds and of many rare and beautiful jewels. They also brought him an elephant and an animal called an *azorafa* [giraffe], and an ass that was striped with one band white and the other black, and many other kinds of beasts and animals. The king welcomed warmly these messengers and did them great honor and sent them very well pleased from there. Then he left Seville and came to Castile; and meanwhile there took place what the *History* will relate.

Notes

1. The *Fuero de las Leyes,* or *Book of Laws,* more commonly known as the *Fuero Real,* or *Royal Law,* a code of municipal law, was probably promulgated in the Cortes of Toledo in 1254. O'Callaghan, *The Learned King,* 30–36.

2. Together with the *Fuero real,* Alfonso X likely promulgated in the Cortes of Toledo in 1254 another law code for use in the royal court known as the *Espéculo,* or *Mirror of the Laws.* An amplified version of this, known as the *Siete Partidas,* or *Seven Parts,* stressing the king's role as emperor, was completed between 1256 and 1265. O'Callaghan, *The Learned King,* 36–37.

3. The Romance version of the Bible may be an allusion to the *General Estoria,* which freely adapted the Bible for its account of world history from creation to the birth of Christ. O'Callaghan, *The Learned King,* 140.

4. Various works of science and astrology were composed under the king's direction, but they cannot simply be attributed to the year 1260. O'Callaghan, *The Learned King,* 141–44.

5. The participation of Ibn al-Ahmar in the anniversary of Fernando III on May 31 should be probably be dated in 1260 or 1261. O'Callaghan, *The Learned King,* 206.

6. The King of Egypt was probably the Sultan Kutuz (1259–1260); he

bore the honorific title al-Muzaffar, which the *Chronicle* distorted as Alvandexáver. The arrival of his envoys in Seville has to be dated between December 1259 and November 1260, the dates of his reign. O'Callaghan, *The Learned King,* 207. For a detailed treatment of the beasts and birds, see John E. Keller's article, "The Depiction of Exotic Animals in *Cantiga XXIX* of the *Cantigas de Santa María,*" in *Studies in Honor of Tatiana Fotitch* (The Catholic Univ. Press, 1972).

Chapter 10

※

How This King Alfonso, While a Prince, Took Murcia and Its Lands, and How After He Became King, the Moors Living in Those Regions Rose up Against Him, and What Came of It

In the ninth year of the reign of this King Alfonso, which was in the Era of 1299, and it was the year 1261 after the birth of Jesus Christ, among the things that happened in the time of King Fernando the *History* states that King Alfonso, while still a prince, conquered the kingdom of Murcia. They say that at that time Aben Huxel ruled in Murcia, and this should be placed among the feats of this King Alfonso. And because it is found written in other places that Aben Huxel was not ruling in Murcia, what the historian found written states this:[1]

That in the Era of 1264, after Aben Hud had died, Mohamed Aben Alhamar was elevated to the kingship of Arjona. After King Fernando had won the city of Córdoba and the cities and towns of the Bishopric of Jaén, he helped this Mohamed Aben Alhamar to recover the kingdom of Granada and Almería.[2] This time, those of Murcia, not wanting Aben Alhamar as their lord, made Alboaquez king. Fearing that he would be unable to fend off Aben Alhamar since King Fernando was supporting him, they sent their messengers to his son Alfonso, still but a prince, to tell him that they would give him the city of Murcia and all the castles that are from Alicante to Lorca and Chinchilla. And this King Alfonso, still a prince, as soon as he received this message from the Moors of Murcia, went there under orders and with the will of King Fernando, his father. They received him as lord and surrendered the city and all the castles. All of the fortresses stayed in Christian hands, and the city of Murcia and all other places remained inhabited by Moors. It was thus that King Fernando and his son Prince Alfonso took half of the income, and Alboaquez had the other half. This Alboaquez was King Fernando's vassal all of his life, and later on that of Prince Alfonso during the time he ruled in Castile and León. When this King Alfonso was in Castile in the ninth year of his reign, the Moorish kings of the kingdom of Murcia and all the other territories he had conquered took counsel together and sent their messengers to Aben Alhamar. They agreed that all of them at once would rebel against King Alfonso, and on that day the King of Granada should begin to wage the greatest warfare he could, and each of them should do the same.[3] Having made this decision, King Alboaquez and all of the other Moors who had remained in the kingdom of Murcia rebelled against King Alfonso and took some of the castles that were in Christian hands. Likewise, the Moors who had remained in Jerez and in Arcos, and in Lebrija, and in Utrera,[4] rebelled against King Alfonso; and the King of Granada started to wage a very sustained war. At that time, a knight named Garcí Gómez Carrillo held the *alcázar* of Jerez, and a knight-priest of the Order of Calatrava named don Alimán held the tower of Utrera. The Moors of Jerez, realizing that there was time in which the king would not be able to stop them from what they intended to do, besieged the *alcázar* of the town and Garcí Gómez Carrillo and those who were there with him, fighting them very fiercely night and day so that they did not give them time to rest. Other Moorish people from Algeciras and Tarifa came to the aid of these Moors, and though the Christians did much to defend themselves, the Moors entered the *alcázar*. Garcí Gómez Carrillo and some five or six squires who were with him sought refuge in the principal tower of the *alcázar*, and all the other Christians were killed. The Moors went to the tower that Garcí Gómez Carrillo held, and they fought so hard for it that they burned the doors and killed the men who were with him in the tower. Garcí Gómez Carrillo defended the door with all his might so that they could not enter, and the Moors, refusing to kill him on account of his great nobility, brought iron hooks so that they might capture him. Although they hooked his flesh in places, he let himself be torn rather than be taken captive. The Moors made such efforts that they took Garcí Gómez Carrillo alive as prisoner with those iron hooks, and they took control over the *alcázar* and were in possession of everything. The Moors of Utrera likewise were anxious to capture don Alimán, who kept the tower of Utrera secured. But while they were talking to him, he realized very well exactly what they wanted to do and took refuge with some of his men in the tower. The Moors had Alimán under siege for a long time and fought him for the tower, but he defended it so well that they could not take it from him. The Moors did the same in every place to the castellans who held the fortresses on behalf of King Alfonso, particularly in the kingdom of Murcia. And in this same manner, the castle of Arcos was lost, which was in Christian hands then. Henceforth, we will relate what King Alfonso did when he learned of this.

Notes

1. Aben Huxel (the *Estoria de Espanna*, ch. 1060, mocked his inferior status by calling him Abenhudiel), or Aben Hud, or in modern usage Ibn Hûd, the Muslim king of Murcia, pledged homage to Alfonso X while still Infante when he came to take possession of the kingdom of Murcia in his father's name in 1244–1246. O'Callaghan, *The Learned King*, 16.

2. Córdoba surrendered in 1236, so the date given "in the Era of 1264"— i.e., A.D. 1226—is off by ten years. Ibn Hûd was murdered in 1238 and was succeeded by his son al-Watiq, whom the *Chronicle* called Alboaquez. Mohamed Aben Alamar, who was proclaimed king in Arjona and later became King of Granada, is Ibn al-Ahmar, the first of the Nasrid dynasty.

3. The revolt of the Mudéjars, or Muslims, under Christian rule in Jerez and the surrounding regions in Lower Andalusia and in Murcia, urged on by the King of Granada, occurred in May through June 1264. O'Callaghan, *The Learned King*, 182–83.

4. For Utrera, one should read Matrera.

Chapter 11

◉

*How King Alfonso Built Villa Real and
Settled It While on His Way to the Frontier*

In the tenth year of the reign of this King Alfonso, which was in the Era of 1300, and the year 1262 after the birth of Jesus Christ, news reached him in Segovia of how the King of Granada had broken the truce that he had with him. He learned as well that in the kingdom of Murcia, his vassal King Alboaquez had also risen against him and, moreover, that the Moors of Jerez had taken the *alcázar* and imprisoned Garcí Gómez Carrillo and had besieged don Alimán, who held the tower of Utrera, and other castellans he had left in other towns and castles of the kingdom of Murcia. So King Alfonso had letters sent to the princes and high nobility and all the counselors of his kingdom in order for them to come right away to him at the frontier.

He departed from Segovia and went to Toledo, and from there to the frontier. Passing through a place called El Pozuelo de don Gil—which is in the bounds of Alcaraz—while the forces he had sent for were arriving, he ordered the men of the district to come and commanded that a town be populated there and ordered them to name it Villa Real.[1] He then laid out the streets and indicated the points around which the walls would go. Then he had a gate built of stone—this is the one that is on the road from Toledo— and he ordered the townspeople as to how they should build the walls. Then he departed and went to Córdoba, and from there to Seville, and he ordered war waged against the Moors and sent men to make the castles along the border secure. In this year, nothing else is found to tell about in the *History*.

Note

1. Villarreal, modern Ciudad Real, was founded in 1255, not in 1262. O'Callaghan, *The Learned King,* 81.

Chapter 12

⊞

How King Alfonso Laid Waste to the Vega of
Granada and Its Lands, and of the Gifts and
Freedoms He Gave to Those in Andalusia

In the eleventh year of his reign, which was in the Era of 1301, and the year 1263 after the birth of Jesus Christ, this King Alfonso, being hard-pressed so much in the war with the Moors, was encouraged by all of the princes, great nobles, knights, and advisors that he had sent for to go immediately and lay waste to the land of the King of Granada and to do the greatest possible damage that he could. King Alfonso thereupon sallied forth from Seville with all his forces and went to Córdoba. From there he entered the land of the Moors, and from there arrived at Alcalá de Benzaide. From there he went throughout the Moorish lands, ravaging and burning and doing them great harm and damage.

On his departure, the king went to Seville. From there he sent don Nuño and don Juan González, Master of Calatrava,[1] with part of the army in relief of don Alimán, who was besieged in the tower of Utrera.[2] The Moors who were there fled, for they did not dare to wait. The Christians resupplied it with men and food, and the tower and the grange remained in the power of Christians. King Alfonso divided these forces so that they could be in all the border towns and castles fighting the Moors.

The King of Granada also waged the hardest war he could with the Christians, and he ordered his men to destroy the land if they could do no more against the foe; for he said that largely war came down to "the enemies are here, or the enemies passed this way."

King Alfonso, seeing that he had begun this war with the Moors, in which many horses were being lost, and also that many townsmen excused themselves from service in the annual call to frontier duty (during that time everyone would go and serve for three months with what they owned, since the king gave them nothing from the military tribute), and because there were more men from Extremadura in his service than from any other towns of his kingdom, and so that they might have cause to maintain and raise horses and be ready to come when he called them, King Alfonso ordered the governors in all of Extremadura to hold to this policy:[3] that any man who kept a horse and weapons be exempted from the Saint Martin's Day tax and from the military tribute; and that his overseers, millers, gardeners, ploughmen, butlers, and servants be exempted as well; and that he therefore ordered that they be obliged to serve on the frontier whenever the king might ask, without other compensation for the three months' service. This decree the king made with the consent of those from Extremadura who were with him there, and he dispatched it to the cities and towns and villages of Extremadura. This decree was created for farmers, knights, and any others who wished to maintain horses and have the dispensation for themselves and their exempted followers. Now we shall say no more of this; we shall leave off this and shall tell what the King of Granada did to protect himself in the war he was in.

Notes

1. Juan González was Master of the Military Order of Calatrava from 1267 to 1284.

2. The king's invasion of the plain of Granada and the relief of Matrera (*not* Utrera) probably occurred in the summer of 1264, certainly not in 1263. O'Callaghan, *The Learned King*, 183–85.

3. The king published the Ordinance of Extremadura regulating the military service obligations of the towns of Extremadura on April 15, 1264. O'Callaghan, *The Learned King*, 85, 93.

Chapter 13

How the Moors Came Over the Sea to Assist the King of Granada, and of the Feats That Were Done Concerning This

The King of Granada, seeing the great fierceness of the war he was in, sent to beseech Aben Yuzaf to send some troops in his aid.[1] Yuzaf sent the king a thousand knights, and as their leader came a Moor who was blind in one eye, said to be among the most powerful men there were beyond the sea. According to what was written, they relate that these were the first mounted knights to come over after Miramamolín was defeated.[2] Although at the beginning, the arrival of these knights from overseas was a great advantage to the Moors, and even though it greatly frightened the Christians, who reported many more Moors, great damage came to the King of Granada from their coming. He rewarded them excessively; in order to keep them satisfied, he gave them high wages; and what he should have paid his own men, he paid them. Seeing this, the leader of Málaga and the leader of Guadix warned the king not to damage his own men for strangers.[3] The king gave them a harsh reply, about which they were very displeased. For this reason they sought a way to destroy the foreign Moors, as the *History* will relate subsequently. Now we shall cease discussing this and shall turn again to what King Alfonso did in this war.

Notes

1. Abû Yûsuf Ya'qûb (Aben Yuzaf in the *Chronicle;* Jacob Aben Yuzaf in ch. 14), the emir of the Marinids (or Benimerines), of Morocco, sent three hundred knights, probably late in 1263, in response to the King of Granada's appeal for help. O'Callaghan, *The Learned King,* 181–82.

2. Alfonso VIII of Castile (1158–1214) defeated the Almohad caliph of Morocco (whom the *Chronicle* called Miramamolín—*amîr al-mu'minîn,* or prince of believers) at Las Navas de Tolosa in 1212.

3. As members of the Banû Ashqîlûlâ, the *arraeces,* or governors, of Málaga and Guadix were longtime rivals of the King of Granada.

Chapter 14

How King Alfonso Retook Jerez and Other
Towns That Had Risen Against Him,
and What Came of That

In the twelfth year of his reign, which was in the Era of 1302, and
the year 1264 after the birth of Jesus Christ,[1] while King Alfonso
was at war in Andalusia and had about him all the men of his kingdom and of his menage, thinking on how the Moors of Jerez in his
own realm rebelled and captured the *alcázar,* he sallied forth from
Seville with his army and went to besiege the town of Jerez. As soon
as he arrived, he ordered many siege engines raised around the
city, engines which bombarded the towers and the wall, doing se-
vere damage. The siege of this city lasted five months.

The Moors, feeling hard-pressed by the army due to the nu-
merous injuries it was doing them with so many siege engines, sent
to tell King Alfonso that should it please him to spare their bodies,
they would surrender the town and the *alcázar.* Even though the
king was very angry at what they had done in the great conflict with
the King of Granada and with the Moors from overseas, and also
because he had news that King Jacob Aben Yuzaf of Morocco was
preparing to cross the sea with all of his strength in order to retake
the city, he considered it wise to occupy Jerez before that should
transpire and let the Moors leave unharmed. As soon as the city
was handed over, he manned it with knights and gentry and other
companies. From there he went on to Vejer, Medina Sidonia, Rota,
and San Lucar, and the Moors who held those towns turned them
over to him. Then he colonized Puerto de Santa María. Thereafter
he came through Arcos and Lebrija, which had revolted against
him, and expelled the Moors, and they yielded the castle of Arcos
to him. He peopled them with Christians and supplied them with

food, weapons, and other things that they needed. Then he went back to Seville to plan how he would wage the war. Because it was almost winter, he ordered some of his troops back to his realm so that they all might come to him in the month of April to continue the war with the Moors.

Note

1. The chronicler assigns to the year 1264 the fall of Jerez after a siege of five months, but this did not occur until October 1266. O'Callaghan, *The Learned King*, 187–88.

Chapter 15

◉

*How King Don Alfonso Sued the King of
Granada and Recovered Murcia and the Land
That Had Rebelled Against Him*

In the thirteenth year of his reign, which was in the Era of 1303,
and the year 1265 after the birth of Jesus Christ, King Alfonso,
desiring to carry out with vigor the war under way with the Moors,
had all his vassals summoned by letter as soon as the month of
February had come. Before they arrived, messengers came from
the chiefs of Málaga and Guadix, who were very powerful. The
messengers asked the king, by his grace, to help and protect their
leaders and said that they had towers and castles and many knights
with which their chiefs would serve King Alfonso against the King
of Granada. The king was greatly pleased with the communica-
tions, and he sent the chiefs a very good reply in which he told
them that he would defend and protect them and that if the King
of Granada should besiege some towns or castles that they had, he
on his part would go to succor them and breach the siege. And
concerning this he immediately sent don Nuño with a thousand
knights. He also sent his charters of assurance so that the chiefs
would be sure of it.[1]

With Alfonso's vassals having come to the king and wishing to
begin to lay waste and to make war and do harm and damage to
the Moors, the King of Granada saw himself hard-pressed in the
war with the Christians. Seeing that the chiefs were causing him
harm and damage, the King of Granada sent his messengers to
King Alfonso to say that he might consider it well if Alfonso would
grant him a truce and cease his support of the chiefs. He also said
that he would remove his support from the kingdom of Murcia,
which had rebelled against Alfonso, and from Alboaquez, their king,

and he would support King Alfonso against them so that King Alfonso might seize the land for his own realm. King Alfonso made this information known to the princes and nobles and knights who were with him, and he summoned some counselors to the meeting. It was agreed that King Alfonso should meet with the old King of Granada, who came with Alamir, his son, who would hold the kingdom after him. So both of these kings had meetings near Alcalá de Benzaide and established their truces by agreement and contract.[2] The agreement was that Aben Alhamar and his son, when he should reign, would give King Alfonso two hundred and fifty thousand *maravedís* in the coinage of Castile each year, that the King of Granada would help King Alfonso to take the kingdom of Murcia, and that King Alfonso would forsake the chiefs. With the treaties signed, the King of Granada pleaded earnestly with Alfonso not to kill Alboaquez when he recovered the kingdom of Murcia. Though what the King of Granada asked of him grieved him greatly, Alfonso could not avoid granting it to him. King Alfonso asked the King of Granada to concede the chiefs a truce for one year to see if during this period of time he [Alfonso] could reconcile them, and if not, he would not help them any longer. The King of Granada granted this truce, and they left the meeting.

King Alfonso returned to Jaén and moved with all of his army to the kingdom of Murcia. As soon as he learned that the King of Granada had forsaken him, that both kings were coming with great armies against him, and that King Alfonso had promised not to kill him, Alboaquez, King of Murcia, came to San Esteban del Puerto to place himself at Alfonso's mercy. King Alfonso went on to the city of Murcia, and this Alboaquez and the Moors who were in the city gave it to him. The king left the *alcázar* to his brother Prince Manuel and went from there to all the other places that had rebelled, and they handed those places over to him. King Alfonso appointed governors in all of the castles and gave parcels of land to many Christians who came to take it. But because the territory was large and he could not immediately get so many people to settle it, he allowed many of those Moors who lived there before to remain. He deposed King Alboaquez but refused to have him killed because of the promise he had made. He ordered him to dwell among the Christians and gave him a fixed income to live on. And because King Alfonso wanted to have kings as vassals, he ordered that Mahomad, brother of Aben Hud, rule in Murcia and contribute one-third of the income of the kingdom of Murcia.

And concerning matters that took place, no others that need to be recounted are found in writing.

Notes

1. The chronicler neglects to mention that Alfonso X, then fully occupied with the uprising in Andalusia, called on his father-in-law Jaime I of Aragón to subjugate the rebellious Muslims of Murcia. Jaime I completed his task by January 31, 1266. The Muslims of Murcia formally renewed their allegiance to Alfonso X on June 23, 1266. Only after he had concluded peace with Granada in 1267 was Alfonso X able to journey to Murcia to begin the task of settling the region with Christians. O'Callaghan, *The Learned King*, 185–86, 191–95.

2. The meeting between Alfonso X and the King of Granada at Alcalá de Benzaide probably took place in June 1267, rather than 1265. O'Callaghan, *The Learned King*, 188–89.

Chapter 16

*How King Alfonso Made an Agreement
with the Chiefs of Málaga and Guadix,
and How Some Knights of Castile Established
a Friendship with the King of Granada*

In the fourteenth year of his reign, which was in the Era of 1304, and the year 1266 after the birth of Jesus Christ, after King Alfonso had gotten the lands of the kingdom of Murcia, he remained in this kingdom the entire year, having the towns and castles very well and strongly fortified. He settled the land with as many Christians as possible, making especially great efforts to people the city of Murcia, the town of Orihuela, and the town of Lorca with Christians. Because he could not have enough subjects from his own lands to populate them, many of the Catalans who had come to populate the kingdom of Valencia came and settled in Murcia.[1]

Since the expiration of the truce that the King of Granada had granted the chiefs was close, this King of Granada came to Alfonso in Murcia and earnestly entreated him to be pleased to carry out what he had agreed upon—to forsake the chiefs so that the King of Granada might have compensation from them and might recover the lands with which they had risen against him. King Alfonso, realizing that with the help of these chiefs he could always keep the King of Granada under such pressure that he could take the greatest portion of his realm, or that he would always serve him with its income, refused to forsake the chiefs[2]; rather, he said he would protect and defend them so that they could rule themselves and not obey the King of Granada or any other. For this reason the King of Granada took leave of Alfonso very angrily: on the one hand, because he had not kept the agreement he had with him, and on the other, because he saw that King Alfonso wanted to keep him in perpetual servitude. While the King of Granada was in his tent, Nuño González, son of don Nuño, came to speak with him and told him that King Alfonso had done some wrongs and injustices to don Nuño and to Juan Núñez, the brother of this Nuño González, and that if they should find the King of Granada disposed to help and reward them, he would persuade his relatives to help the King of Granada. When the King of Granada heard this, he was greatly pleased. He talked with Nuño González, telling him that the chiefs held this territory of his by force and that they were doing him much harm, and that King Alfonso was doing him a very great wrong by not keeping the agreement he had made in Alcalá de Benzaide. He said that if Nuño González could speak to don Nuño, his father, and with don Juan Núñez, his brother, and with other lords of the realm who wished to help him, he would help them in such a fashion that King Alfonso would make amends for all of the wrongs he had done them. Concerning all this, the King of Granada gave Nuño González some of his jewels and shared with him some of his gold coins, and then left for Granada.

King Alfonso, seeing that the territory of the kingdom of Murcia was being populated by Christians and that they were working on fortresses in which they had begun to settle, left men to finish them and came to Villa Real, and from there to Toledo, where he dwelt for some time.

Notes

1. Jaime I had settled many Catalans in Murcia. O'Callaghan, *The Learned King*, 186, 191–95.

2. The *arraeces* of Málaga and Guadix feared that the King of Granada would use the Marinids (or Benimerines) of Morocco to ruin them. Ibn al-Ahmar visited Alfonso X at Seville, not Murcia, in June 1268. Alfonso X did not go to Murcia until February 1271 and returned in the late summer/early fall of 1272. O'Callaghan, *The Learned King*, 195–96.

Chapter 17

*How King Alfonso Asked the King of France
to Give His Daughter as the Wife of His Son
Don Fernando, and of How the Empress of
Constantinople Came to the King's Court to
Petition King Alfonso to Free Her Husband,
the Emperor, Who Was Captive*

In the fifteenth year of his reign, which was in the Era of 1305, and
the year 1267 after the birth of Jesus Christ, this King Alfonso, seeing that Prince Fernando, his son and heir, was of age for having a
wife, while in Toledo sent messengers to Saint Louis, King of France,
asking him to give him the hand of his daughter doña Blanca so
that she might marry his son Prince Fernando.[1] This doña Blanca
was the daughter of Saint Louis and sister of don Felipe, and in the
year here cited, Saint Louis was yet alive, as he died in the year of
our Lord 1270. The messengers having been sent, King Alfonso
went to Burgos and from there to Vitoria to meet with the King of
England and with the queen, Alfonso's sister.[2] However, they sent
to tell him that they could not meet with him, so he tarried in
those lands for a few days and then returned to Burgos, where his
nephew Edward, son and heir to the King of England, came to
meet him.

Being in that city, Alfonso heard that an empress from
Constantinople whose husband was captive in the land of the Sultan was coming to see him,[3] and with her came thirty ladies-in-
waiting, all dressed in black. King Alfonso came out to welcome
her with a large number of people and did her great honor. In
Burgos, he had her stay in his dwelling with Queen Violante, his
wife, and the queen did her great honor and was very pleased with
her. She ordered the table set so that she and the empress might

dine. The queen told the empress to sit at the table to eat. The empress told her that God would never order her to sit at table with her. The queen marveled at what she said and asked why she said that. The empress said: "You have your honor, and may God preserve you in it, because you are in your own land, with your lord safe and sound. May God protect him and keep him from harm! I am away from my land, and my lord is not in his right, for he is captive in the land of the Sultan, and his ransom is set at fifty quintals of silver. I went to the house of the Pope of Rome to see if I could find help in him, and he gave me a third of this amount. I went as well to the King of France, and he gave me another third. There I heard tell of the nobility and goodness and generosity that there is in your lord, so I have come here to ask his help to free my husband, the emperor, from captivity, and until I have an answer in this, I shall not eat." Queen Violante sent for King Alfonso and told him everything the empress had said. The king entreated the empress to sit and eat, and she answered that she would never eat from a tablecloth until she had enough to free her husband the emperor. The king asked her: "Why don't the people of your land free him?" She replied that it was customary that they give nothing for him, for her people said that they were doing much by not taking another emperor while he lived. The king took her hand and seated her at the table and told the empress: "Eat, for I promise you that twenty days from now, I shall give you the wherewithal to free your husband." And she said: "Consider what you are saying, King, for you know not the price of his prison." The king asked her what sum was set, and she said it was fifty quintals of silver but that the King of France had given her one third and the pope another third. King Alfonso took the empress by the hand and went to seat her at the table, and he gave her his hand, promising her that in twenty days he would give her the fifty quintals of silver. The empress said: "Now shall I eat from a covered table, for my lord is free." Twenty days later, the king gave her the fifty quintals of silver, and he ordered her to give back what she had taken from the pope and the King of France, and she returned what was theirs, telling them how it happened with King Alfonso. All of those who heard it greatly esteemed this King of Castile. And when this emperor emerged from captivity he proclaimed the kindness and nobility of King Don Alfonso. This tale having spread through all countries, it happened that the Emperor of Germany died and the electors came together to decide whom they would make emperor. Amid dispute, some of them elected King Alfonso as emperor and agreed to send for him to come and receive the empire.[4] But although this was to the great and good repute of King Alfonso in other lands, this and other matters the king did brought great impoverishment to the kingdoms of Castile and León.

Notes

1. A pact providing for the marriage of Infante Fernando de la Cerda and Blanche, the daughter of Louis IX of France, was concluded on September 28, 1266. The marriage was solemnized on November 30, 1269, during the Cortes of Burgos. Louis IX died on August 25, 1270. O'Callaghan, *The Learned King*, 76, 237.

2. The future Edward II, the son of Alfonso X's sister Leonor and Edward I of England, came to the Cortes of Burgos in 1269, where the king knighted him. O'Callaghan, *The Learned King*, 65.

3. Marie de Brienne, Empress of Constantinople, came to Castile in 1258 to seek help in securing the release of her son Philip of Courtenay, held by the Venetians as a pledge for the repayment of a loan made to the Emperor Baldwin II. O'Callaghan, *The Learned King*, 204–05.

4. Richard of Cornwall was elected Holy Roman Emperor on January 13, 1257, and Alfonso X on April 1. O'Callaghan, *The Learned King*, 200–202.

Chapter 18

*How the King of France, Saint Louis, Sent His
Daughter to the King's Son Prince Fernando
to be Married, and How Messengers from
the German Empire Came to the King*

In the sixteenth year of the reign of this King Alfonso, which was in
the Era of 1306, and the year 1268 after the birth of Jesus Christ,
the King of France sent doña Blanca, his daughter, to Castile in
order to wed Prince Fernando, the king's first-born son and heir.
With her came don Felipe, her brother, who later was King of France
and was father of Felipe el Bel.[1] Likewise with her came prelates
and counts and nobles from the kingdom of France. King Alfonso,
who was in Burgos, left as soon as he learned of the arrival of these
people and went to welcome them in Logroño. With him went his
nephew Edward, son and heir of the King of England, who had come
to be knighted by King Alfonso, and Prince Pedro, brother of Queen
Violante, who later was King of Aragón. Likewise, Princes Fadrique,
Manuel, and Felipe, his brothers; and Princes Fernando, Sancho,
Pedro, Juan, and Jaime, his sons; and Prince Sancho (of Aragón),
Archbishop of Toledo, came, as well as many prelates and lords and
gentry of the kingdom. Then from Logroño they all came to Burgos,
and many people from both within and without the realm came
together there and celebrated with many festivities.

Before the wedding, King Alfonso knighted his nephew Edward, who was later King of England. Also, Edward knighted counts,
dukes, and other high-born men who had come with him from the
kingdom of England and the Duchy of Guienne. On the day that
Prince Fernando was to be wed, Princes Juan and Pedro, Fernando's
brothers, along with many other nobles and knights of Castile and
León, counts and dukes from France, and other gentlefolk of that

land who had come there, received knighthood from him. After they were knighted, Princes Juan and Pedro knighted others. King Alfonso wanted Prince Sancho to receive knighthood from his brother Fernando that day, but Sancho, as soon as he learned of this, refused to wait in the king's house and went to the house of Prince Pedro of Aragón, his uncle. The Marquis of Monferrand, who was married to Alfonso's daughter Beatriz, and whose daughter later married Prince Juan, also came to the wedding.[2]

The Emperor of Germany had died at about this time,[3] and the electors of the empire could not agree on a new emperor from the land of Germany. Because King Alfonso was renowned in all the lands of the world for his greatness, kindness, and generosity, while he was in the city of Burgos messengers came from the counts and dukes and other people of Germany saying that they had elected him. They had been sent to tell him that, knowing of his great nobility, some of the electors had chosen him as Emperor of Germany and that he should go and claim the empire, since many were ready to receive him as emperor. The pope, too, sent his letters about this, assuring him of this fact. King Alfonso, having heard these messages, spoke with the princes—his brothers and his sons— and with all the nobles who were there with him and made a positive reply to the messengers, which pleased them. Then he rewarded them liberally from his wealth and sent them off. Afterward, he consulted with those closest to him concerning how he would go to the empire. To remedy this difficulty, the king requested from those of his land, until the matter of the empire could be concluded, that they grant him each year two sums of money in addition to the tributes and taxes they had to give. All the great lords and nobles, knights and councils of the cities and towns of the realm approved this.

At these wedding festivities and ceremonies of knighthood, those personages dwelt a great part of the year in the city of Burgos, and King Alfonso incurred great expenses maintaining those of his realm while they lived there; and many robes and many horses and all manner of other things he gave in great measure from his fortune to all those departing who had come from outside of the kingdom.

While King Alfonso was in the city of Burgos, Nuño de Lara and Lope Díaz, son of don Diego, made pacts of friendship and acted covertly against Alfonso. During this time, they assembled all the best friends they could get and went to San Andrés de Arroyo, where they married don Lope Díaz to Prince Alfonso de Molina's daughter doña Juana, the king's first cousin, who was there at the monastery.[4] Although Alfonso found out about it, he did not see the disservice that came to him later, nor did he make them think they should be wary of him, since he had need of them in the war with the Moors and for the matter of the empire. And because they told him that the King of Granada wanted to move against him—particularly, that he had begun to cause harm and damage to the chiefs who were in his service—King Alfonso departed from Burgos and went to Seville. With him went Princes Fernando, Manuel, Fadrique, and Felipe, and don Nuño, don Lope Díaz de Haro, don Esteban de Castro, and other great lords. Now the *History* will tell the events that took place in this city while the king was there.

Notes

1. The wedding of Blanche, the daughter of Louis IX of France, and Fernando de la Cerda took place at Burgos on November 30, 1269. Her brother, the future Philip III, attended as did the future Edward II of England. O'Callaghan, *The Learned King*, 65, 76, 237.

2. William, Marquis of Montferrat, married Alfonso X's daughter Beatriz at Murcia in August 1271. The marquis's daughter Margaret was betrothed to Infante Juan. O'Callaghan, *The Learned King*, 210–11.

3. When the *Chronicle* speaks of the death of the German Emperor, that was probably Richard of Cornwall, Alfonso X's rival for the Holy Roman Empire, who died in April 1272, rather than William of Holland, whose death in 1256 resulted in the double election of 1257. O'Callaghan, *The Learned King*, 222.

4. Lope Díaz de Haro, the son of Diego López de Haro, and Lord of Vizcaya, married Juana, the daughter of Alfonso X's uncle Infante Alfonso de Molina.

Chapter 19

How King Alfonso Gained Cáliz, and of How
He Removed the Tribute That Portugal Gave
to Castile, and of What Grew Out of This

In the seventeenth year of the reign of this King Alfonso, which was in the Era of 1307, and the year 1269 after the birth of Jesus Christ, while the king was in Seville, he found out that in the town of Cáliz,[1] which is a harbor on the other side of the sea, the people were so confident that they never guarded the town's gates during the day, nor did they close them at night. The king was told that if he sent the fleet with his men, they would capture that town of Cáliz. So the king had his fleet prepared during this time, and its admiral was Pedro Martínez de Fe. Also with the king was a nobleman, his vassal, whom they called don Juan García. The king ordered don Juan García and Pedro Martínez, his admiral, and other knights and squires to board the fleet and to capture the town of Cáliz. So don Juan García and Pedro Martínez and the others whom the king sent with them went on that fleet, and in one day, at dawn, they arrived at the port of Cáliz. Because the people were confident and had the town's gates opened at night, the Christians captured the town. At the entrance they killed some Moors, and more would have died if they had not cared to flee; none cared to defend it. The Christians captured the wall's towers and the town's gates, and don Juan García entered the town and ordered them to capture the fortresses and to station very strong guards at the gates, and he forbade that they steal or seize anything that was in that town. Pedro Martínez, the admiral, remained on guard with all the sailors, and don Juan García and those who stayed with him took possession of the town and had it under their power for four days. In spite of don Juan García's order, during these four days, they took whatever they wanted from it, for there were many goods, and gold and silver, and other things of very great value, and they put them on the ships and galleys. Learning that all of the land was uniting and that a very large number of Moors was assembling to come there by sea and land, and knowing they had their own support very far away, they departed from the town. They brought from there many Moors and everything they wanted to bring, and they came to Seville without any conflict. And King Alfonso, as soon as he knew of this, was very pleased.

While he was there in this city, don Deonis, son of King Afonso of Portugal and grandson of this King of Castile, came there.[2] This prince was young in age—twelve or thirteen years old—and very handsome, and he requested from King Alfonso, his grandfather, the favor of making him a knight. Because this prince was the king's grandson—and also because other princes, heirs of kingdoms, had come to receive knighthood from him—King Alfonso was very pleased with him and with his coming, and he did him much honor, and also did him much honor with his knighthood. As soon as this happened, the prince spoke apart with his grandfather and asked him for the favor of removing the tribute that the kings of Portugal were obliged to make to the King of León, namely, that they were to come to his help every time he asked them and also to give him some cavalry each time that the king went to war with the Moors. King Alfonso said that he could not do it on his own, but that he would have the princes and noblemen who were there with him called, and would speak about it before them, and that if they were to advise it, he would gladly do it. The next day, King Alfonso ordered summoned Princes Manuel, Felipe, and Fadrique, his brothers; and he also had don Nuño de Lara, son of Count Don Gonzalo, and don Lope Díaz de Haro, don Esteban de Castro, and other noblemen and knights who were with him there. He ordered Prince Deonis, his grandson, to tell them the request he had told him, and because Deonis was young and had no embarrassment when he was telling the request, King Alfonso ordered him to be seated like the other princes who were at his feet on the dais. The king ordered a nobleman of Portugal who came with Prince Deonis to request it on his behalf. The nobleman began his plea in this fashion: "Lord, the Prince of Portugal came to you on the one hand, in order to see you and because of the family ties he has with

you, for he is your grandson; and also, he came to receive knighthood from you because you are the noblest king that there is in
the world. And notwithstanding that, Lord, other princes, sons of
kings, came to receive knighthood from you and you did much
favor and honor to them; but Lord, because of the family ties the
prince has with you, you should more fully favor and honor him
than any of the others. And Lord, the favor he requests from you is
that you consider it good to remove from King Afonso, his father,
and from Prince Deonis—from the time he rules until his days are
over, and from others who will rule after them in Portugal—the
tribute that they are obliged by you to pay on behalf of the kingdom of Portugal to you, Lord, who are King of Castile and León.
And although he requests acquittance and favor from you now so
that men can see your disposition toward the prince and do him
honor and good because of the family ties he has with you, nonetheless Lord, you shall always have King Afonso, don Deonis, and
the kings who shall come later at your support and for your honor."
     Once the plea of the Prince Deonis had come there and was
told, King Alfonso ordered the princes and noblemen of his council who were with him there to speak to him and advise him about
what he should do about this. But all of them were silent, and they
were a long time without saying anything. The king again asked
them why they did not answer to the plea that was spoken by the
prince and became angry with all of them; but he showed more
anger against don Nuño than against any of the others who were
there. So don Nuño on this account rose to his feet and said: "Lord,
I held back from giving you my advice about this for a good reason. For the princes—your brothers—who are here and don Lope
Díaz de Haro and don Esteban should tell you first what is best for
your service; but Lord, since you consider it well that I answer you
about this, I shall do it, Lord. That you do much honor and much
good to Prince Deonis, your grandson, giving him whatever it is
from your fortune, and many gifts, and many horses, is very just,
and you should do it because of the family ties he has with you and
because he came to be your knight. And even if your help in whatever is necessary is sufficient, you are obliged to do the same for
him and for his honor as if he were one of your sons. But Lord,
that you take away from the Crown of your kingdoms the tribute
that the King of Portugal and his kingdom are obliged to give to

you, I shall never advise you." As soon as don Nuño said this, King Alfonso showed that what don Nuño said did not please him, and the king ordered the others to speak. And don Nuño left the meeting and went from the palace.

Realizing how the king was angered by what don Nuño had said, Prince Manuel and all others who were there told the king how the tribute that the King of Portugal and his kingdom had to make to the King of León was very small, and that because Prince Deonis had such great family ties the king should do more for him than this, and that if he did not it would not be a good thing. In regard to this, the others who were there told the king that he had cause to grant the prince what he was requesting. Thus, the king granted it to him and ordered him given his charter. And he gave him from his gifts what he considered as good. The prince then departed from Seville and went to Portugal, and King Alfonso remained in Seville. While he was in that city, don Nuño and don Lope Díaz and don Esteban criticized what the king was doing, saying that it would be best not to consent to them and that because he was going to the kingdom of Murcia, they should go to Castile and do something about it so that these things could not happen in such a fashion.

Later, messengers from King Aben Yuzaf came from beyond the sea about the issue of the seizures that don Juan García and those who went with him made during their entry into Cáliz. The king gave them a good answer, but they delayed a while, and they did not have their freedom, because two knights—one named Serpia and the other, Pero Núñez—were prisoners beyond the sea. Aben Yuzaf had ordered them imprisoned because they said they wanted to enter Tremecén in support of Gomarazán.³ Don Nuño spoke with these messengers of King Aben Yuzaf to see if he could have those knights freed, and the messengers said that Aben Yuzaf would do whatever they were sent to demand from him concerning this. So don Nuño sent him his letter concerning this, and the messengers sent word to Aben Yuzaf, telling him they had realized that there was disagreement between King Alfonso and his nobles and that if he sent his letters to the knights, they believed he would have them at his service. The king departed from Seville to go to the kingdom of Murcia,⁴ and Prince Fadrique went with him while Prince Fernando and Prince Manuel remained in Seville; and

Prince Felipe, don Nuño, don Lope Díaz, and don Esteban came to Castile. King Alfonso went to the kingdom of Murcia through Villa Real, and Prince Felipe, don Nuño, don Lope Díaz, and don Esteban went with him that far. There, don Nuño spoke to the king and to don Pero Lorenzo, Bishop of Cuenca, who was also there, and don Nuño told King Alfonso that never had he such willingness to serve the king as he had then and that he asked a favor: not to believe anything they said about him. Then he took leave of the king, and Prince Felipe, don Lope Díaz, and don Esteban did the same, and they departed from there and went to Castile. And the king departed from Villa Real and went to the kingdom of Murcia. Henceforth, the *History* will relate the other things and how they happened.

Notes

1. The chronicler has confused Cádiz (spelled Caliz in the text) with Salé, a port on the North African coast, plundered by a Castilian fleet in September 1260, commanded by the magnate Juan García de Villamayor, whom the king had named as *adelantado de la mar,* or admiral, and Pedro Martínez de Fe. O'Callaghan, *The Learned King,* 172–74.

2. Dinis (Deonis in the *Chronicle*), heir to the throne of Portugal, was the son of Alfonso X's illegitimate daughter Beatriz and Afonso III. He probably visited Seville in late 1266 or early 1267. O'Callaghan, *The Learned King,* 160–61.

3. Yagmurâsan b. Zayyân (Gomarazán in the *Chronicle*), the ruler of Tlemcen (Tremecén) in Morocco, was a chief rival of Abû Yûsuf, the emir of the Benimerines.

4. Alfonso X went to Murcia in February 1271. O'Callaghan, *The Learned King,* 195.

Chapter 20

❖

How Prince Felipe Began to Have Meetings and
Agreements with the Noblemen Against the King,
and of What They Sent to Tell the King

In the eighteenth year of the reign of this King Alfonso, which was in the Era of 1308, and the year 1270 after the birth of Jesus Christ, since King Alfonso had gone to the kingdom of Murcia, Prince Felipe and don Nuño, and many noblemen and knights, and those of noble descent, and all others got together in Lerma and made a pact and agreement: to assist each other in opposing King Alfonso,[1] harming him however they could if he did not grant and fulfill to them the things they would go and demand (which we will relate further along). Notwithstanding that some of them had sent their letters to the King of Granada, they determined there, because the King of Navarre was also in disagreement with King Alfonso of Castile,[2] that Prince Felipe should go to meet with him (Alfonso). They also determined that if they found in King Alfonso what was convenient to them, it would be best for all to go to him and not to the King of Granada. One reason was that they were closer to his lands, and the other, in order not to embolden the Moors, who through their efforts might come to harm the Christians. They agreed that meanwhile they might assure King Alfonso in this fashion so that they could sign these treaties before he might return from the kingdom of Murcia. For this reason don Esteban Fernández, as soon as King Alfonso departed from there, went to him, taking care to reach an agreement with him so that he give him doña Aldonza Rodríguez, granddaughter of the King of León, to whom don Esteban said he was betrothed.[3] The king answered him that notwithstanding that this doña Aldonza Rodríguez was related to him, for her brothers and parents had given her to him, if don Esteban was engaged to her, he should ask the Holy Church for her, and if approved, it would please King Alfonso to give her to him. But don Esteban Fernández was not pleased with this answer and said that he desired to go to Galicia. The king, having suspicions about that meeting, ordered him to abandon his trip to Galicia and to go and wait for him in Toledo, where the queen and the Princes Sancho, Juan, Pedro, and Jaime were.

Also, Prince Felipe, after he departed from there to win over King Alfonso, had him told through his letters that don Fernán Ruiz de Castro wanted to take away his wife, who was the sister of that don Fernando Ruiz and heiress of Santa Olalla and other regions that she expected to inherit from Queen Mencía of Portugal,[4] whom they called de Paredes. Prince Felipe did this with the support of the noblemen who met there, and for this reason he had to come to that meeting, and he asked the king to consider it and not allow it. Also don Nuño, in order to assure King Alfonso, sent two knights, his vassals, to him—one of them named Pero Ruiz de Villegas and the other Garcí Prieto—sending them to tell Alfonso that it was their will to serve him faithfully. The king, thinking that it was so, sent to thank them; but people from so many regions sent to warn him, telling him that the meeting was for his great harm and great disservice, that the king immediately sent his letters and his messenger, who was Fernán Pérez, Dean of Seville,[5] to Prince Felipe. Through this messenger Alfonso informed Felipe that he was certain that the King of Granada had sent for his tribes of Moors and for other Moors beyond the sea to wage war against him; he begged Prince Felipe to come to him immediately, for he had been told that Felipe and the noblemen of his kingdom were united in Lerma with don Nuño González and that they made pacts of which he knew nothing, and he begged him to send along with that dean what their meeting and pacts were all about. Prince Felipe sent to tell him that he could not go to him, because the monies that he had from him, from the land, were not paid. Concerning the meeting the noblemen had with him, he answered in this fashion: that King Alfonso knew well that the friends he had until then were don Juan García, don Alfonso Téllez, don Juan Alfonso, and don Rodrigo Flórez,[6] in whom he had very great trust because of the many good things he had done for them; and that because they were deceased, he could find himself without any friends who might help him and advise him, and that this was the reason why he had come to that meeting. The Prince gave the messenger other such reasons from which he was able to gather what kind of agreements they had made among themselves.

Dean Fernán Pérez went to don Nuño and don Lope Díaz and spoke with them, but they denied that they had any agreements. He had King Alfonso told everything, and in order to know more about this matter, he remained in Castile. As soon as Alfonso knew Prince Felipe's answer, and likewise how matters were, he wanted to come immediately to correct matters that were at hazard in the kingdom of Murcia on account of the many Moors who were settled there. Also, because of the war he wanted to wage against the King of Granada, and keeping in mind that those men would not attempt to do anything against his service, King Alfonso sent don Enrique Pérez de Arana to Castile,[7] making sure to show that he sent him to speak on his behalf with don Lope Díaz and to grant a truce to Diego López de Salcedo, whom he considered untrustworthy in the king's court that he held in Castile.[8] Alfonso ordered him to speak secretly with don Nuño and to tell him that notwithstanding it was difficult for him to believe what he had been told, he could not forgive him for the things he was hearing from everyone: that he was doing to the king's disservice and the diminishment of his honor. And that because he thought that no other man should do more to protect the king's affairs than don Nuño, that he was surprised about what they told him, and that it seemed to him so unreasonable he could not believe; it notwithstanding that Prince Fernando, his son, had sent to tell him that don Nuño sent him to express some complaints about King Alfonso, and he considered strange that he had complained to his son or somebody else and not to the king.

And that notwithstanding that don Nuño had communicated through his messengers that he was truly at the king's service, Alfonso knew he had had discussions and meetings with all the noblemen and many knights who were against the king because of the wrongs and downright injustices they said he was doing to them; and that don Nuño could not do more against law, since in that lay disinheritance, and that all other evil could come to him, and that he was surprised that he promoted such uproar among his kingdoms and their inhabitants, encouraging enmity between them and him, and that he erred much in this, the king having done to him all the good he had done him. And that if don Nuño had done some wrong to him in the marriage of don Lope Díaz, he should correct it with service so that the king might forget the dissension rather than do something to increase it. And that if don Nuño was doing this in order to frighten the king, he should know that wrongfully and pridefully one ought not to be afraid, but instead one should make an effort to put an end to it. And that if he did it in order to have more goods than he already had, by serving the king he could quickly gain more. And that if he did it to please some other kingdom, he should know well that he would not receive from anyone as much good and as much assistance as from the king, and that for none of these reasons, nor any other, should he do such wrong against the king; and that Alfonso begged him as friend and ordered him as a vassal to soften his heart and serve him as he had done before.

As soon as Enrique Pérez arrived in Castile, he found out that don Nuño was in Palenzuela. So he went to don Nuño and found out that don Simón Ruiz de los Cameros, and don Lope Díaz, Lord of Vizcaya, and don Fernán Ruiz de Castro were there. Since don Nuño had heard the message, he was somewhat displeased on account of it, fearing that some harm and evil would come from the king for this reason. In order to reassure the king, don Nuño said that it was true that he had sent to tell Prince Fernando that he was lacking some of the *maravedís* that he used to get from the king, but he had not had any other meeting nor agreement against his service. If the king wanted to order another service to those that were ordered in Castile or Extremadura, it pleased don Nuño and those noblemen who were there, and from that service King Alfonso should order them all to pay their debts as to what they received from him in granted land; with this they would satisfy the councils of some of those who were unhappy. This don Nuño said for two reasons: one, in order to be able to sow enmity among those of the land, and the other, so that they could have money to be able to do what they had agreed to do. Enrique Pérez had the king told the answer that don Nuño had given him, and later on don Nuño sent his messengers to the king, who were Garcí Prieto and Garcí Gómez Carrillo,[9] by whom he had him told many excuses about the things don Enrique Pérez de Arana had said on the king's behalf. Likewise, he sent to ask that the king order through letters so that they could pay him some of the sums he was lacking from the land he, don Nuño, had from him. Meanwhile, he gathered as many men as he could to harm and do disservice to the king.

While King Alfonso was in the kingdom of Murcia populating the land and building and repairing the castles, don Nuño's messengers returned to him with the answer concerning that for which they went. While the king was verifying their excuses, many letters from many regions of Castile and León reached him, telling the king that don Nuño and his sons, don Juan Núñez and Nuño González, were fortifying themselves against him, and that they were making pacts and allegiances with some noblemen, particularly with don Lope Díaz de Haro; don Esteban Fernández; don Nuño Ruiz de los Cameros[10]; don Fernán Ruiz de Castro; Álvar Díaz de Asturias; Diego López, don Diego's son; Fernán González de Saldaña; Fernán Ruiz, son of Rodrigo Álvarez; Gil González de Roa[11]; Lope de Mendoza; Juan García; and other knights. They sent to ask for King Alfonso's favor and advise him to come to Castile to calm these noblemen and said he should know that all of these treaties were being made to his great harm and disservice. For this reason the king departed from the kingdom of Murcia in order to go to Castile. Henceforth, we will continue relating other matters and how they occurred.

Notes

Part II of the *Chronicle,* according to Procter, begins with chapter 20.

1. The assembly of nobles at Lerma took place in 1271. O'Callaghan, *The Learned King,* 77–80.

2. Henry I (1270–1274), King of Navarre.

3. Esteban Fernández de Castro wished to marry Aldonza Rodríguez, the daughter of Rodrigo Alfonso, an illegitimate son of Alfonso IX of León (1188–1230).

4. Mencía López de Haro was the widow of King Sancho II of Portugal.

5. Pope Alexander IV confirmed Fernán Pérez as Dean of Seville on January 29, 1255.

6. Juan García de Villamayor, Alfonso Téllez de Meneses, Juan Alfonso, and Rodrigo Froilaz (Flórez in the *Chronicle*) were all magnates.

7. Enrique Pérez de Arana was the royal *respostero mayor,* or butler.

8. Diego López de Salcedo was *adelantado mayor,* or governor, of the Basque provinces of Álava and Guipúzcoa.

9. Garcí Gómez Carrillo, one of Nuño's envoys, was likely the same person whom Nuño had left to defend Jerez in chapter 10.

10. For Nuño, read Simón Ruiz de los Cameros.

11. Fernán González de Saldaña, Gil Gómez (not González as in the *Chronicle*) de Roa, and Lope de Mendoza were all leading magnates.

Chapter 21

How Juan Alfonso Carrillo Came to King Alfonso with Letters from Don Nuño and the Noblemen in Which They Excused Themselves from What Others Were Telling About Them

In the nineteenth year of the reign of this King Alfonso, which was in the Era of 1309, and the year 1271 after the birth of Jesus Christ,[1] the king was getting ready to go to Castile because of those letters sent to him. Juan Alfonso Carrillo came to him there with letters from don Nuño, don Jimeno Ruiz, don Lope Díaz, and don Fernán Ruiz de Castro in which they asked him, by his grace, to do what he had said on their behalf. And as for their credence, Carrillo told the king that these noblemen and all of those from Castile and León had granted him their service and that they had never made an oath or pact against the king with the Moors nor with the Christians that might do disservice against him. And also, that at no time had they served him in better fashion than then, and that they asked his favor to order the granting of their sums as payment for the properties they had from him. They said that if the king needed them for his service to wage war against the King of Granada, he should have them summoned and they would immediately come to his service against the Moors or against the Christians whenever he ordered them to do so. They also said that if he did not need them now for the war against the Moors, to have them told if he wanted them to go somewhere else, for they would be available. Since the king heard what Juan Alfonso Carrillo told him on behalf of the noblemen, he took counsel with the queen, who was with him there; and with Prince Fadrique, his brother; and with the bishops of Córdoba and Cáliz[2]; and from Juan

González, Master of Calatrava[3]; and don Día Sánchez de Frias[4] and don Enrique Pérez de Aranas; and from the Archdeacon Don Juan Alfonso,[5] appointed in the Church of Santiago; and don Gregorio Yáñez de Aguilar[6]; and Master Gonzalo, Archdeacon of Toledo,[7] Notary of Castile; and from don Jofré de Loaysa.[8] King Alfonso, having sought advice from them, trusting what the noblemen had him told in regard to the services they were promising him, ordered don Gómez de Monzón and don Sancho Pérez, who were the collectors of rents for all the kingdoms, to go, and take, and collect that sum of money. He sent don Pero Lorencio, Bishop of Cuenca, to the noblemen to speak with them and to tell them that if he granted those things that Juan Alfonso Carrillo had said on their behalf, exempting them from the sums they had from him, for he did not need them for the war against the Moors then, that he thought that now, with those sums he then ordered given them, some of them would prepare to go with him to the empire where he wanted to go, and the others would stay to serve Prince Fernando however he might need them. The bishop went to Prince Felipe, who had returned from the meetings in Navarre, and to the other noblemen. They granted everything Juan Alfonso Carrillo had promised the king on their behalf. So Juan Alfonso Carrillo, don Gómez, and Sancho Pérez collected the sum of money and gave them all their money. After the prince and the noblemen had collected the sum that the king ordered given them, they divided it among their vassals, and they gathered as many men as they could have as knights. With those sums they supplied themselves with weapons and horses, and many of them wandered throughout the land and seized food from many places they should not have, and they did great damage in the land. Then they sent their messengers to the King of Granada and to the King of Morocco, and they also sent letters to the King of Portugal, in order to encourage them to wage war on Castile. Prince Felipe once again went to have meetings with the King of Navarre so that he could make firm with him the things that were being discussed. And henceforth, the *History* ceases here to relate what Prince Felipe and the noblemen were doing and will relate what the king did after he ordered them given the sums.

Notes

1. These events occurred in late 1271 and early 1272. O'Callaghan, *The Learned King*, 214–15.

2. Fernando de Mesa, Bishop of Córdoba (1257–1274) and Fray Juan Martínez, Bishop of Cádiz (1267–1278).

3. Juan González was Master of the Order of Calatrava from 1267 to 1284.

4. Dia Sánchez de Funes (Frias in the *Chronicle*) was *adelantado mayor de la frontera*, or governor of the Andalusian frontier.

5. Juan Alfonso, Archdeacon and Archbishop-Elect of Santiago, never became archbishop, as the pope appointed Gonzalo García in 1272.

6. Gregorio (correctly, *Gonzalo*) Yáñez de Aguilar, a noble and a poet.

7. Master Gonzalo García Gudiel, Archdeacon of Toledo and notary for Castile, became Bishop of Burgos and then Archbishop of Toledo (1280–1299).

8. Jofré de Loaysa, an Aragonese, had served as tutor to Queen Violante.

Chapter 22

❖

How King Alfonso, While Wanting to Depart
for the Empire, Received Letters Written in Arabic,
Which Are Found in This Chapter

After King Alfonso, as the *History* has narrated, had sent the bishop to his noblemen, he wanted to meet with the King of Granada and appease him while he went to Castile to win over those noblemen and prepare the journey to the empire. The King of Granada had Alfonso told to come and meet with him in the city of Jaén. Therefore, King Alfonso departed from Murcia to go to the meeting; and being in Alcaraz,[1] letters from Prince Fernando and from Prince Manuel, who were in Seville, arrived in which they had King Alfonso told that a large army of Moors, which the King of Granada had sent for, had crossed from beyond the sea and had overrun the territory and killed and captured many men. They had attacked the castle of Béjar and seized from there cattle and everything else they found. Therefore, King Alfonso had all of those from the border ordered to wage war on the King of Granada; and because he was aware of what the noblemen were doing in the land, from there he went to Huepte in order to go to Castile. From there he sent letters to Prince Felipe and to don Nuño, and to don Lope Díaz, and to don Jimeno Ruiz, and to don Esteban Fernández, and to Fernán Ruiz de Castro, and to all of the noblemen of Castile and León, in which he had them told how the Moors were waging war against him, and that he ordered and begged them to go immediately to succor and serve Prince Fernando, who was at the border. Prince Felipe and the noblemen had him told through their letters that they could not go immediately to the border, but that all of them as one, and with their vassals, would go to Alfonso and speak with him about some things they had to tell him. The king being in Cuenca, a Jew whom they called Aben Nazar came there and told Alfonso that don Nuño sent him to advise the king to go to Castile, and that it would be to his service and great advantage. But the king refused to believe it, since it was being said by that Jew. A day later, a cleric from the Church of Burgos named Pedro Jaime came and brought another letter of credence from don Nuño and told him the very same thing. So King Alfonso departed from Cuenca and returned to Huepte, and while being there, Fernán Gudiel de Toledo came to him and brought letters in Arabic that he had seized from Lorencio Rodríguez, don Nuño's squire, who had carried them. Alfonso Pérez de Toledo and Vasco Gómez translated them, and they said as follows:[2]

"In the name of God, the holy and merciful, and of King Aben Yuzaf, the Elder of the Moroccans, profuse and elegant greetings to the son of King Fernando, the illustrious monarch recognized in blessings and in all good qualities, and truthful in speech. This letter is from Ali Aben Yuzaf, the King of Morocco. May God grant you goodness over and above what I, by rights, should grant you. My messengers made it known to me that all the noblemen met with you so that you might help them to take away the wrongs which he [Alfonso], your brother, is doing to them. And this pleases me, because the wrong deserves righting, and the towns and vassals should not consent to it. It is well that you are helping to reveal their right and to remove the wrong he is doing them. And I desire to have you know how much I love you, and that if from me you have need of money or men or knights or weapons, I am able to help you, if God wills it. And what I want from you is for you to write, with your trusted messenger, everything you want, God willing, as to what you wish. And I beg you heed the greetings of my messengers upon whom God's mercy is."

Letter by Abdiluait, son of Aben Yuzaf, for don Felipe:

"May God grant you over and above what I, for justice's sake, should grant you. Know that my father, Aben Yuzaf, my brother, and I love you and await your letter, since the honorable king wrote you. Write everything you want, and if you want land, or goods, or men; all of this shall reach you safely, and for God's sake; let my messengers be heeded, and that you send to tell everything you want, because my father wants to cross there to

Andalusia and is awaiting your letter, in the name of God, the answer. And I am letting you know that I am holding Pero Núñez and Serpia as prisoners, for they wanted to do me treason and go to Gomarazán.³ I forgave Pero Núñez. And I send my greetings to you, and God's mercy over you."

Letter of Aben Yuzaf:

"Don Nuño, you should be aware that your letters reached me, and I was pleased with them. And I marvel at your nobleness and at how you outdo your kindness. And my messenger made known to me that you have complaints against don Alfonso, who required wrong claims and who took from you false sums, and who broke the good statute you used before, for your estates decreased and things increased in price, and destroyed the markets. And that he did not do a good deed to your son, whom he exiled from the land for treason; and all of this grieved me. I beg you to send your son, and I shall place him with my son Abdiluait in Morocco, and I shall appoint your son King of the Christians and Lord of the armies. And if you do not send me don Juan Núñez, send me one of your sons, and I shall place him in my son's place. And this I am telling you because I love you, and do not expect anything belonging to Alfonso, for I, if God is willing, shall give you ten times as much love as the love of Alfonso. And do instruct me to send you funds, or horses, or safe passage, or whatever you want to let me know, and I shall send it to you and it shall reach you safely. And I quickly let you know that my son Yuzaf is in Tremecén, and that I have in my power Serpia, the knight, but that I gave Pero Núñez his freedom because he said he was your relative. And send me an answer as quickly as possible, for I have all my armies at sea, and I await your answer about everything."

Letter from Abdiluait for don Nuño, asking him to send one of his sons, and to let him know what he wants from beyond the sea, and that he shall send it to him, and that he wants him to know that Aben Yuzaf wants to cross hither.

Letter from Aben Yuzaf for don Lope Díaz:

"It has come to me by word from my messengers that the King of Castile required much from you, and tricked you and cheapened the currency, and that all of you are joining don Felipe until he rectifies the coinage and corrects the damage to hearts and wills. I love you and wish to speak with you through my letters. And whatever you want of my money, or men, or horses, have it requested from me in writing. And write from there so that everything will reach you. And I want you to send your letter quickly by whatever messenger, and for God's sake, the answer concerning where the crossing will take place before I cross over."

Letter of Abdiluait, son of Aben Yuzaf, to don Lope Díaz concerning the very same thing, and in which he finally says that he begs him not to have him told if it is not true.

Letter from Aben Yuzaf to Jimeno Ruiz, in which he says that he had sent his letter to don Jimeno before he took Morocco, but that after he had it, he did not send it to him. And that he begged him to come to him, and that he shall do whatever he wants, and to let him know what he wants and that he shall give it to him. And he had him told how Yuzaf, his son, had besieged Tremecén, and that Gomarazán was lying imprisoned inside. And that when he had Tremecén, he shall cross over to him.

Letter of Abdiluait for don Jimeno about this affair.

Letter from Yuzaf to don Esteban Fernández, who they told him was in disagreement with King Alfonso, and that he was good and chivalrous, and that he wanted to have his affection, and that if he needed any assistance, to let him know and he shall send it to him. And that if he wanted to come there, that he is awaiting him and that he shall do what Miramamolín never did. And that he wants to go hither completely, and that he would have already gone if don Esteban Fernández were there, who had departed with his son from Morocco.

Letter from Aben Yuzaf to Gil Gómez de Roa, in which he tells how he saw the letter in which he let him know that he wished to do him service. And that he would be grateful, and that if he were to come, he would have him as one of his sons. And that if he wished to serve him in Granada or in Algeciras or beyond the sea, that he will increase his salary twenty times, and that he begs him to send his knights immediately.

Letter from Abdolhat Trigrama to don Jimeno and don Esteban Fernández, in which he tells how much Aben Yuzaf and his sons love them, and in which he begs them to do that which Aben Yuzaf requests them to do, and in which he says that he shall give them

whatever they ask for. And that if they immediately send their letter with their credence, the one they know about, that they know
he shall immediately come with all they require. And that they protect his messenger and free him quickly.

King Alfonso, having seen these letters, came to Guadalajara,
and don Juan Núñez, son of don Nuño, came to him there. Don
Juan spoke with the king, warning him about how Prince Felipe
and the noblemen wanted to make a pact with the King of Navarre
against him. In regard to this, Alfonso sent don Juan and the Bishop
of Cuenca on his behalf to tell Prince Felipe and those noblemen
how the King of Navarre was his enemy and the enemy of the whole
kingdom, and that with such a man they should not make a pact of
agreement against their natural lord—they being his vassals and
having from him the rents of his land—and because he gave them
their sums, besides having with them a good friendship as they
knew well. He begged that they would not refuse to do it. Also, he
had the knights, his vassals, and all others who were with them
instructed to consider what they were doing in that matter, for they
knew well that it was against the loyalty to which they were bound
and that they should preserve it. After these messengers were sent,
one of don Nuño's knights, named Diego Ordóñez de Castejón,
came to King Alfonso and he told the king that don Nuño was
sending to ask him for mercy and to advise him to go immediately
to Burgos or Valladolid, and that if he should do so, he would realize that no vassal ever gave better service or advice to his lord. On
that day, a knight, another of don Nuño's vassals, named Lope
Suárez de Fermosilla, arrived with his letter. He told Alfonso that
he knew well how don Nuño had agreements with him, and that
he never made a pact with Christians nor Moors without letting
him know it, and that until that time he would observe this; but
from then on, he wanted to do it. The king, in order to know which
one of these reasons he would consider as truth, immediately sent
his messengers to don Nuño, and they were Gregorio Ruiz de
Atienza and Juan Ruiz de Río Cerezo.[4] Once these messengers were
sent, Nuño Fernández de Valdenebro immediately arrived there
with a letter from don Nuño. He told the king on don Nuño's
behalf that don Nuño was sending him to ask for mercy and to beg
and advise him to come immediately to Castile, and that all the
uproar and evil that were throughout the land would be removed.

And now let us cease to relate this, and we shall relate the answer that Prince Felipe and the noblemen gave to the Bishop of Cuenca and to don Juan Núñez concerning what they told him on the king's behalf.

Notes

1. The king left Murcia on his journey to Burgos, stopping at Alcaraz on June 23, Huepte on July 8, and Cuenca on August 1, 1272. O'Callaghan, *The Learned King,* 214–15.

2. See O'Callaghan, *The Learned King,* 19–20, for a discussion of the letters of Abû Yûsuf and his son 'Abd al-Wâhid. See page 19, note 41, on Fernán Gudiel de Toledo, Alfonso Pérez de Toledo, and Vasco Gómez.

3. Gomarazán, correctly, is Yagmurâsan b. Zayyân, the ruler of Tlemcen (Tremecén) in Morocco.

4. On Gonzalo (Gregorio in the *Chronicle*) Ruiz de Atienza, one of the most active royal messengers (*mandaderos*), see above, page 20, note 43. Juan Ruiz de Río Cerezo is less known.

Chapter 23

※

On the Pacts That Passed Between King Alfonso and the Noblemen of His Kingdoms

Don Juan Núñez, don Nuño's son, and the Bishop of Cuenca went to Prince Felipe and to these noblemen.[1] They spoke with them on King Alfonso's behalf as they had been ordered to do. And Felipe and his noblemen answered them that they had a certain deadline they had to meet with the King of Navarre, and that they would not relinquish going there for any reason. With King Alfonso having come back to Roa,[2] since he was going to Burgos, the Bishop of Cuenca and don Juan Núñez came to him with the answer that Prince Felipe and the noblemen gave. Also, Gregorio Ruiz de Atienza and Juan Ruiz de Río Cerezo came there with the answer for the two messages don Nuño had sent, and they told the king to authorize both. Nuño Fernández de Valdenebro also came there with a command from the prince and from all of the noblemen, in which they sent to tell Alfonso that they had him in their favor because he was coming to Castile, and he should consider it well that he should stop on the way and that all of them would come to him to welcome him as their king and natural lord. For this reason Alfonso spent five days in that town, and from there he went to Tordesandino, and from there to Lerma. While he was hunting along the road with don Fadrique (his brother) and with don Sancho, don Pedro, and don Juan (his sons), don Nuño and don Lope Díaz and don Jimeno Ruiz and don Esteban Fernández and don Álvar Díaz de Asturias, with a large number of mounted men, met him on the road. They all came armed and with a great crowd, and don Felipe did not come there, because he had gone to the King of Navarre. When the king saw that they were coming in such fashion, he considered it very strange, because they were not coming as men who go to their lord but like those who come to look for their enemies. And on this day, the king remained in Lerma, and from there he went to Burgos.

Those armies were telling the king many things and promising him many services. And as soon as he arrived at the city, they refused to enter with him there, and they told him that they would come the next day to settle with him those matters. The king waited for them in the city, and all the noblemen who were in that action came to the wasteland of Burgos and with men on horses and on foot. In the same manner, they sent to tell the king that he should come out and that they would speak with him, for they did not want to enter the city due to the suspicion they had of him. So the king sent don Fadrique and don Luis, his brothers, and the Bishop of Cuenca to them, and through them he entreated the noblemen not to continue that uproar and to come under safeguard to him. But the noblemen refused to do it, and from there they went to the surrounding villages where they were staying, and they had the king told that if he wished to speak with them, to have them told through his messengers.

Because the king's messengers told Alfonso that these noblemen were telling the knights and those of noble descent of the kingdoms that he refused to grant their statutes and their offices and their traditions as they used to have them, to make these knights and nobles understand that it was not like what they were being told, the king agreed to send his messengers with his letters of credence to the vassals of each one of the noblemen. He decided that there were to be two of those of noble descent and someone from the city. To the vassals of don Nuño as messengers: Gonzalo Ruiz de Atienza and Rui Fernández de Cuenca and don Martín de Burgos. And to the vassals of don Lope Díaz the messengers were Juan Ruiz de Río Cerezo and Velasco Jiménez de Ávila and Gil Pérez de Burgos. And to the vassals of don Fernán Ruiz de Castro the messengers were Juan Núñez de Leyva and Fernán Gil de Burgos and Rui Pérez de Sepúlveda. And to the vassals of don Jimeno Ruiz the messengers were Rui González de Agociello and Juan Pérez, a cleric of Burgos. And to the vassals of don Esteban Fernández the messengers were Esteban de Moya and Rui Fernández de Zamora. The king ordered these, his messengers, to tell that if anyone had told them that the king refused to preserve their statutes—which they had during the time of King Alfonso, his grandfather, and in the time of his father, King Fernando—they were not to believe it, for he wanted to have his agreement with them and preserve it for them fully, trusting that they would also preserve the statute and right he had with them. Also, that if some of them had a complaint against him, he wanted to compensate them, and that he would accept as judges those vassals belonging to the noblemen to make clear the statutes of Castile, and that he sent word to them that because they were such judges, they wanted justice and loyalty just like those from whence they had come desired it. He ordered that these things be told to them while all of them were dining with their lords, because at that time they would find them together, and the messengers did it that way.

As soon as the knights heard what the king sent to inform them, they said they would have an agreement and they would send the king their answer along with eight knights. Don Nuño came there, and the king spoke with him before his knights and told him he knew well he had never done anything to him or to the other noblemen by which they should be as upset as they were, and that they were doing him a great wrong. Don Nuño told King Alfonso that Felipe and the noblemen, the knights, and the others of noble descent from Castile perceived themselves to be wronged by the king in some matters, which were these: that the statutes the king had given to some cities in which those of noble descent ruled were oppressive to them and to their vassals and that they had been forced to adopt the statutes; and also that the king did not keep in his court governors from Castile who might judge them. The other reason for which they perceived themselves to be wronged was due to the disputes that the king and his sons received from the noblemen and those of noble descent, because they remained disinherited. The other request they were making of him was that the services, which were authorized, should amount to fewer years and that they be given ordinances that would not demand these services of them, neither by statute nor for a longer period of time. Also, those of noble descent were angry about the tax they were paying in Burgos, called the *alcabala.* Another complaint they had was about the royal judges, collectors, and magistrates, because they said that they were causing them much harm; also that the noblemen and those of noble descent of the kingdoms of León and Galicia were very angry about the towns the king was building in some regions of those kingdoms, because they said that on this account they were losing what they had. They said that if the king corrected these things, all of them would serve him gladly. King Alfonso told them that he wished to reflect on these matters and would send them his answer. And don Nuño went to the other noblemen who were staying in the villages; and henceforth, we will continue relating the other things that took place concerning these matters.

Notes

1. Pedro Lorenzo, Bishop of Cuenca (1261–1272).

2. The king was in Roa on August 27, 1272. From there he went to Tordesandino, Lerma, and reached Burgos in September 1272. He was in Burgos at least until November 4, 1272. O'Callaghan, *The Learned King,* 216–17.

Chapter 24

◾

How King Alfonso, Being in Burgos,
Replied to What the Noblemen
of His Kingdom Were Demanding of Him

The *History* tells that after don Nuño had left Burgos, King Alfonso held a council concerning these demands with don Fadrique and with don Luis, his brothers; the Bishop of Cuenca; Gil García de Sagra; Gutier Suárez; Diego López de Salcedo[1]; and with other knights of noble descent who were with them so that they could come and hear the king's reply at his court or at Santa María de Burgos. But they refused to do it, and instead, they came armed to the wasteland with all of their men. The king went there where they were and gave his reply in this fashion: Concerning the complaint about the law, he responded that those of noble descent could have their laws according to how they had them during the times of other kings, and that if the king had given a law to some city or town bordering their lands, those of noble descent should not be judged by it if they did not wish. To what they said about the governors, he replied to them that despite the fact that he had appointed capable governors, he considered it a good thing to appoint others who were from Castile. Concerning the disputes, he responded that it was a law and custom for men to dispute with whomever they wished and that in this he could not remove the right his sons had, but that as far as he was concerned, he could not accept the idea that any nobleman should judge him. Concerning the services, he replied to them that they had granted such services to him because of the many expenses he had incurred in the war against the Moors and in order to give them their salaries[2]; also, so that he could collect some money so that he could travel to the empire. Concerning their fear that he would require the services by law, King Alfonso responded that they did not give them by law, nor was he willing to adopt it as a law, and as to this he would give them his charter. To what they requested about the privilege of the *alcabala* they paid at Burgos,[3] he answered that they were there when he granted it to the Council of Burgos for the construction of walls and all had agreed to it then, and that since they were angry regarding this, he considered it right that the nobles not pay it. Concerning what they were saying about the royal judges, magistrates, and tax collectors, he replied that he would rule as to this and as to what the nobles had done that they should not have, for he would reprimand and make them act justly. To what they said about the towns of the kingdoms of León and Galicia, he answered them that he would not order a town built on someone else's property and that if they built towns on their own lands, he would not encroach on anyone. He said that because they considered it wrong, he would place it in the hands of the knights of noble descent, townsmen, and the clergy, and that if they were to find that other kings had not built them and that he should not build them, then he would destroy them.

Over and above all of these things, the king promised them that if any noblemen, knight, or another of noble descent had any complaints about him, he wanted to do justice according to the old law that other kings held with their nobles. He said that this should be examined by some of those knights who were there with the noblemen, and that during the time of deliberation they should not be vassals of the king or of any other. Because they had told King Alfonso that those noblemen were saying the king was impoverishing the land by giving wealth to men of other kingdoms and also for the matter concerning the empire, he told the nobles that if he was giving wealth to men of other lands, it was to bring honor to the people of his kingdoms, and that because of it, those of his realm were the most loved and valued men of his realm that ever lived in the whole world. Concerning the empire, the king informed them that the pope had appointed him as emperor and that the electors sent him their letters confirming it. He said that he would pursue this for the honor of his realm and that if all of them would help him well in it, he would be very honored. Moreover, he begged them not to allow such a good king to have such ill fortune, for he wished to do good, but he did not have any funds with which to accomplish it. For they knew well that there never had been a king in this land who had done so much good and so much favor to them as he had, and that they never were as wealthy or as well supplied, nor possess as many horses or as many weapons as they did during his time.

After King Alfonso had pronounced all of these reasons, don Nuño called apart some of the noblemen, who were these: don Lope Díaz and don Jimeno Ruiz, don Fernán Ruiz de Castro and don Esteban Fernández. Having reached an agreement about it, don Nuño told the king on his behalf and on behalf of all others that they found grace in the reply he gave them and that they were very pleased with what he said. They said that because of this, they were obliged to serve the king wherever he ordered them, but they asked his favor that he assemble a royal court and tell them those things in the court. The king immediately replied that he would be glad to do it, and he then sent for the prelates and attorneys of all the towns of the kingdom to go to Burgos until Saint Michael's Day.[4] He entered the city, and the noblemen went to the villages where they were staying. King Alfonso thought he had appeased them with this, but then they sent word that they could not excuse themselves from going to meet with the King of Navarre due to the agreement this king had made with Prince Felipe. The king had them shown many reasons for which they should not do it, but they did not desist from it on this account. While on their way to Navarre, they met Prince Felipe, who was coming from there and who had broken the agreement since the King of Navarre was asking for things that implied the disinheriting of King Alfonso, particularly that they should help him recover all of Burgos and up to what belonged to Navarre. As soon as the noblemen learned those things that the King of Navarre was demanding, they thanked Felipe for breaking off the meeting and they all returned to stay in the towns where they had stayed before, for it was time for the *cortes* that the king had organized. Henceforth, we will relate other things that took place concerning this affair.

Notes

The *Chronicle's* account of the discussion between Alfonso X and the nobles in September 1272 is distinctly favorable to the king, who is praised for being in the right. O'Callaghan, *The Learned King*, 217–18.

1. The persons with whom the king took counsel were all trusted royal servants: Pedro Lorenzo, Bishop of Cuenca; Gil García de Azagra, *mayordomo mayor* in 1272; Gutierre Súarez de Meneses, as *adelantado mayor* of León; and Diego López de Salcedo, *adelantado* of Álava and Guipúzcoa.

2. The king's response to the nobles seems to be taken from a contemporary document.

3. The *alcabala* was a sales tax.

4. The feast of St. Michael (Michaelmas) fell on September 29.

Chapter 25

⊞

How the King and the Noblemen Who Were
Angry Met at the Hospital of Burgos,
and What They Discussed There

During this year that the *History* has related, after the princes and
prelates, noblemen and knights, those of noble descent, and attorneys of the council who had to come to the *cortes* were assembled
in Burgos,[1] the king sent to tell Prince Felipe and don Nuño, and
the other noblemen who had joined them, to come and that he
would speak to them before the whole court about those things he
had told them the other time. They sent word that they feared the
princes and noblemen who were with the king and they wanted
him to grant them a truce, and that as soon as he had granted it
they would come armed to the court with all of their knights and
men and horsemen. Because the king realized that they said such
a thing without any cause—for in his court all men were safe and
they had no reason to demand a truce or come armed—he sent
his messengers to them, who were: Diego García,[2] brother of don
Juan García; Gonzalo Morante[3]; Fernán Pérez, Dean of Seville;
Gonzalo Ruiz de Atienza; don Marcos de Ávila; Gómez Cerra de
Segovia; and don Juan de Soria. And he ordered the messengers
to speak with them on his behalf and to do whatever they could to
make them desist from that uprising. Don Nuño and the noblemen, having heard the king's message, refused to come there until
the truce had been granted, and later on they all came armed to
the Hospital of Burgos, and King Alfonso went there with all those
from the land to speak with the noblemen. After the king had spoken and granted before all those who were there what he had promised, and for which he had assembled the royal court at their
request, they made new demands, which are these: that no one be

granted authority to judge them except a man of noble descent, that there be two judges of noble descent in his court, and also that the towns he had ordered built in Castile be destroyed. Since the king had appointed his royal judges to administer justice in the districts of Castile and León, they asked him to remove these judges and to appoint governors. They also demanded that he abandon the tithes of the harbors, which he ordered collected from the goods that were brought to the kingdom, and that he order them not to collect the sums of money from their vassals. And don Lope Díaz, don Fernán Ruiz, and don Diego López asked him to order Urduña and Balmaseda, which they said belonged to their inheritance, handed over.

King Alfonso replied to them immediately concerning these demands and said that it pleased him and that he saw as good that they demanded to have judges of noble descent who would judge them, notwithstanding that none of the kings who were before him ever brought into his court a governor of noble descent, nor did the kings ever grant the other offices to those of noble descent as he had done. To their demand concerning the towns, he replied that he was not doing anything illegal to anyone and that they should be judged by those who had the authority to judge in the towns of León and Galicia. To what they asked about his replacing the royal judges he had appointed with governors, he answered them that he would see it as good to do it when the land had been made calm with justice. To their statement that he should not collect the tithes, he told them that the kings who were before him did much to increase the rents and that he should do the same. And that even they, who each day asked the king's favor to give them what they were demanding, should not want the rents of the kingdom reduced but increased. To the demand that he should not demand service from their vassals, the king answered that he did not deny that he should not favor those who requested it of him with service, and that notwithstanding his having their charters in which they granted him the service, those who said they did not wish to grant it should not do so.

To what don Lope Díaz, don Fernán Ruiz, and don Diego López said of Urduña and Balmaseda, which was their inheritance, the king replied that this and the complaints that some other noblemen had against him for reasons of inheritance, which they claimed

he seized from them by force, he wanted handed over to his vassals' knights, and to those who were with don Felipe and with the
noblemen, and also to the hands of good townsmen. Further, the
king said that some clergymen, religious men, and knights should
abandon their vassalage while they were judging the disputes, and
that all of them should make an oath to tell the truth and to judge
according to the law. He said that these judges should also judge
the complaints the king had against the noblemen, and that once
the truth of the matter had been made known—notwithstanding
he was the King and Lord of Castile according to the law—and
before he received any emendation, he wanted to mend any wrong
if he had done it, and afterward they should mend the wrongs they
had committed against him. The king argued so well concerning
these matters that all of those who had assembled there understood that he was just and lawful and that don Felipe and those
noblemen were causing the uprising unjustly.

As soon as don Felipe, don Nuño, and all the noblemen heard
what the king told them, they did not respond. They all left the
palace and departed in the midst of their rebellion, even though
they were armed. On another day, they sent their messengers, who
were Rui Pérez de la Vega and Sancho de Velasco, to the king with
word that they wanted to leave for their lands. King Alfonso, thinking he could convince them to abandon their rebellion before they
left, sent don Fray Tello, minister of the Friars Minors of Castile;
Garcí Jofré de Loaysa[4]; and Juan González de Fuente Alméjir to
them. He ordered them to speak with the rebels and to let them
know all of those things the king had said to them and granted
them, first in the wasteland of Burgos and then in the courts; and
that because he wanted to preserve their laws and rights, he begged
they should preserve their service and the king's right in all things,
for he would send a charter with his messengers and with his seal
concerning everything he had told them before. As soon as don
Felipe and the noblemen heard what the king had sent to tell them,
they said they saw that the king was being gracious in what he was
telling them and that they would send their messengers to him.
And concerning this Juan de Almazán, don Felipe's vassal, and Pero
Ruiz de Villegas, don Nuño's vassal, came to the king in Burgos
with an answer concerning what the king was sending to tell them.
Because of what the king perceived from this message—that don

Felipe and the noblemen refused to put an end to their rebellion and return to his service—he sent don Fray Tello and Gonzalo Ruiz de Atienza to them once more. Don Felipe and the noblemen refused again to hear anything of what these messengers had to say, for they said that they could not agree among themselves. Together they departed from the towns where they were staying, which were near Burgos, and they left for Campos. And now we will cease here to relate this, and will return to tell the other things that happened in Burgos, in the court where the king was.

Notes

1. The Cortes of Burgos took place around Michaelmas, September 29, 1272, not 1271. O'Callaghan, *The Learned King*, 218–20.

2. Diego García, brother of Juan García de Villamayor.

3. Gonzalo Morante, on his mother's side, was a half-brother of Alfonso Fernández, el Niño, an illegitimate son of Alfonso X; he had served as territorial administrator (*merino mayor*) of Léon.

4. Garcí Jofré de Loaysa served as royal *copero mayor,* or cupbearer.

Chapter 26

◉

How the Prelates of the Kingdom Attempted
Among Themselves to Bring Discord
Between the King and the Noblemen
So That King Alfonso Would Grant Them
Certain Things They Demanded of Him

The prelates of the kingdom who were there with the king during the *cortes* attempted to cause a division between the king and those noblemen, and they were pleased that both parties could not reach an agreement.[1] The *History* even tells that don Felipe and the noblemen only left that city on the prelates' advice; and they acted in this fashion thinking that the king would grant them everything they requested. All of them united gave the king their complaints and made demands that had never been granted by other kings. King Alfonso, realizing the things that the prelates were doing and why they made those demands, wished to expel them from the kingdom. But in order to protect the land from more turmoil, and to prevent the rebellion from growing even larger, and in order not to have the pope against him, the king replied to the prelates in this fashion: that they should show their power through their knights, and that if they had any power to mend the complaints the king received from them, and to receive compensation for what they had told him, they should appoint four of their knights for this dispute, and that he would appoint princes, noblemen, knights, religious men, and townsmen. Those appointed to dispute the affair of the noblemen and the requests of the prelates were these— on behalf of the king: Queen Violante; Prince Fadrique; don Gil García; don Juan Núñez, son of don Nuño; don Diego López de Salcedo; don Gutier Suárez; don Diego García, son of don García;

and don Ruy González de Cisneros; for the knights: Gutier González Quijada, Gonzalo Ruiz de Atienza, Juan Ruiz de Río Cerezo and Ruy Díaz de Valdetovos; for the prelates: the Archbishop of Toledo Don Sancho,[2] the Bishop of Palencia,[3] the Bishop of Cuenca,[4] and the Bishop of Calahorra[5]; for the clergymen: the Dean of Seville, the Archdeacon of Cuellar, Master Esteban, and the Abbot of Cuevas Rubias; and for the Orders: Friar Tello, minister of the Orders of Saint Francis, Friar Diego Ruiz, and Friar Juan Reveca; and for the Dominicans: Friar Martín, Doctor of Palencia and Friar Domingo; for the townsmen: Velasco Núñez de Ávila; Sancho Íñiguez de Ávila; Ruy Pérez de Segovia; Gómez Cerra de Segovia; don Nuño de Arévalo; Aparicio Ruiz de Medina; Ovieco Sancho de Medina; don Gómez (who was a judge in Cuellar); Gil Sánchez, also from Medina; Diego Pérez de Valladolid; Ruy Pérez, also from Valladolid; Juan Fernández, Governor of Palencia; Ferrand González de Burgos; don Martín; don Gil de Sepúlveda; and Diego Fernández. And for all of them to examine the demands those prelates were making, and that whatever they found that he had to right, he would compensate them for it, and likewise, they should right that for which they were at fault with him. Concerning their demands, he said he would grant those things that were granted to them during the time of the king whence he came. Meanwhile, King Alfonso during those *cortes* discussed with the noblemen, knights, and attorneys from the council, who were there with him, what he thought was of benefit for his kingdom.

Notes

1. O'Callaghan, *The Learned King,* 57, 220–23.
2. Archbishop Sancho II of Toledo (1266–1275) was the son of Jaime I of Aragón.
3. Alfonso García, Bishop of Palencia (1265–1276).
4. Pedro Lorenzo, Bishop of Cuenca (1262–1272).
5. Vivián, Bishop of Calahorra (1263–1273).

Chapter 27

⊞

How Prince Felipe and the Noblemen
Who Were with Him Took Leave
of the King to Go to Granada

Prince Felipe, don Nuño, don Lope Díaz, don Esteban Fernández, don Fernán Ruiz de Castro, don Jimeno Ruiz de los Cameros, the noblemen, and knights of noble descent who were there with them sent their messengers to take leave of the king and to request from him a truce of forty-two days so that they could leave the kingdoms,[1] and also to request from him keepers in whose hands they would put the castles that some of them held. Afterward, they left Campos and stole many things without any right or reason, and they went over the Duero in order to go to the land of the Moors. When the messengers arrived at Burgos, the queen kept them from speaking to the king for two days, thinking that the king and the noblemen might reach an agreement. Once the king learned about it, he departed from Burgos and went to Villa Gonzalo, and there those messengers from the noblemen spoke with him and took leave of him, requesting the forty-two-day truce. The king, who had come to Burgos hoping to appease them, taking into account how they were taking leave of him, granted the forty-two-day truce so that they could leave the kingdom. The messengers also requested guards to whom to turn over the castles that some of them held from the king. The king granted them the guards, and he wished to go after them so that they could not do more harm or damage in the land, for he thought that the noblemen and knights who were at his service and the Councils of Extremadura, which were ready as he had ordered, would go along with him. Because he realized that this was not as certain as he thought, he sent Gil Ruiz de Caracena and Juan Íñiguez de Mora, his governor, with them and with his letter. He ordered these men to guide the noblemen and to give them quarters with his money. The king left there and went to Toledo, and from there he sent the archbishop and the bishops of Palencia and Segovia to Prince Fernando and Prince Manuel,[2] that all of them together might meet the prince and the noblemen and speak with them to see if they could make them return. These knights went along with them up to the boundaries of the kingdom, protecting and guaranteeing that they could not harm those from the land. They also pleaded with the noblemen that because the king was doing what they wanted, they should not cause nor order any harm or damage done to the land during those forty-two days of the truce. But they refused to abide by this truce, and instead they stole much cattle and all other things they found and set fire to some unfortified places and demolished some churches. Because of what they did during this time of the truce that the king had granted them, later on, some of them were excluded from the trials because they did not keep that truce. And some of their goods were confiscated because of those evil deeds they had committed then. While these armies were approaching Atienza, two of the king's messengers, named Gonzalo Ruiz and Sancho Pérez, arrived with letters of credence, and they communicated to them the king's message, as will be told in this chronicle.

Notes

1. The nobles apparently left the Cortes on their journey into exile in November 1272. The king was in Burgos on November 4; in Madrid on December 9–10, 1272; and in Toledo on January 22, 1273. O'Callaghan, *The Learned King*, 223.

2. Fernando Velázquez, Bishop of Segovia (1265–1278/9).

Chapter 28

▣

How the King's Heralds Came to Don Felipe, and About What They Told Him

"Lord and Prince Felipe, noblemen and knights of noble descent, lords of the towns who are here from the kingdoms of Castile and León: You know well that while the king was in Murcia, you sent word to him that he order sums be given to you and that you would go and serve him wherever he thought you should. And he ordered them given to you; they gave them to you by his command. And because Prince Fernando, his son, was at the frontier, he ordered you to go and serve him and you refused to do it. And well do you know that although you were his vassals and have partaken of his sums—and besides, you held a great portion of the rents of his kingdom each year—you failed to do what you were ordered by law of Castile and León, and you waged war and rebelled. Because of your refusal to go where he ordered you, now he sends word and orders that you go and serve him in exchange for the sums he gave you. He also sends word that you are aware, as it is law in Castile and León, that when any man of noble descent commits any evil deed and seizes food as he should not, he would be brought to justice before the king and his judges. You know how many robberies, crimes, and evils you have committed in the land, and the king orders you to send guarantors to pay for the evil deeds that you have committed. He also sends word to you of how because of your pleas and counsel he came to Burgos, and of how as he approached Lerma, you came to meet him armed, not as to your lord but more as if you were seeking your enemy. Afterward, when he wished to speak with you in order to win you back into his service and favor, you refused to enter the city with him but came armed with all of your men to speak to him. Also, in the hall of the Hospital of Burgos, where the court was assembled, you left there without providing him with an answer to what he was telling you, and you did not free yourselves from the offenses that they reported to you. In these matters you showed great ingratitude for the many favors and benefits he did for you more fully than any of the other kings who lived in Castile and León by rearing you, wedding you, in granting inheritances, and giving many sums to you from the tributes that you held from his land. And also by excusing you from much violence, great wrongs, and disorders that you, Felipe, and the noblemen committed against those of noble descent of his realm and against the Orders, which he let you get by with and did not banish you from the kingdom for, though capable of doing so. Moreover, you asked him to grant you forty-two days so that you could leave his kingdom, and the king granted this to you and sent men from his house to give you money for your rations and to tell you on his behalf not to harm the land and its people. During this forty-two-day period that was established as a truce between the king and you so that you would be careful not to do evil and damage, you ravaged and caused much damage; and because of this, you should be able to realize what the king can do to you by law in this matter. Now that we have told this message to all the others, we shall tell each of you what is required of us on the king's behalf."

Chapter 29

※

Of the Explanations That King Alfonso's Heralds, On His Behalf, Gave to Prince Felipe

"Sir Prince Felipe, your knight whom you sent to the king told him that due to the outrages and disinheritances you had received from him and the wrongs in the land you have done, you therefore distanced yourself from him. And you know that during the time in which you were a clergyman,[1] you said many times to your brother the king that you wanted to abandon the clergy; and he always pleaded with you and advised you not to do it, for while you were the Archbishop of Seville and Abbot of Valladolid and of Cuevas Rubias, with other benefices you held, you lived with much honor. On one occasion when you returned from Paris, where you were in school, you told the king that you wished to abandon the clergy, and he told you that he was not pleased by it but that because you wished to do so, it would be better if you were to do it outside the kingdom since you were not a native. Afterward, when you abandoned the clergy, it was not under his advice, but when you showed him what you had done, because of the good will he had toward you and to do you honor and favor, he gave you as wife Princess Cristina, daughter of the King and Queen of Norway. Even though some of his other brothers requested her hand in marriage before you and because you asked for her, he right away gave you a great portion of his rents from wherever you wished, which is all of the tax payable on Saint Martin's Day of Ávila, and the toll of the Jewry of that city, and all the other privileges that the king held in that city. He also gave you all the tributes of the Archbishopric of Toledo and of the Bishoprics of Ávila and Segovia, and other sums of his rents that he granted you as land you would receive from him.

And he gave you as inheritance Val de Corneja, which included four towns—el Barco, Piedrahita, la Forcajada, and Almirón—something that no other king was ever willing to grant to any of his brothers, nor to any of his sons, nor to anybody else from any of the territories of Extremadura. Moreover, you took the food you needed from the land of Ávila and Segovia when you were there, because of which those from Extremadura were very angry at the king. The king also gave you as inheritance Val de Porchena, and notwithstanding that it was neither his nor yours, he gave you each year from its rent.

The king did this for you and did not take anything away from you. And you—being his brother and vassal and always promising that you would serve him—sent word to tell him that he was disinheriting you, particularly in the territory of the land of León, and King Alfonso did not disinherit you due to this. For you know that Queen Doña Mencía adopted Prince Fernando, and at the time of the death of that doña Mencía, Diego de Corral entered all of the inheritance without the king's permission but by order of Prince Fernando on account of the adoption that she made; and if you have any complaint about this, you never manifested it to him. Regarding what you told the king, that he acted illegally in Castile and León, he never did it nor was it his will to do it; and even if any of his officers committed any wrong, he always regretted it and exiled that officer for it. But you, Sir Prince Felipe, illegally deprived the kingdoms of Castile and León, stealing and seizing from those of noble descent and from townsmen and monasteries of the Orders all you could seize. And besides the king's doing these favors and these honors, and giving you sums from his rents so that you could serve him wherever he ordered you to do it, and having sent word to you that he was in need of your service in the war against the Moors and that you should go to be with Prince Fernando, his son, you refused to do it.

Now he orders you to return the sums that you took from him and the land that you hold from him, that you send him guarantors for the crimes you committed in the land; and if not, he considers that you were disobedient; and because of what you have said, he cannot avoid what is the law in Castile. Moreover, he sends word that they told him you were going to the kingdom of Granada to be on its side, knowing that the King of Granada is the enemy of

God and of the Faith, and of the king and his kingdoms, and the enemy of all of noble descent who there are in Castile and León, and of all of those from these other kingdoms. And you, being the son of King Fernando and of Queen Beatriz, and brother of King Alfonso, he considers that you ought to protect better the lineage from which you come and the duty you have toward him. In all of these things you deprived the land and you disinherited yourself, and he did not deprive you nor is he disinheriting you."

Note

1. Infante Felipe, the third of Alfonso X's brothers, was originally intended for the archbishopric of Seville, but opted for a lay career and led the rebellion against his brother. He died about 1274. O'Callaghan, *The Learned King*, 9, 75–77, 223.

Chapter 30

Of the Answers That the Heralds of King Alfonso, On His Behalf, Gave to Don Nuño

"Don Nuño[1]: Your knight whom you sent to King Alfonso told him that you were leaving him because while you were serving at Málaga, he took away the land you held from him, and also because he was encroaching upon the rights of Castile and León. You know that you received from him much honor and favor, more than any man of your station ever received from any other king. For being a child, you grew up with him, and being Prince, when he began to rule, because of the love he felt for you, he placed Gonzalo Nuño, your brother, under his protection and favor. When King Fernando refused to make you a knight or give you land and had no wish to do you good but instead wanted to harm you and all your lineage, Count Fernando and Count Álvaro, your uncles, and Count Gonzalo, your father, who lived when he began to rule, rebelled and waged a great war against him. But King Alfonso as a prince gave you Écija contrary to his father's will, which you held through him, and it was the first thing King Fernando gave to his son in Andalusia, being a prince. The first time that King Alfonso went to the kingdom of Murcia, being a prince, he granted you land and later on pleaded and asked King Fernando, his father, to give other holdings, to make you a knight, and to give you in marriage doña Teresa Alfonso, his first cousin and granddaughter of the King of León. King Fernando, because of his son's plea, granted against his will these favors to you. Afterward, you started a dispute with don Diego concerning the estate of the mountain. And notwithstanding that King Alfonso knew that you were wrongly demanding it, he behaved with you in such a fashion that the estate remained yours, worrying his father, the king, because King Alfonso favored you more than anything else. After this, you, don Nuño, brought your conniving to Castile, and King Alfonso, being a prince, gave you so many friends in that time that you preserved your honor. After King Alfonso recovered all the realms, so great was the good he did you that don Diego asked him many times not to do it, for everything he did for you was to his disadvantage. But the king did not cease on account of this to do you favor and more than ever, granting so great a portion of the rents of the kingdom and many offices to you and to all of those you favored that don Diego left the kingdom; and the king gave you his land, which was an honor to you and a very great loss for don Diego. Due to this, the king was never able to have don Diego in his service, but instead don Diego did him disservice with Prince Enrique and with all of those he understood wished to harm the king. If you do not remember anything except this, you should understand how much the king did for you in losing someone like don Diego in order to make you the best in his kingdom. Moreover, you know that he granted that you hold Seville, which is the most honorable possession of all of his kingdoms, and along with that city great wealth and possessions greater than what he had given to any other. In addition, he granted you all of the rents he held in Burgos and Rioja and a great portion of the other rents of his kingdom. And you took all of the rents of Old Castile, and he allowed you to do so, and of as much as you possess he never took anything away from you. You know, don Nuño, that thanks to the king you held Jerez, which the Moors took, and that after the Moors had won it the king gave you from his rents the equivalent of the rents from Jerez at the time you held that city; and without blaming you if from some fault of yours came the loss of Jerez. But wishing to do you favor, he gave you as a holding the city of Torre de Lobatón with its towns, and he also granted you holdings at the frontier and in other places when you requested them from him.

In your time, the king gave land to your sons don Juan Núñez and Nuño González, and to grant holdings to the sons while the father still lived was something that was never done during the time of any other king, and many from the kingdom had much to say about this. Later on, when your son don Juan Núñez went to

Palestine with the King of Navarre, King Alfonso protected his land so that it could not be given to anyone else. And you, don Nuño, know that the favors and honor the king did you were great, and that you came to have three hundred of the best knights of the nobility living in Castile, León, and Galicia as your vassals. Thus, you were the most powerful and honorable man that any lord had in all of Spain. To what you say, that the king took away the land you held from him: he never took it from you, but instead he increased it so much that there never was a wealthier man in Spain who held so much land from his king or lord. And as to what you say, don Nuño, that the king encroached upon the rights of Castile and León, it was you who encroached upon the king, the noblemen, the royal estates, and all of the abbatials, and it was you who imposed taxes in all of the land in which the king left you in charge while he was at the frontier.

Don Nuño, you know that the king asked you whether the taxes you imposed in his land were legal, and you said no but that others imposed them before you and that for this reason you had done it. And the king told you that because this was not the law, it was force and robbery; and the king forbade you from ever again committing such outrage that you had done, and you promised him that you would put an end to it.

Afterward, and disregarding his prohibition, while the king was in Seville, you dispatched another requirement on all those of noble descent, knights and squires, and ladies and damsels in his royal holdings, and in his Orders, and you seized food and collected the taxes payable to him on Saint Martin's Day without his authority and ordinances. You had it collected in a very disorderly fashion, and thusly, you broke the laws of the land. All of those of noble descent who accompanied you and these noblemen who were with you there dishonored themselves, their sons, and their relatives because of the taxes that you imposed, and if those here with you are being dishonored, it is because of you. Even though at the *cortes* you demanded on their behalf that the law should protect them, not taking into consideration that the king upheld the law before and after that, you deprived them and did them much harm, as we have already told.

And you, don Nuño, having incited all the noblemen to rise against the king, you sent to tell him to come to Burgos and said you would advise him on how to appease all of his kingdom. As the king approached Lerma, you came to him with a large number of men-of-arms, not like those who go to meet their lord but like men who are seeking their enemies. Afterward, you came to speak to the king about that matter near Burgos, where you told him the matters in which you thought the king was doing you wrong; to which the king replied to you that he wished to mend them according to which facts were found, as well witnessed by some of the knights who were with him. As to this, you asked him permission to assemble the *cortes* and said you would put an end to this matter, and the king considered it proper. Then you came with a large number of men-of-arms and made other new demands, notwithstanding that the king gave you good answers; and then, having left there without telling him anything, you pillaged and stole all you found around Burgos. Moreover, being the king's vassal and having his money, you made a covenant and a pact with the King of Granada, and now you go to serve and assist him against King Alfonso, your lord, whose vassal you are. You know that the King of Granada and his Moors are God's enemies, the enemies of the Faith, of the king, and of all of those of noble descent of Castile and León—for there is not anyone in the kingdom who does not have a dead relative—and you want to serve that man who has lied and broken the treaties and agreements that King Alfonso had with him. And so you encroached upon all of the kingdom and should ponder what might come to you from this deed."

Note

1. Nuño González de Lara was head of one of the principal Castilian noble houses and had enjoyed the king's friendship and patronage for many years before turning against him. O'Callaghan, *The Learned King*, 72–73, 75–77, 223.

Chapter 31

❖

Concerning the Replies That the King's
Heralds Gave to Don Lope Díaz

"Don Lope Díaz[1]: The king sends to tell you that the knight you sent to him when you took leave of the king said that because the king had disinherited you and was not granting you the land that your father and your grandfather used to hold, you considered yourself even more disinherited, although not of the land that your father had left you. And this is why you say that the king encroached upon the rights of Castile and León and why you were leaving him. Don Lope Díaz, you know how many favors he did you, for when your father, don Diego, died—notwithstanding that he was doing disservice to the king—you came to him later on and he welcomed you in his home; and he honored you much and commanded that on his wedding day his son Prince Fernando make you a knight; and he gave you much honor and money, which he ordered given to you each year. And when don Nuño wished to take from you Durango and other regions you held, for which he claimed to have a right, the king ordered him not to do it; and because he refused to obey this order, the king sent to your assistance don Juan Sánchez de Salcedo and other knights, who went on the king's behalf to protect your land so that don Nuño could not take it from you. In this manner, the king acted for you so that you remained on your land, and don Nuño was not able to seize anything from you. So many favors and so much help the king did for you in this that it is one of the major complaints don Nuño holds against the king, even though don Nuño makes them wrongly—for Alfonso always told him to demand the land from you, as he should, and said he would make just payment to don Nuño on your behalf. The king would not allow that he use force against you, being young and in his power. On this account you received Vizcaya, because if he had not protected it for you, you would have lost hereditary right to it. In this and in other things the king did much good and honor, trusting you; and you, promising to serve him, placed your friendship secretly with don Nuño against him, and you married doña Juana, daughter of Prince Alfonso de Molina,[2] against the king's will. Afterward, you came to him in Úbeda and made many assurances that you had not made a treaty against him, nor did you consider that he would take offense on account of that marriage. And the king being in Murcia, you sent word promising to serve him, and while you felt very confident, he found out about the words that don Nuño and you made among the noblemen and those of noble descent of the kingdom and that you had challenged Diego López de Salcedo because of the justice that he carried out in Álava and Guipúzcoa.

To what you now sent to tell the king (that he was disinheriting you), we reply, don Lope Díaz, that the king never disinherited you and that if you are disinherited, it is because those under whose authority your father, don Diego, placed you have disinherited you. For bringing you along with them after you departed from the king's court, you pillaged the land and ordered many places burned, and many places were burned and pillaged and ruined.

To what you say, that Urduña should be yours and that King Alfonso's father, King Fernando, your lord, granted it as a gift to your grandparents, don Lope and doña Urraca, it is true. But you waged war on the king for it, and thus you caused much evil in the land, and it is the law in Castile that if anyone wages war against the king and harms the land on account of a gift he has granted, then the king is lawfully allowed to seize it.

And to what you say about Balmaseda, you know well that being there with your mother, your uncles, and your vassals, you plundered the land and did a great deal of harm to it. Therefore, the king had to station some of his vassals to protect that land. And you left Balmaseda, and the king regained it and holds it because of the evil acts that your mother and you committed in the land against the king. The king did not disinherit you, but you disinherited yourself and those who hold you under their authority and protection, for the king could not avoid doing what was lawful and just.

And as to what you say, that the king encroaches upon the rights of Castile and León: he does not do it, nor is it his will to do it, for he favors and has favored in his court many men of noble descent, and he arranged marriages for them, made them knights, granted them lands, and did many good things for them, more than any other king who was in Spain until his time. You have treated Castile and León outrageously and done many unlawful things in the land, dishonoring those of noble descent and their wives, parents, and many other relatives, among whom are many of those of noble descent. Besides, you know that the king, being in Murcia, sent to tell you about how the Moors were waging war and that because you had seized his monies, he ordered and begged you go to be with his son Prince Fernando in that war, but you refused to do it. Although in this fashion you disobeyed him, he now sends to beg you to go to the frontier with Prince Fernando and serve your king with the land and monies that you seized from him. If you refuse to do this, he sends to tell you to go to give him securities in exchange for the evil acts that you committed so that you could pay for them as the law demands it, and if not, the king will order that they be paid from your wealth, according to the law of Castile. Also, you know that when the king, your lord, came to Burgos in order to lull you back into his service, you came forth at him supported by many armed men on foot and on horses as those men with whom you have come against their king and sovereign lord never came. And you and the other noblemen demanded from him whatever you wished, and the king granted it to you. About this, he assembled the *cortes* at your request so that he could grant, before all, what he had promised you. And the king being at the palace and before his court, you made other demands and left the palace where he was without speaking to him and with a great number of armed men, and you pillaged the land. Now they have made him realize that while you were his vassal and while you were holding his land and monies, you made a treaty against him with the King of Granada. You know that the King of Granada is an enemy of the Faith, of the king, of you, and of all of those of noble descent in Castile and León, and that you do a disservice to the king by making an alliance with such a man as this, who has lied to him and broken whatever treaties he made with him and who has broken truces. In all these things we have said, don Lope Díaz, you have trespassed against the king and all of those of noble descent in Castile and León, all of those of noble lineage, all the abbatials, and what you do is against the law and against justice. You cannot say that the king trespasses against you, for you trespass against yourself: you took away horses and weapons that you purchased with the money he gave you with which you should serve him. And you are going to do him a disservice in it. And you should consider what may come to you from this deed."

Notes

1. Lope Díaz de Haro was head of the Haro family, who were lords of Vizcaya on the northern borders of Castile. O'Callaghan, *The Learned King*, 74–74, 77–78, 223–24

2. Infante Alfonso de Molina, brother of Fernando III and uncle of Alfonso X.

Chapter 32

⊞

Of the Answers That the King's Heralds
Gave to Don Fernán Ruiz de Castro

"Don Fernán Ruiz de Castro[1]: The king sends to tell you that the knight whom you sent told the king that you were abandoning him because King Alfonso has disinherited you from the territory of León. Don Fernán Ruiz, you know well that the king favored you and made his father grant you the land he held that belonged to Ruy Fernández, your father, when you were a child of four—which he was not accustomed to do for any nobleman, because the land of the one who died he customarily granted to the son who was old enough to administer it. Moreover, because your grandmother, Countess Elo, wanted to sell Santa Olalla and the estates of Toledo and the other inheritances she held so that she could dispossess you of them, the king purchased them and gave them to you. Later on, after you had pawned all of it to a Jew from Toledo, don Abraem, whom they called Doctor of Law [*alfaquí*]—even the rings and precious stones that belonged to don Pedro Fernández, the governor—the king recovered them and returned them to you, and he granted you much more land than that which your father used to hold; and in order to honor you more, he wed you to doña Urraca Díaz, the daughter of don Diego de Vizcaya, whom they would not have given to you had it not been for him. While he trusted you and you promised to serve him, the king learned that you had made treaties with don Nuño and others against the king, but he refused to believe it until you manifested it through the deeds in which you are now engaged.

As to what you say concerning the disinheritance of the royal estate: you know that Queen Mencía, to whom it belonged, had as a son Prince Fernando, and when she died she bequeathed it to don Diego de Corral in Palencia on the order of the prince, the king not knowing it. And so the king did not disinherit you, but he favored you and he deeded it to you, just as we have said, and he knighted you.

As to what you say, that the king encroached upon Castile and León, we say that it is you who encroaches upon them, according to what we have already told each one of the others. With you holding land and money of the king, whom you ought to serve, you take these to his enemy so as to serve him, and you act against law and against justice, and this is wrong for you. Moreover, you did him evil deeds in the land and refused to rectify them. If the king had done to you what is law in Castile, you should understand that the guilt is yours."

Note

1. Fernán Ruiz de Castro, the head of the Castro family, was lord of Cigales. O'Callaghan, *The Learned King,* 70.

Chapter 33

⊞

Of the Answers That the King's Heralds, At His Bidding, Gave to Don Esteban Fernández

"Don Esteban Fernández[1]: The knight whom you sent to the king told him that because it had been a long time since he gave you your monies, and because he kept you away from your wife, Aldonza Rodríguez, by force, and because he was encroaching upon the laws of Castile and León, that for this you were parting from him. The king tells you that you hold from him his well-cared-for land, which he was able to give you, and the rest that you hold in money; and that his letters command you to give him firm proof that you hold this; and that even though well-requited, you deserted him. You know how he had given you the governorship of Galicia, and notwithstanding that the king took away the governorships of Castile and León, he refused to take away from you the governorship of Galicia. He trusted you in this and in many other things and did you much good, and you always gave him to understand that you were pleased with him and with the favors he was doing you.

At what you say concerning Aldonza Rodríguez, that she is your wife and that the king has her under guard: you know that the king sent to tell you that he would give back Aldonza Rodríguez to her relatives, who entrusted her to him, and that they might take her back to the house from whence they took her, and that they might leave her there, and that she might be assured by treaty that you would not take her by force; and if she is your wife, you should request her through the Church, as it should be requested, and that if justice were on your side, it would please the king that you might have her as wife, and he would not keep her from you nor would he allow anyone to keep her away from you, and he now sends to tell you the same.

Regarding what you say, that King Alfonso encroaches upon Castile and León, he did not do it nor would he wish to do so. But, the king doing for you all of these benefits that we have mentioned, you took leave without cause and without justice or law, and you do to him disservice with the greatest enemy he has. And you damage the realm and act against God, the law, and against your liege lord, and harm the kingdoms from whence you have dominion. And we urge you on the king's behalf and of the kingdom not to do it."

Note

1. Esteban Fernández de Castro, lord of Lemos and Sarria, was *adelantado mayor*, or governor, of Galicia. O'Callaghan, *The Learned King*, 70, 77–78, 215–17, 223–24.

Chapter 34

◩

Of the Explanation That the King's Heralds Told Don Juan Núñez

"Don Juan Núñez[1]: Your squire told the king that you were parting from him, and he considered it a great surprise—on the one hand, because he never did anything to you so that you ought to part from him, and on the other, because he always cared for you and did you good. Even when you went overseas, he always refused to take away the land from you, and he gave it to your son, and today you hold it through him. Even now, in good faith, he has it in his heart to give you more, and for this reason he is surprised that this was the motive for which you parted from him; particularly because in this matter of the noblemen, he confided in you, for you were a messenger between them and him. He also thought that you would serve him in this and that you would not disservice him with them."

Don Juan answered them immediately, and later on told them secretly that he asked the king's grace that he not consider it wrong that he took leave of him and went with his father. Since even though everything they were saying was true, his father had done him so much good and showed so much love for him, it would not be that he would not be with him. And for this reason he asked the king's grace so that he forgive him for it, for he could not do otherwise there.

Note

1. Juan Núñez de Lara, the son of Nuño González de Lara, played a prominent role in the later dispute over the succession. O'Callaghan, *The Learned King*, 77, 239–40.

Chapter 35

❖

Of the Answers That the King's Heralds Gave to Don Álvar Díaz

"Don Álvar Díaz[1]: The knight whom you sent to inform the king that you were departing his service said that you were doing it because the king took away land from you without any legitimate reason, and also because he illegally encroached upon the land of Castile and León. About this we tell you that the king did not take away the land from you, but that, as you know, you went away from the kingdom and abandoned the land you held, and furthermore that you acted very wrongly. Because of the King of Aragón's plea, he welcomed you back into his land and forgave you, and had pleasure in favoring you, even when you requested it with service as you should. Before, you promised him that you would serve him because you had his love and grace; and now you go to disservice him in a very bad mode and in a very wrong manner. See how it is for you, for this is not the way that you might receive his favor and grace, but instead it is the way to lose them. If you say that the king encroached upon Castile and León, we have told you and the others that he did not do it nor did he wish to do so; but you promised before the King of Aragón that you would serve him and that you are his subjects and have the right to do so, and yet you go to that one who is God's enemy and the king's. The depravation and the wrong came from you, and from you it comes to the king and the kingdom, and you cannot say it is just."

Note

1. Álvar Díaz belonged to the Álvarez de Asturias family. O'Callaghan, *The Learned King,* 72, 77, 217, 233.

Chapter 36

❂

Of the Explanations That King Alfonso's Knights Told to Don Nuño González, the Younger, and to Don Diego López de Haro, and to the Other Noblemen Who Were There

"To all you of noble descent and knights who are here and to those who are not here,[1] we tell you on the king's behalf that you should ponder all the things that the king sent to say to these noblemen about what he wanted to do for them and what he wanted to fulfill for them again and now. And they never did want to accept it or receive it, doing him many wrongs and many insolences. For if they demanded rights, he gave them and granted them through his word in the courts and through his privilege. Other things they told him that they advised him to do, which were for the land's benefit, and he tried to do them just as the noblemen of Castile and León advised. He sent for them many times, telling them that he needed their advice and their service for this and other things; and they always refused to come to him in such fashion that it was not good for their honor or their welfare. You know how the king gave them good and large territories and many *maravedís* so that they could serve him with them; and now, with that which he gave them for you, in this fashion they take it to the enemies of God, of the Faith, and of the king. And with the very same wealth, which the king ordered them to give you so that they could serve him, with that [money] they take you to where you can disservice him, without God nor reason. See how it is for you and for them and what it is that you should do there: for we tell you on the king's behalf that those from whom you descend always considered loyalty and justice—particularly to the liege lord—and you should do the same. Because the king wants to do right under the law and in the other things that they requested from him, they have no reason to go to disserve him, nor do you. Thus, going with them wrongfully, with insolence you want to leave him; we say that you should not go with them against your liege lord. As for what they gave you because you are his vassals, the king gave it to them, and you did not give them from their inheritances; if they did not give you something, you would not be his vassals, nor would you be with them for reasons of kinship nor because of the debts you owed them. And since the matter of the vassalage which they have over you is due to the monies they gave you, from which the king gave them, because of these sums you have to render service, particularly to your liege lord. Therefore, we tell you to consider loyalty and justice and the law and to do so in order that neither God nor man may have anything to question you about."

Notes

Nuño González de Lara, the Younger (*el menor*), was the son of Nuño González de Lara, one of the leaders of the nobility. Diego López de Haro was a brother of Lope Díaz de Haro. O'Callaghan, *The Learned King*, 77, 195, 219, 239–40.

1. *Infanzones* and *caballeros fijosdalgo*, or noble knights, were nobles ranking below the magnates and were usually their vassals.

Chapter 37

❖

Of the Answer That Prince Felipe Gave to King Alfonso's Ambassadors

After Prince Felipe, the noblemen, and the knights had heard what the king's messengers told them, they withdrew in order to reach an agreement, and they sent for the king's messengers and gave them this answer:

"Don Gonzalo Ruiz and don Sancho Pérez: We have heard what you said to all of us together on the king's behalf, and understanding it very well; we cannot respond to each matter, for the explanations are very long, but we answer you concerning the two most important things.

As to what you say, that the king gave us his land and his *maravedís* so that we ought to serve him, you speak rightly; and we are sending to tell him that if he wants our service, we shall serve him. But asking it of us now is at a time in which we are not able to do so.

As to what you say concerning the matter of the evil acts: we did not give guarantees nor make compensations to him; the king knows that it is the law in Castile that concerning matters such as these he should provide investigators and order an investigation made, and according to what he finds in the investigation, he should order them to execute it. And we say likewise that he order his investigators to conduct the investigation, because we left good properties there; and according to what they find in the investigation, they should order them handed over. And to all the matters we do not answer now.

If he desires to do us favor, he also shall do so there as well as here where we are, and we want his good and his grace. And may the king do there as he considers proper, because since we do not live with him nor have his favor, we cannot avoid searching for a place where we may live."

Note

The royal letters to the nobles and their response to him probably all were dated in November–December 1272. O'Callaghan, *The Learned King*, 223.

Chapter 38

❖

How Prince Felipe and the Noblemen
Went to the Bishopric of Jaén

In the twentieth year of the reign of this King Alfonso, which was in the Era of 1310, and the year 1272 after the birth of Jesus Christ, Prince Felipe and the noblemen gave this answer and departed for Atienza. And they made their way to the Bishopric of Jaén in order to go to Granada.[1] Along the way, they committed great robberies and arrived at Sabiote, near Úbeda, with all of the plunder they carried along with them—which was more than five thousand horses, and clothes, and cattle, and other things. Prince Fernando, hereditary prince; and Prince Sancho, Archbishop of Toledo; Prince Manuel; the bishops of Palencia, Segovia, and Cáliz; the Masters of Uclés, Calatrava, Alcántara; and don Día Sánchez went there, and these princes, prelates, and masters spoke with them, telling and showing them the error and wrong that they were committing, and doing what they could in order to convince them not to go on that journey. No matter how much they said to them, they were not able to stop Prince Felipe and the noblemen nor return them to the service of the king, even though they promised many things. And because they were not able to convince them in this fashion, they showed a writ they had taken to the archbishop, the bishops, and to Gonzalo Ruiz de Atienza, which was sealed with the king's seal.

Note

1. The journey of the rebellious nobles from Atienza to Sabiote near Úbeda in the diocese of Jaén probably took place in December 1272–January 1273. O'Callaghan, *The Learned King,* 224.

Chapter 39

◙

*Of the Things That the Queen and
the Archbishop of Toledo Requested
the King to Grant to the Noblemen*

"These are the things that the queen, the archbishop, and the bishops asked of the king through his grace so that he might grant
them to Prince Felipe and the noblemen concerning the demands
they made.[1]

Regarding the statutes, may he grant them his statutes and their
uses and customs, just as they had them in the time of King
Fernando and he granted it to them; and if there is anything he
needs to execute, he will fulfill it.

Regarding the tithe of services, may he remove it; and since
these noblemen of the land return to his favor, they shall look for
a way to serve in such fashion that the king can accomplish his
affairs and that the land may bear it—and may this not be by law
nor by custom.

Regarding the men who petitioned for don Felipe, don Fernand
Ruiz, don Álvar Díaz, Juan Núñez, Nuño González, Diego López,
and Rodrigo Rodríguez, may he grant it to them so that they not
be imprisoned. And the king authorized so that he would grant it
to them from what he had and could grant it now, and from those
who sought to fulfill their affairs. Also that don Felipe may regain
his inheritance and the land he held. Regarding don Nuño, may
he hold the land he has, and may he hold that which he had at the
salt mines of Castile before don Zag seized them.

Regarding don Lope Díaz, may he give up his inheritance, just
as the queen, the archbishop, and don Fernando should decide
how much he should do. As to the six thousand *maravedís* that don

Lope Díaz demands—three thousand in land and three thousand in cash—let them give the cash to him, just as stated above, and may he be granted the land in those regions in which the archbishop might advise him.

Regarding don Esteban Fernández, may the king give Aldonza Rodríguez to the relatives who entrusted her to him. May they place her in her house, and may they let her be reconciled. Also, may don Esteban Fernández assure the king that he not come by force or might for her, but request her through the Church; and if he were to win her, or if she were to be granted as his wife, may he have her. Regarding the land that don Esteban Fernández requested: the king had granted it to don Fernando, and he is not able to give it to him, but he shall give to him from his monies what it was worth.

May he also grant a truce to the King of Granada from this Christmas for a year, and may the King of Granada grant the truce to him, and may the Moorish chiefs grant it to the King of Granada, and may Alfonso keep the treaties with the King of Granada, except in the case of the chiefs, so that he may act there according to what the queen, the prince, the archbishop, and the bishops will advise is good for him.

All of these things the king grants to them so that they go along with him to the empire and so that they may serve him just as they promised him."

And the prince and the noblemen, having heard and seen the writ regarding what don Fernando and the other good men who were there with him told them, they were not satisfied by what the king was sending to tell them. And they had a letter written concerning the things that they requested the king do for them, and they gave it to the archbishop and to don Manuel. And they departed from Sabiote and went to Granada, carrying along all they had seized from Castile. And now we shall relate what they sent to ask for and the reply that the king gave them regarding this.

Note

1. The text "These are the things . . . " ["*Estas son las cosas . . .*"] appears to be a contemporary document inserted in the *Chronicle.* O'Callaghan, *The Learned King,* 224.

Chapter 40

⬛

How King Alfonso Sent His Ambassadors
to Prince Felipe, and of the Answer

Prince Sancho, Archbishop of Toledo, and Prince Manuel arrived at Toledo where King Alfonso was,[1] and they related to him how Prince Fernando and they, and the prelates, and masters spoke with Prince Felipe and with those noblemen, who said that they refused to do anything of all that they told them nor did they wish to forsake the journey because of what the king was sending to tell through his writ, sealed with his seal, and that they were sending him another, which reads as follows:

"Firstly, may the king grant statutes and privileges, uses, and customs to the Orders, to the churches, to those of noble descent, to the Christians, and to the Jews and Moors, just as they had during the time of his father and grandfather.

Secondly, that he abrogate the tithe that was collected when entering and leaving from his kingdoms.

Thirdly, that he forsake the service tributes, which is a damage to all of the land, which becomes wasteland because the vassals are unable to comply.

Fourthly, that he not allow to be taken out of his kingdom by sea nor land, except those things that used to be taken out during his father's time.

Fifthly, that the salt and iron return to that condition it used to be in his father's time.

Sixthly, that he not collect the money except every seven years, just as his father, grandfather, and those of his lineage collected it, and that he never demand other taxes nor have the money count for more than the man who has been taxed ten *sueldos* and three coppers for ten years.

Seventhly, that in the king's court there may not be a governor except from Castile and León.

Eighthly, that the contributions for the pastures be not taken as they should not be, that they be collected as they used to be during King Fernando's time, and that the tributes of the cattle not be collected; moreover, they ask his favor that he grant the land to those of Castile and León, and that he favor others from the money in his treasury.

Regarding the *maravedís* that these good men have, since they hold them in established sites, may he order that the *maravedís* be given to them as the tribute that is now collected in the kingdom of Castile. And to those who do not hold them in established sites, may he order given to them from beyond the Duero.

If these good men caused any grief to the king after they parted from him, they ask him that through his grace he may forgive them and order them given his writ regarding this.

And may the king eradicate the towns of León and Castile that are detrimental to the king and lead to the dishonor of the knighthood of Castile and León."

As soon as the archbishop and Prince Manuel had spoken with the king about this and had shown him the writ, notwithstanding that it seemed to the king very strange to grant these things the noblemen sent to demand from him, and that it was very grave to authorize them—particularly because they requested them in arrogance—nonetheless, he handed this matter over to the queen, and to don Fadrique and don Manuel, his brothers. And the king sent them his letters in this fashion:

Letter from the king: "Don Felipe, don Nuño, don Lope Díaz, don Ferrand Ruiz, and don Esteban Fernández[2]:

Be aware that the archbishop came to me in Toledo and showed me those things that you were demanding, so that I act also for the good of the land as well as for some of your men; he told me that by doing these things you would come under my clemency. The queen, the archbishop, and don Manuel discussed with me that I should grant it, and even though they were very troubled by the fashion in which you were demanding from me, they pleaded with me and insisted so much that I had to grant it. Hence, I tell you that I consider it as a good thing and that it pleases me to do all of those things that they told me, and regarding this I send you my ordinance with legal security for it all."

Also the king sent another letter such as this one to don Felipe, don Nuño, don Lope Díaz, don Ferrand Ruiz, don Esteban Fernández, all of the noblemen, those of noble descent, and knights who were there with them. And he grew more in stature as he did it and granted it, because Prince Fernando pleaded and requested it from him, and he would fulfill it according to what the queen, the archbishop, don Manuel, and don Fadrique were sending to tell him through their letters.

Letter to don Lope Díaz: "Know that the archbishop and don Manuel came to me at Toledo and told me the things that you begged them to tell me on your behalf. Among other things, they told me that upon giving you Álava with Vitoria, you would come to me and would come to do my service. I would have given it to you, but don Fernando holds it on my behalf; but if he gives it away so that you may have it, I grant it to you."

Letter from the king to don Fernando: "I am letting you know that Lope Díaz sent to tell me that by giving him Álava with Vitoria, which you had from me as land, he would come to serve me. But because you held it, I did not give it to him; but if you hand it over to him, I grant it."

Also, the queen, the archbishop, don Fadrique, and don Manuel sent their letters, which said: "Don Felipe, don Nuño, don Lope Díaz, don Ferrand Ruiz, don Esteban Fernández, and all the noblemen, those of noble descent, and knights who are with them: We let you know that we advised, pleaded, and asked the king's grace so that he may desire that you come to his service and have his favor, and that he grant you those things you sent to require from him. The king wants to do them according to what you had sent to tell us in your letter, and they are these:

He grants statutes, privileges, uses, and customs to the Orders, the clergymen, those of noble descent, and to all of those of his kingdom who had them during the time of King Fernando and of his grandfather, King Alfonso [IX].

He abrogates the tributes that they collect at the entrance to and the departure from his realms; also he gives up the services to his land, and he will not take out by sea or by land from his kingdoms, except those things they used to take out during his father's time and that of King Alfonso [IX]. And the salt and iron will be as it used to be before his father's time.

Also, he will not collect the money except every seven years, just as his father and his grandfather collected it. Also, the king grants that in his court there may not be a governor except from Castile and León, and that they be laymen, and that they judge those from the land.

He will collect the contributions for the pastures just as they collected them during the time of King Fernando, and he will not collect the tributes for the cattle.

He also will give the land of Castile and León to its natives. And to what you told him regarding the towns in León and Galicia, he said that when you come to him, whatever we and you advise him to do, he will do.

We also told him on your behalf that because of these goods and on account of these favors that he was granting to those of the land and to you, that as soon as you were as one, you would examine how you would serve him in order to accomplish his deeds in such fashion that the land could bear it—and it should not be done except by law or by custom.

In order to do and fulfill all these things, you ought to come to him if he succeeds in accomplishing them for those who were there with him and with you; and if not, he will have the *cortes* convened in order to grant them forever."

And he granted and promised to preserve and carry out all these matters just as they are stated above.

Notes

1. The king was in Toledo from January through March 1273. O'Callaghan, *The Learned King*, 224–25.

2. The king's response to the nobles was probably taken from a contemporary document. See above, page 223–24.

Chapter 41

◙

Of the Letter That the Queen and the Princes
Sent to Prince Felipe and the Noblemen
Who Were with Him in Granada

The queen, the archbishop, don Fadrique, and don Manuel also sent another letter to don Felipe, don Nuño, don Lope Díaz, Fernán Ruiz, and to don Esteban Fernández.[1] It said as follows:

"Know that we advised, pleaded, and asked for the king's mercy so that he allow you to come to his service, have his favor, and grant you all those things you had sent to ask on your behalf. He grants them to you and wants to do them just as we send to tell to you in this our letter sealed with our seals. The things we are requesting on your side are these: We ask his favor to grant you and give you the lands that you used to hold. The king, in order to do you good and favor, grants them to you and wishes to give them to you just as you used to hold them, and particularly to you, don Felipe, your inheritance of Val de Corneja, and grants you more good and favor.

He also grants to you, don Nuño, your lands, just like you used to hold them in the salt mines and the rents, and to all of the noblemen what was theirs.

We also requested his grace to return to you, Lope Díaz, your inheritance of Balmaseda and Urduña, and he considers it good to do so.

We also told him on your behalf, don Esteban Fernández, that you were requesting your wife, Aldonza Rodríguez, and he granted to return her to her relatives and for them to take her home. And that you and they should protect her, and for you not to commit any violence, and that she should not be sequestered in any of your towns or castles, nor should you encounter because of his ordinance any obstacle, but that he will help you to obtain your right.

Regarding the three thousand *maravedís* that you requested from him concerning the land that don Martín Alonso holds, he says it belongs to don Fernando and that he might give it to you if he so wishes. Also, concerning the agreement through which all of you requested from him the *maravedís*, that because you had them in known regions, he will search where you used to have them and he will immediately grant them to you.

We also asked his mercy in forgiving you if you caused him any grief after you parted from him, and he says that as far as he is concerned, he forgives you. He promises to grant and preserve all of the treaties that were made at Alcalá de Benzaide between Alamir, on behalf of the King of Granada[2] and him, and requests that they likewise keep and preserve them—except in the case of the Moorish chiefs, because he wishes that they be with him during the truce. And because the King of Granada did not keep the treaty this last time, he wants him to pay it all to him in money, just as it might be found as decided between the king and you."

Before these letters were sent, the archbishop sent his squires to the noblemen in Granada with his letter. And we will relate their answer further along. Now, we will relate about the treaties and pacts that the noblemen had with the King of Granada, whom they went to serve and assist.

Notes

1. For the context of Queen Violante's letter, see O'Callaghan, *The Learned King*, 224–25.

2. Alfonso X and Ibn al-Ahmar, King of Granada, concluded a pact at Alcalá de Benzaide in June 1267. See O'Callaghan, *The Learned King*, 189.

Chapter 42

⊞

Where the History *Returns to Relate*
the Facts That Were Between
Prince Felipe and the King of Granada

Because it is appropriate that the deeds that are done by greater men be written before those that are done by lesser men, for this reason we related up to this point how King Alfonso heard what the noblemen had sent to tell him there and the answer he gave them. And we cease to relate the treaties that the noblemen had with the King of Granada, and [now], the *History* relates it at this point as follows: that before don Felipe, don Nuño, the noblemen, those of noble descent, and the knights who were going with them entered Granada, letters were written between them—one in Arabic, and the other in Spanish.

Note

The agreement between the King of Granada and the rebellious nobles was written in Arabic and Latin, but the version given in chapter 43 is in Castilian. O'Callaghan, *The Learned King*, 225.

Chapter 43

❖

Of the Letter and Treaties That Were Processed
Between the King of Granada and the Noblemen

"Let all those who see this letter know that we—Alamir Abboadille
Mahomad Aben Yuzaf Abenasar, King of Granada[1]; Amir Amus
Lemin; and Alamir Abboadille, our son and heir—are making this
treaty with the honorable Prince Don Felipe, son of King Fernando;
the nobleman don Nuño González, son of Count Gonzalo; the
nobleman don Lope Díaz de Haro, Lord of Vizcaya; the nobleman
don Esteban Fernández; the nobleman don Fernán Ruiz de Castro;
the nobleman don Juan Núñez, son of don Nuño González; the
nobleman don Diego López, brother of the aforementioned nobleman don Lope Díaz de Haro, the above-mentioned Lord of Vizcaya;
the nobleman don Álvar Díaz de Asturias; the nobleman don Gil
Gómez de Roa; the nobleman don Ferrand Ruiz, son of Ferrand
Rodrigo Álvarez; and with the nobleman Lope de Mendoza.

I, the above-said Prince Don Felipe, and these above-said noblemen, are united in this that we are doing for you, King of Granada,
Amir Amus Lemin, and Alamir Abboadille, your son, a treaty of
fealty in good faith that we hold for you without that you consider
it evil deceit; and if we were not to keep it with you, we should be
worth less for it before God and all men in the world, as one who
breaks an honorable treaty. Regarding this is the treaty and fealty
that we are making with you, and what you should do for don
Alfonso, King of Castile: Keep the treaties and agreements that he
made with you at Alcalá de Benzaide, and if he were not to keep
them, then we, the aforementioned, should help you with our bodies, our men, and with our might in the war you might wage against

him. If concerning this, don Alfonso, King of Castile, were to keep the aforementioned treaties that were made between you and him at Alcalá de Benzaide, then may you, the King of Granada, and Alamir Abboadille, your son, also keep those treaties that you made with him at Alcalá de Benzaide without any additions. And I, Prince Don Felipe, and these above-said good men grant you that we shall not make peace nor any treaty with the King of Castile unless you do, and may this treaty be during the days of don Alfonso, King of Castile. And I, the said Prince Don Felipe, grant through my authority that this treaty be in effect during the days of King Don Alfonso, Prince Don Fernando, and whomever might be his heir, just as it is stated; and I grant the privilege that was awarded at Alcalá de Benzaide. I, Prince Don Felipe, and the aforementioned good men, promise to help you against all men in the world, Christians or Moors, in war as well as in peace.

We, the King of Granada, Amir Amus Lemin, and Alamir Abboadille, our son, promise you that when we have need of your assistance, we shall send word concerning this so that you can come to our assistance. And I, Prince Don Felipe, and these aforementioned good men, all promise and are obliged to do for you, the King of Granada, Amir Amus Lemin, and Alamir Abboadille, your son, the same as we used to do for the King of Castile when we were his vassals, in all worldly things in which you may have need while we might be with you. And I, Prince Don Felipe, and the said good men, promise to be forever friends to your sons, to your grandsons, and to those who might descend from you.

We, Alamir Abboadille Aben Yuzaf Abenasar, King of Granada, Amir Amus Lemin, and Alamir Abboadille, our son, promise you, the very honorable Prince Don Felipe and the above-said noblemen, that we are obliged by this, and that we are making a treaty of fealty in good faith, without evil deceit; and that if the King of Castile were to seize the land you hold from him or your inheritances, or if he were to deprive you, may we be obliged to assist you with our territories, our men, and our might and wage war against him. If you were to come to us, may our war be one, and if you were to remain in your land, may you wage war on your side and we on ours. And if it were to happen that you join us, may we do for you the same as we did during that time you joined us.

This treaty and this fealty we shall keep, and if either you or we should not keep it, may we be worth less for it before God and all men in the world, just as the one who breaks a treaty of fealty. We, the King of Granada, Amir Amus Lemin, and Alamir Abboadille, our son, promise you, Prince Don Felipe and the said noblemen, that we shall not make peace or treaty with the King of Castile unless you do. We, the King of Granada, Amir Amus Lamin and our son, Alamir Abboadille, also promise you that if you were to seize towns and castles from don Alfonso, King of Castile, from today onward may we be obliged to return them to him when there is peace with him. And I, Prince Don Felipe, and these aforementioned noblemen are obliged from here on to make the King of Castile return to you, when there is peace, your towns or castles if he were to seize them.

We, the King of Granada, Amir Amus Lemin, and Alamir Abboadille, our son, in order that you join us whenever we have war with the King of Castile and that we do for you as we did at this time: we order more for you, the aforementioned prince and the noblemen, that we be always friends to you and to your sons and your grandsons and to those who descend from you. We, the King of Granada, Amir Amus Lemin, and Alamir Abboadille, our son, so that it be resolute and that no one may doubt it, write with our own hands this treaty. And I, Prince Don Felipe, and the above-mentioned noblemen write it on our appended seals."

After these treaties were signed between the prince and the nobles with the King of Granada, they went to Granada, and the King of Granada and his sons went forth to receive them with a great company. They all entered the city, and they gave them lodgings, food, and other things the prince and nobles needed, and they dwelt there for a few days.

Later on, the King of Granada begged them to go and harm and damage the chief of Guadix. The prince, the noblemen, and the knights who went there with them seized foods and other things they needed and went to wage war against the chief and came to the town of Guadix, and they lived there a month, felling the orchards and doing them great evil and harm. The chief and those who were with him fought back as much as they could, so that the damage was not so great that the chief considered himself overly oppressed. As soon as the companies arrived there, the chief sent to complain to King Don Alfonso concerning this, and the king sent to the nobles a messenger by whom he sent to say that whatever damage they did to the chief, his vassal, he would compensate him from his own wealth. This compensated for a great portion of the harm that they had done to the chief.

Because the King of Granada was very old and was weak from illness, he sent to them to beseech that they come to Granada. A few days later, after they had arrived there, King Abboadille died. The noblemen of Castile and León who were in Granada did him much homage, for they took him to be buried. But some of the Moors refused to accept Alamir Abboadille, his son, as king, for many of them clove to his brother. Some wanted to take one of the chiefs of Málaga or Guadix so that they could remove them from King Alfonso's vassalage. And the noblemen of Castile and León took their plea to Alamir Abboadille and made him the king. Now, we cease to tell about this, and we shall turn to relate the answer that Prince Don Felipe and the noblemen gave to King Alfonso.

Note

1. The emir Abû 'Abd Allâh Muhammad Ibn Yûsuf Ibn Nasr, more commonly known as Ibn al-Ahmar or Muhammad I (1232–1273), was the founder of the Nasrid dynasty that ruled Granada until 1492. The title *amîr al-muslimin* meant prince or ruler of the Muslims. He died on January 22, 1273, and was succeeded by his son, the emir Abû 'Abd Allâh, usually known as Muhammad II (1273–1302). Alamir is *al-amir*, the prince. O'Callaghan, *The Learned King*, 225.

Chapter 44

Of the Letters That King Don Alfonso Had From Prince Don Felipe and the Noblemen Who Were in Granada

In order to relate the treaties that Prince Don Felipe and the noblemen had with the King of Granada, let us relate what they sent to reply to the queen, the archbishop, and to Prince Manuel. The *History* relates it here and as follows: that after Prince Felipe and the noblemen saw the letters from the queen, the archbishop, and don Manuel, they sent an answer to the archbishop, in which they said to him that they were very grateful because he beseeched the king to grant them those things that the *History* has related that he granted to them. Because of his affection for the archbishop, the king sent to ask that they consider a truce for one month between the Christians and the Moors and to let the chiefs take part in this truce. He also begged them not to make another treaty with the King of Granada besides the one they had made. They also said that by the time the letters arrived, the King of Granada had died, and that they made his son Alamir the king, and that they spoke with him concerning the truce. The King of Granada [Alamir] answered them that he very much wished to serve the King of Castile and that it pleased him to have a truce with the Christians, but that he would never have a truce with the chiefs. And that although everyone failed him, he would rather give the land to Aben Yuzaf than to grant a truce to the chiefs. Regarding this, he showed the letters to the King of Castile of how he should not help them even though all of his Moors so advised him. But if the King of Castile refused to help the chiefs, then the King of Granada would serve him. They also sent to tell the archbishop that the king's messenger, who was to come to sign the treaties, did not come and to consider it as good for this messenger to come without delay. When this answer reached the archbishop, the king, being in Toledo, found out about the treaty and pact that Prince Don Felipe, don Nuño, don Lope Díaz, don Fernán Ruiz, don Esteban Fernández, and the noblemen who were in Granada had made with the Moors. He was very grieved about this, particularly because they were asking him to forsake the chiefs who were men with whom he could pressure the King of Granada. The king immediately spoke with all of the noblemen and masters who were there with him, and he told them he had learned what the noblemen did in the treaties they had made with the King of Granada and how they were sending to tell him to forsake the chiefs. On account of this, he decided not to have an accord with the noblemen; and he sent as many people as possible to Prince Don Felipe, who was in Córdoba, so that he could wage war against the King of Granada as much as he could and assist the chiefs.

While the king was in this meeting in Toledo, don Juan Núñez, Nuño's son, and Gregorio Ruiz de Atienza, arrived from Granada, and don Juan Núñez brought a message from don Nuño. At this, don Juan Núñez learned how things were, and he spoke with the king and told him that notwithstanding that those noblemen had made treaties with the King of Granada, not having been able to avoid it—for they were parting from the kingdom of Castile and were going to the kingdom of Granada—in that treaty they preserved their service to the king. And that since they departed for Granada, they had to go against the chief of Guadix, and that in that they kept their service to the king—for they did not do to him as much damage or harm as they could. And that while they were waging war and doing harm, as soon as they saw the king's letter that he sent them, they departed from there. Also, that none of them nor any of their men had trespassed into the king's land or caused any harm; hence, the king should not abandon the matters that were discussed, so that the prince and the noblemen could return to his service.

Henceforth, the *History* will relate the other things that don Juan Núñez discussed with King Alfonso regarding the message with which he came.

Note

This can be dated between January and March 1273. O'Callaghan, *The Learned King*, 225.

Chapter 45

How the King of Granada Spoke with Don Nuño
So That He Would Take a Petition to the King
in Order to Make Peace

The King of Granada, realizing that the chiefs were very powerful in his kingdom, and that with the noblemen he could not do against them what he wanted because of the great support that King Don Alfonso was giving them, and moreover, because he realized that the noblemen were sending messengers each day to the king and also that they were receiving letters from the queen and princes, he understood that they wished to come. The King of Granada spoke with don Nuño so that he might send his son don Juan Núñez to the king that he might take with him a tribute for the king, and to say that the King of Granada wanted to give King Alfonso some part of the land he held, and to ask that he forsake the chiefs and help him conquer them so that he could recover the territories they held. Regarding this, don Juan Núñez spoke with the king, and the two having discussed this matter, the king answered don Juan Núñez that it concerned him greatly to forsake the chiefs, for some plans could be attempted there that would satisfy King Don Alfonso, the King of Granada, and the chiefs so that they could remain on good terms. These are the things that the king and don Juan Núñez discussed in these talks and that the king ordered him to discuss with don Nuño and the King of Granada:

Firstly, that the King of Granada give the harbors of Algeciras, Tarifa, and Málaga to King Alfonso, that he give Guadix to the chiefs, and that in exchange for this, he would cancel payment of the tribute money the King of Granada had to give him for ten years—including in this account the money he owed him for the last two years. And that if he were to be offended by this agreement or if he refused to come and make it, he may consider another so that the King of Granada retain Málaga and Tomarque, and that he give the chiefs Baza and Guadix with their boundaries, and that he give the King of Castile the harbors of Algeciras and Tarifa; and that in exchange, King Alfonso would excuse the funds the King of Granada had to give him for six years. If they could not negotiate this treaty, it was possible to offer him another: that he give to the King of Castile the harbors of Algeciras and Tarifa, and that the chiefs deliver Málaga, Guadix, and Tomarque to the King of Granada; and that the King of Granada grant some land to them from which they could live, and that the King of Castile would grant the chiefs land from what he held near the land that the King of Granada might grant them; and that the King of Castile would subtract the revenue that the harbors of Algeciras and Tarifa produced from the tribute that the King of Granada ought to give him each year. But if the King of Granada said the king had to forsake the chiefs according to the treaty he made with him in Alcalá, he should come to his court to manifest it, and that if they justly found that he had to forsake them, he would immediately forsake them. But if they found that he should not forsake them, he would not forsake them.

And concerning this, King Alfonso said that he would give assurance so that the King of Granada could be certain that the King of Castile would comply. Once the treaty concerning the chiefs had been resolved in this fashion, may the King of Granada give him immediately all the wealth he had to give him from past times, and may he give the king a great loan from what was to come for the journey to the empire. And that if the King of Granada gave the King of Castile some land on account of these treaties, may he grant inheritances in it to those noblemen of Castile who were in Granada as he considered it appropriate.

Concerning the matter of the empire, don Nuño and don Juan Núñez said that they would go with the king and would bring with them five hundred knights if the king would give them whatever was arranged, and that don Felipe and don Lope Díaz would bring the other five hundred; or if not, may the king bring them along from his body of armed men.

Concerning the territories of those noblemen and the other

requests that don Juan Núñez made on their behalf, the king answered him well, for which he was very pleased.

Because he had received good answers to these matters, the king decided that he would be in the kingdom of Jaén or in Córdoba for three weeks, and don Juan Núñez took all of these things in writing and departed from Toledo. Gonzalo Ruiz de Atienza went with him and later carried the king's letters to don Felipe and to each one of the noblemen who were in Granada—letters in which the king sent to tell them that they should be aware that he wanted their well-being and service and that he was grateful to them for it and for loving and serving him, that he would right the injustices they said he had done them, and that he would do them favor. He also sent another letter to the knights of Castile who were with them and another letter to the knights of Toledo, Talavera, Zamora, Toro, and Salamanca, in which he sent to tell them that they should be willing to come to his grace and to serve him, and that he would not deprive them nor do anything for which they should part from his kingdom. And because their lords had gotten them involved in the turmoil that they wanted, he would pardon and do favor to those who were to come to him, and they should believe Gonzalo Ruiz on his behalf. And don Juan Núñez and Gonzalo Ruiz went to Granada with his messages.

Henceforth, we will relate about the battle that the noblemen fought with the Moors while they were in Granada.

Note

This can be dated between January and March 1273. O'Callaghan, *The Learned King*, 225.

Chapter 46

⊛

How Prince Don Felipe Defeated the Chiefs,
and How He Seized the Bounty
They Carried with Them

The *History* has related that during that time in which they made Mahomad Alamir Abboadille the king, some Moors wanted to have as king his brother. This brother of the king and those who favored him fled Granada and went to Málaga. And the leader of Málaga, who was an enemy of the King of Granada, welcomed them, and they assembled as many armies as they could and went to rob the land of the King of Granada. As soon as don Felipe, don Nuño, and the other noblemen who were in Granada knew about this, they took all of their armies and those of the King of Granada and went to that region where the Moors were. They found them in a place named Santiago, where they came to the boundary of Antequera. The king's brother, the leader, and the Moors who came with them were defeated, and don Felipe's men seized the booty they carried, which was very large, and a very large number of Moors died there. Don Felipe and the noblemen returned to Granada with honor, and the king welcomed them very well and gave them some of his possessions.

And now the *History* ceases to relate about these noblemen, and will relate the meeting that the king held in Almagro, in the Order of Calatrava's territory.

Note

Infante Felipe's defeat of the governor (*arraez*) of Málaga probably occurred in late January or early February 1273. O'Callaghan, *The Learned King,* 225.

Chapter 47

◼

How the King Held a Meeting in Almagro,
and of the Things That Were Accomplished There

Notwithstanding that Prince Felipe, don Nuño, don Lope Díaz, and the noblemen who were in Granada requested that the king grant them statutes, uses, and customs according to what they had during the time of the other kings who were in Castile and León, the king was aware and knew of many others who were with him and served him who claimed that they were querulous about this. Among these were men of noble descent, prelates, noblemen, knights, and many others from the cities and towns of his kingdom. They particularly considered themselves wronged by the tributes the king collected each year, for they said that the land was being deprived. Also, because of the tenth parts the king ordered collected from all the things that entered his kingdoms, cloth and other things that people needed to buy were in short supply. The king, in order to remove these complaints and those of his kingdoms, ordered them summoned so that they all could be with him at the meeting he wanted to hold in Almagro, a region in the territory of Calatrava. He held the meeting in that place firstly so that Prince Don Fernando and those who were with him at the frontier could come there and not be too far removed from the war in which they were engaged. Also, so that as soon as the noblemen who were in Granada knew about this meeting, they could send their messengers to speak with him, or observe what he was discussing, or become witnesses to the granting that the king wanted to do to all who were there assembled with him; and also so that as soon as they found out, they would come more quickly to an agreement among them. To this meeting came his first son and heir, Prince Fernando; his brothers don Fadrique and don Manuel; the Masters of Uclés, Calatrava, and Alcántara; and from the Temple, the Prior of San Juan, don Jimeno Ruiz; don Día Sánchez; don Fernán Pérez Ponce; don Alfonso Téllez; don Diego López de Salcedo; don Rui Gil de Villalobos; don Rodrigo Rodríguez de Saldaña; don Pero Álvarez de Asturias; don Fernán Pérez, Dean of Seville; don Jofré de Loaysa; and other noblemen, those of noble descent, knights of noble descent, and other knights of noble descent from the cities and villages whom the king had summoned for this. Before all, he manifested that while all of those from his kingdoms were assembled in the city of Burgos during the *córtes* and during the great meetings, that they—realizing what he needed for the great preparations he had to make in order to go to the empire—should agree that for a certain period of time each year, he should have a tribute in all of his kingdom. And that now that he had become aware that some of them were complaining about this tribute he collected each year—for they said he was depriving the land on its account and because they considered this an injustice—he could not avoid but to gather some funds for the journey. He considered it right that for the four years remaining in which he had to collect the tribute, he remove the tribute from two and collect the tribute during the other two, or in one year, if they so wished. Likewise, that the tenth parts he had to collect in order to pay for the great sums he had to give to the princes, noblemen, and knights from his realm be preserved so that they could be available for the war against the Moors. Likewise, he also granted that he would give something to all of those who had to go with him to the empire, and that he would collect it for six years, and that from then on he would abandon it. He also granted to all of those who were with him there statutes, uses, and customs just like those they used to have during the time of other kings who were before him in Castile and León, and that they keep for him those same statutes that the natives of those kingdoms kept during their time.

As soon as all those who were there and were with him heard these reasons, they considered it a favor, and they granted him to have the two tributes during the two years, or during one, if he wished it. Likewise, that he might have the tenth parts during the six years, according to what he had said. And because the *History* has related in which fashion this meeting in Almagro was conducted and about the things that were done, now we will relate the answer that the King of Granada gave concerning the message that don Juan Núñez conveyed.

Note

The assembly at Almagro in the modern province of Ciudad Real took place in February 1273. After returning to Toledo, Alfonso X issued a charter on March 28 confirming the agreement with the nobles. O'Callaghan, *The Learned King*, 225–26.

Chapter 48

◉

Of the Messengers That the King of Granada,
Prince Felipe, and the Noblemen
Who Were with Him Sent to King Alfonso

As soon as don Felipe, don Nuño, and the other noblemen who were in Granada had seen the writ that don Juan Núñez brought and the letters that don Gonzalo Ruiz brought, and having heard what they told them, don Nuño spoke with the King of Granada concerning those treaties that King Don Alfonso sent to order him to communicate with them. But the King of Granada did not give an answer to any of them, for he thought King Alfonso would not request of him such a great thing as the harbors of Algeciras and Tarifa, and that if he wanted something, the king would be pleased if he gave him one or two castles located near the Christian border; and even more, because he wanted this treaty with the condition that the chiefs be conquered and destroyed, yet he realized that King Alfonso wanted the chiefs to be powerful lords in his land. Nonetheless, he answered in this fashion:

He said that his will was to serve the king more than any other man in the world, and to consider well to keep the treaties and agreements they made together in Alcalá de Benzaide. He would give him the sum he owed him from the last two years, minus the tithes of Málaga, of Guadix, and of the other land he did not hold and that the chiefs held. In addition, he would give him as tribute two hundred and fifty times a thousand *maravedís* for the journey to the empire; and he would give him in silver what he could and would give him the rest in gold coins at the rate of seven *maravedís* per gold coin. He would also come to the king's court and make him understand how much he was willing to serve him. But for this, he needed a letter from the king in which he forgave him all of his previous wrongs. The noblemen also asked the King of Granada that because there was a treaty between King Don Alfonso of Castile and him, they should not welcome back any noblemen or knights who were in discord with their king. They also asked the King of Granada to let them destroy the written treaty that they had with him so that they could keep this treaty with King Alfonso and so that the nobles could go without shame. Notwithstanding that he was worried about this demand when they told it to him, he answered that if the king kept the treaty of Alcalá, he would do it in order to have King Alfonso's favor and benignancy and in order to satisfy what he agreed upon with him.

Don Felipe, don Nuño, don Lope Díaz, and the other noblemen sent their letters concerning this matter to the king, and they gave this answer to Gonzalo Ruiz. In order to examine what the king was granting concerning this, they sent their messengers with their letters of credence, who were these: Don Felipe sent Lorenzo Venegas de Talavera; don Nuño sent Pero Ruiz de Villegas; don Lope Díaz sent Sancho Ruiz de Linares; don Fernán Ruiz de Castro sent Gutier Díaz de Sandoval; don Esteban Fernández sent Nuño Fernández of Seville. All of these came to King Alfonso in Almagro while his son don Fernando, his brothers don Fadrique and don Manuel, and the Masters of the Orders were with the king. Before all of these men, Gonzalo Ruiz told the king the answer that the King of Granada had given, which he brought in writing, and which was related in this chapter. While these messengers were there, Rodrigo Álvarez de Saldaña came from Granada to the king's favor; and the knights who were vassals of don Felipe and of the noblemen told the king that the noblemen who were in Granada were sending to ask his favor to grant the King of Granada what he was requesting—according to what Gonzalo Ruiz told him, which was written in the document he brought—assuring that all of the noblemen would return to him and that they would serve him wherever he thought it proper. Furthermore, they told him that those who were in Granada were the men in the world, except for Prince Fernando, who wanted the most to love, serve, and advise the king. Regarding this, the king said that he would have a council with the queen and with those princes, masters, and noblemen who were there. And none of those princes, masters, and men who were there said anything contrary to what those knights had said. Prince Fernando departed from Almagro in order to go to Córdoba, and the king sent with him as many knights and men as he could.

Note

The response of the nobles to Alfonso X should be dated in February or early March 1273. O'Callaghan, *The Learned King,* 226.

Chapter 49

◼

How King Alfonso Sent His Messengers
to the Nobles Who Were in Granada

The king, having taken counsel concerning these matters, decided to send don Juan González, Master of Calatrava, to the nobles with his message, and decided that Gonzalo Ruiz de Atienza might go with him to Granada and sign with the nobles the treaties he had agreed to, so that they might send to petition Prince Don Fernando to send them to the Master of Calatrava; and to send another trusted messenger with whom to discuss the treaties.

The king told the master to speak with them and tell them that the nobles were not speaking correctly in demanding the treaty of Alcalá from the King of Granada to take away the allegiance they had made, since they could not render allegiance to an enemy of the king, [they] having the duties that they had; and with King Alfonso not taking land away nor doing any other damage to them through which they were against him; and even if he did so, though he did not, and since he ordered them told that he would make amends to them for it and in all other matters that they requested of him, then they could not make an allegiance against the king nor agree to it nor preserve it; and yet they were doing so.

Likewise, because the allegiance they had rendered was weak, it did not state that they were traitors nor treacherous if they were to depart from him [Alfonso]; and if they said that the agreement was worthless, they should not abide by it. And when there might be some pittance of harm, it was better that it be with their liege lord than with the Moors, to whom there was nothing owed. Moreover, they wanted to keep the pact with the King of Granada, though he and his son were not keeping it with them. But with King Alfonso rendering them assistance and much benignity, it was contrary to the chiefs who served him well and loyally, and they endured a great deal in his service so that King Alfonso would not abandon anyone who served and helped him. Notwithstanding all of this, what pride and madness they demanded as to inheritances in which they had no right, and to lands that he had given as privileges to those who served him for it, where the others disserved him! They demanded of him that he grant it to them, and they demanded that he give them more lands and that the king relinquish the service and a great part of the rents he had in the kingdom, and the matter of the empire, which they were promising more faintly than ever and with so much effort that they could not comply; and the service given by the King of Granada was so small that it would not be able to outfit four hundred knights; moreover, they requested of him that he strive mightily in the land so that they could get it and let King Alfonso lose by this action the support of the communities.

King Alfonso realized that and understood that they did not wish to grant a treaty, except to his harm and dishonor, which he considered a very great injustice; firstly on account of the station from which he stemmed, who he was, the station he held, and the rest because he was correct about what they were doing; and he was just concerning the above-mentioned matters they desired, which they ought not to. But he considered how they were his people and the relationship they had with him, and decided that if they wanted him to withdraw from that pact in which they so un-reasonably had involved themselves, then let them not request the other parts of the pact unless they remain under his clemency. He agreed to keep the pact they were asking him to keep with the King of Granada and to abandon the chiefs on the condition that they see that the King of Granada and his people serve him as to the empire with as many knights as the king thought he needed, and that it be immediately; and that if they did not desire this, he would carry out all the other matters they had requested of him and that he had granted them, and they should separate them-selves from the King of Granada and come immediately to his ser-vice. He ordered the master that if the rebellious nobles did not want any of these pacts, he should not consider any other proposal from them. And if any of these were to be signed, he would send his charters of established powers to Prince Don Fernando so that he might sign these pacts. Likewise, so that peace would be signed and a treaty formed with the Moors across the sea, and on this side of the sea, and with others that this treaty concerned. And the king departed from Almagro and pursued his daily marches until Ávila. And concerning this year, other matters that pertain to the *History* are not related.

Note

As already noted, after leaving Almagro, the king went to Toledo, where he drew up a charter for the benefit of the nobles on March 29, 1273. From Toledo he went to Talavera on April 6. O'Callaghan, *The Learned King,* 226.

Chapter 50

❂

*About the Assembly That the King Convoked
in Ávila, and About How Don Fernán Ruiz
de Castro Came Under His Grace*

In the twenty-first year of the reign of this King Alfonso, which was in the Era of 1311, and the year 1273 after the birth of Jesus Christ, this King Alfonso came to Ávila with those of the kingdom of León and Extremadura who were united there through the letter of his summoning. Being there and showing them the making of the treaty that he had with the Moors, and likewise, the wrong and outrage that don Felipe and the nobles who were in Granada had done him in departing to his enemies and pillaging the land from him, and proclaiming all the other things that they had done to him (as the *History* has related), don Fernán Ruiz de Castro, who had parted from the King of Granada and the friendship of the nobles, came to his protection. He came with many knights from there, and the king was greatly pleased with them and received them well and favored them greatly.

Likewise came there Gonzalo Ruiz de Atienza, who had taken the message of the king to the rebellious nobles. He reported to King Alfonso that he told those matters, as the king had ordered him to in Almagro, to Prince Don Felipe and the nobles who were in Granada. They forced him to repeat it before the King of Granada, and they stated that they did not wish to be a part of the treaty Gonzalo Ruiz had told them about on the king's behalf; and they said that they had sworn to go with him to the empire, but now they were refusing to go. Concerning the *maravedís* they were paying to the King of Granada so that he would give them to King Don Alfonso for the journey to the empire, they said that King

Don Alfonso should give the *maravedís* to them because they had lacked sufficient since the time they departed from him in the Hospital of Burgos until the present. Likewise, they wished that Gonzalo Ruiz tell, before all those of his court, that King Alfonso should abandon the chiefs and should promise in good faith to assist the King of Granada against them; and also they wished that King Alfonso give his letter in which he would forgive all the wrongs the King of Granada had done without making amends. Although don Felipe had it proclaimed not to do harm to the chiefs, in order to make Gonzalo Ruiz think that he had them on his side, that was not so, for the chiefs were in King's Alfonso's service.

As soon as the king heard these answers, he became very angry and was very concerned by it. He immediately ordered called with those who were there all of those from his kingdoms, and for them to go with him to war against the King of Granada. In order to have more men at his disposal so that he could cause greater harm to the Moors, he agreed to meet with the King of Aragón and his son Prince Pedro so that they would invade the Moors' territory on one side, while King Alfonso would invade the other side. With this and with what the chiefs would do, the King of Granada would realize that the noblemen of his kingdom who were there with him would not protect him. He also immediately sent his royal judges from Castile, León, and Galicia to demolish all the houses that those who were in Granada had.

Henceforth, we will cease to relate this and will relate how the Master of Calatrava went to negotiate a treaty with Prince Felipe and the noblemen as soon as Gonzalo Ruiz had returned to the king.

Note

The king was in Ávila at least from April 25 to May 27, 1273. O'Callaghan, *The Learned King*, 227.

Chapter 51

◧

How Prince Don Fernando Sent the Master
of Calatrava to Discuss Friendship with
the Noblemen Who Were in Granada

Prince Don Fernando, who was in Córdoba, learning of the answer
that the noblemen in Granada had sent Gonzalo Ruiz to tell his
father, the king, and also finding out that those noblemen were
seizing food and other things for which they had need, and that
those and the mighty ones of the King of Granada wanted to invade and overrun King Alfonso's territory, particularly the Bishopric of Jaén, don Fernando held a council with the Masters of Uclés
and Calatrava,[1] and with his brother don Alfonso Fernández,[2] and
with other noblemen who were with him there on what he should
do about these deeds. All of them advised Prince Don Fernando
that he should send the Master of Calatrava to speak with those
noblemen and grant them, on behalf of the king and the prince,
that the king would keep the treaties of Alcalá de Benzaide with
the King of Granada; and to promise it in council, although later
on he should not do it; and to agree with them in all other matters
the best he could.

The Master of Calatrava left Córdoba and went to Porcuna,
and from there he sent messengers to the prince and the noblemen in Granada who were there: Pedro Gómez Barroso[3] and Friar
Espinel,[4] with whom he sent to tell the prince and noblemen that
they should send knights to guide them. The noblemen sent to tell
him that if he did not bring that treaty, which they gave to Gonzalo
Ruiz signed, there was no point in going there. However, don
Esteban came to him in the guise of a friend and not in the guise
of one with a message from the others. He spoke with the master

about their friendship and told him how the noblemen and the might of the Moors had departed from Granada and that they were going to do harm in Christian territory. The master begged him that both of them should go and talk with them. So they left from there and went to speak with them in Alcalá de Benzaide.

They found them all there assembled, in order to enter Christian territory, and the master spoke with them about other matters that Prince Don Fernando ordered him to discuss. He informed them on behalf of the king and don Fernando in this fashion: that the king should forgive the King of Granada those complaints he held on behalf of his father and himself, and that he was granting him all of the treaties that were made in Alcalá de Benzaide, and that the king and the prince should preserve them according to the writ that the King of Granada had. He said that King Alfonso should not help the chiefs nor any men from his land, nor give them bread nor food, and that the King of Granada should be the king's vassal and observe all the treaties and agreements he had with him.

Concerning the statutes, the inheritances, the towns, and all the other things that they were requesting, the master signed with them the treaties as best he could, but not according to what King Alfonso wanted. Afterward, the noblemen and the Moors who were with them returned to Granada, and the Master of Calatrava, don Esteban, and Pero Gómez came to Córdoba.

As soon as Prince Fernando learned how the master had signed those treaties, notwithstanding that he had ordinances from his father, the king, to sign them, even though he did not wish to, he sent to tell the king to carry out what he considered good.

Henceforth, the *History* will relate what the king had Prince Don Fernando told concerning this.

Notes

The king had entrusted Infante Fernando de la Cerda with responsibility for persuading the exiled nobles to return home. O'Callaghan, *The Learned King*, 227.

1. Pelay Pérez Correa was Master of Uclés, also known as the Order of Santiago (1242–1275).

2. Alfonso Fernández, described as "his brother," i.e., the half-brother of

Infante Fernando de la Cerda, was an illegitimate son of Alfonso X; he is often called *el Niño,* the Child.

3. Pedro Gómez Barroso, a Portuguese knight and poet in Alfonso X's service.

4. Friar Espinel, a knight of the Order of Calatrava, held the commanderies of Matrera and Sabiote in the kingdom of Jaén in 1264 and 1268, respectively.

Chapter 52

◙

*Of the Letter That King Alfonso Sent to
His Son Prince Don Fernando Concerning
the Friendship of the Noblemen*

"Don Fernando: I saw the letter you sent me and also those that
the Master of Calatrava sent you, which those who are in Granada
sent him. I also realized that after Gonzalo Ruiz came from there,
they advised you to send the Master of Calatrava to Granada so
that he would grant the King of Granada the treaty of Alcalá de
Benzaide, and to give him my letter in which I promised in good
faith that he consider that you forsake the chiefs in the council,
but that later you should not do it in secrecy; and the Masters of
Uclés and Calatrava advised you on this. Concerning this, you had
your council send there the Master of Calatrava, and he went to
Porcuna and sent to all those who are in Granada to send him
knights to guide him. They sent him their answer—that unless he
carried with him the said treaty signed so that they could have their
monies in Granada, there was no reason to go there.

Don Fernando, when these letters reached me, was in Ávila,
for he was coming there to speak with the councils of the land of
León and Extremadura that I had assembled. I was sick with ca-
tarrh and a low fever, and I was very sorry that it had befallen us at
that time, but I even received more grief when I realized what the
letters were saying. As to what you say that the master advised you,
you should guard yourself from the trickery of the Master of Uclés,
believing such advice as this, for he is one of the men in the world
who advised those noblemen that they do it. Afterward, he sent
word to the King of Aragón not to fail to come to the meetings
with me, for there was peace, and that he would go to him and tell

him how everything was. Concerning the Master of Calatrava, I tell you that notwithstanding that I love him and consider him a good man, I know that he is from Lope Díaz's lineage entirely and that those he loved the most are his. But it greatly surprised me that he gave you such advice, I having told him he should go to Granada to tell them plainly that they would never have my favor unless they ceased to demand these things so unreasonably; and moreover, he having heard what don Juan Núñez and Esteban Fernández told you in Jaén, and yet advising you this.

Don Fernando, now I wish to speak concerning how this matter has reached this point and tell you there is need to keep faith so that you know how better to deal there and to show people how the matter is. These noblemen did not go against me for reason of statute nor for the wrong that I did to them. For I never took away any statute; but even if I had taken it away, I would have authorized it to them so that they would be pleased and happy. Also, I never did them any wrong; but even if I had done the greatest in the world, I wanted to right it for them well within their sight so that they had no cause to demand more. Also, they do not do it for the benefit of the land, for there was no other who wanted to do more than I, to whom the inheritance belongs, and they have little benefit in it but the good that we do them. But the reason why they did it was this: in order to have kings always under pressure and to take from them what is theirs, looking for ways to disinherit and dishonor them like those from where they come have tried before. For though the kings nurtured them, they made an effort to destroy and take away the kingdoms even while some of them were young; and just as soon as the kings bestowed inheritance upon them, they made an effort to disinherit them, first taking counsel with his enemies, then by robbery in the land, taking away what was the king's little by little and denying it to him. And just as kings made them powerful and honored them, they strove to make the kings less powerful and to dishonor them in so many ways, which would be long and very shameful to relate. This is the statute and the benefit for the land that they always wanted.

Now you can understand this, for all things that moved me to do what they wanted, they rejected them—particularly the journey to the empire, which is the greatest—and the fortune that they were to cause the King of Granada to give me so that they could be with me, they tell me to give it to them on account of the monies that I retained from them until now; and besides this that I return to them the lands they held before and that I should give them more of those, and that I should give them inheritances that they request without right so that they could be more powerful than they were before and always do us disservice. Besides, they desire that we be unable to make any kind of agreement with the Moors without them so that they have one firm foothold there and the other here, which will not stand if God is willing. Concerning that which they are rumoring about the treaty with Aben Yuzaf, that he will come over here with great might: now don Fernando, Miramamolín, who held the land now controlled by Aben Yuzaf, by the King of Tunis, and by other kings in between, was more powerful. Moreover, he was lord of all of Andalusia, and the number of knights never surpassed one hundred thousand; even considering that noblemen from this land were always with him, sometimes don Fernán Ruiz de Castro, don Pedro Fernández, don Diego, and sons of kings—Prince Don Pedro of Portugal and even the King of Navarre himself.[1] Each one of these noblemen was of better fortune and better understanding than those who live now. And King Alfonso IX of Castile only held territory up to Toledo,[2] and his son-in-law the King of León pressured him, and even the King of Portugal and the King of Granada as much as they could, and sometimes the King of Aragón. But with all of this, he defended himself very well from Miramamolín, who was never able to seize anything that was his, except the village of Alarcos when it was won in battle, more on account of the fault of those on the king's side than on the Moors' worth. And don Diego,[3] great-grandfather of this Lope Díaz whom they call "the Good," fled with his banner to the village of Alarcos, the king being still in the battle; and afterward, the traitor delivered with his own hands the village to the Moors without his lord's command to do so. But afterward, King Don Alfonso, with what little he had, knew how to avenge himself very well from Miramamolín and defeated him on the field and took away from him a great portion of what he had. Moreover, don Fernando, you should consider how Aben Yuzaf has many wars with Morocco, where they claim he is not their lord, and another with Gomarazán, who wages war against him in the land, and another because he is very despised—for everything he won was through treason and deceit, because of which I believe he cannot cross over, as those who are in Granada are saying. Let's say he wants to cross, where could he find ships to carry across so many knights, and will he bring food to feed those and the others who are here? I cannot believe this could be, nor as much help as they say he will have, for it is a custom among the Moors to write skillful and false letters and to send them to each other in order to obtain some advantages for themselves. This Alamir of Granada probably will have these letters sent to Aben Yuzaf just like his father used to do, and send to tell me to join him, and if not he would do incredible things against me.

Concerning what don Felipe was sending to tell me, that they proclaimed in Granada that they should not harm the chiefs, you can understand it because it was a stratagem that was found to come from there, so that I would hate them, break the treaty, and abandon them. They did not realize there the dishonor and shame that would come to us in doing such a deed as this without telling it, for such a deed like this should not even cross your mind to say it; and whoever advises you in this, he very wrongly advises you like a traitor. Because they so act, when we grant what they want they immediately demand something else. From now on, unless they exert themselves to do all the things that I will order, without land or anything else, and by my grace and measure as I wish it to be done, and unless they employ courtesy with you, let no other thing ever be permitted nor heard. For, don Fernando, I trust in God that we will quickly have great justice over them, for we would not want anything greater. For we hold with the law, and we want to expand it and defend it as much as they diminish it. Moreover, we have justice and truth, which they do not have; but they are in manifest wrong and in falsehood, and we have justice over what is ours, for they want to seize from us to our harm and dishonor, and desire that we give it to them; and that should not be done if the whole world should come against us and we should know that we would die a thousand deaths. Don Fernando, when a man receives harm by force, there is no surprise; but when he does it by his own hand, this is the greatest harm that can be. We should fight to protect ourselves as much as we can, for I trust in God that He will protect us, for He always protected those from whence we came. If we think that they will defeat us for lack of wealth, concerning this

I beg you and tell you that you examine what is the wealth of Granada for them, and what is the wealth of Castile and León for us; and where they have their goods and food, and where we have ours; and where they will have horses, and where we will have them; what is the power of Castile and León for us, and what is the power of Granada for them. If they make us think that they are wise, consider don Nuño, who is considered to be the wisest of them, who did not know how to thank God for the good He had done to him nor serve me in that estate and honor in which I placed him. He knew how to lose it through this madness in which he got involved, and hence, you can see what his wisdom is; moreover, he comes from a lineage of those who always lost what they had and for this reason died in misfortune.

About my brother, don Felipe, I do not have to talk about his wisdom, for you know well what he did to God and what he forsook that he had from the Holy Church, and what he did to us, in which he fully manifested his wisdom—and he appears as he is today. Concerning don Lope Díaz and Esteban Fernández, I tell you that I do not believe that they are as wise, nor should you, to have such bad fortune that they could outwit us; and if they calculate that they are many noblemen, you know well that they are no more than don Felipe, don Nuño and his sons, don Lope Díaz, and Esteban Fernández, and count as noblemen Lope de Mendoza and Fernán Ruiz. And here, I shall give you eighty who are all sons of noblemen and good men; moreover, I give you don Fernán Ruiz de Castro and Rodrigo Rodríguez de Saldaña, who came from there. If they speak of aristocracy, ours is much greater, for those who are theirs are ours, and the best ones are with you. Moreover, a great number of them returned to us and will return to us every day; first, because they know they do wrong by being there, cognizant of the good I did them; secondly, by coveting the good I will do to them; and more, because by being there they are ill-fated, and they will even be more unfortunate each day. But, don Fernando, you know how much it grieves me that you have three men for each one of theirs and better than theirs—without all of those at the frontier—and those who are advising you to put them in the castles, and that you have them scattered and they are not doing anything right. You cannot accomplish anything that is necessary to do with those armies you have there. They also say that the Moors have foot soldiers and men, but these they have are very few and bad, and you have more good men at the frontier than there are in any other territory. I think that if you join those who are placed as frontier guards in the castles with those you have with you and with the foot soldiers you can have on the frontier, you could go now to the Vega of Granada, while the wheat is green; you will take it away from them, even if you do not cause them any other harm except trampling the wheat. And if they should lose that small quantity of wheat, with the other harm they would receive in the agricultural fields and in the vineyards, and with the harm that those who are in Granada have done to them, I believe the war would last very little. But it does not seem to me that there is anyone to tell you this.

But they tell you that they are many and very good, and that the Moors will cross from overseas, and that your men have served their time and will go immediately. On the other hand, they tell you that you do not have any money to give them and that I do not have anything with which to assist you. By telling you false things in this fashion, they are making you afraid in order to encourage you to do the worst, for it is necessary that you examine whether you err now on these beginnings of yours, since when later on, should you wish to right them, you will not be able to. You should have been wary of the advice that they gave you a year ago—that if you had gone to the King of Granada and if the chiefs had gone with you, you would have lost your head and your honor forever. They made you go to Algeciras, making you a believer that Aben Yuzaf's son was there, and in that way you did not have profit nor honor. I also think that the first thing you should have examined was how the galleys might be readied, for if they were now in the strait, neither Aben Yuzaf nor any other could cross even if they wanted to. I also think that since you departed from the Vega, you should have divided the men—some with one chief and the others with another. And when the King of Granada might go against one, the other would enter his territory. There also would go those who might be with you; and with this, and with the other men from the frontier, you could wage such war on them in such fashion that they would do what we wanted. For the King of Granada does not dare to separate himself from the Christians for fear that later on he would be dead. They also tell you that the chiefs refuse to have among them the noblemen and knights you send them unless they carry food to eat. They are telling you the truth, and you should seek for more things to give them than the ones you are giving them here so that they could be there for one month. On the one hand, you should subsidize the chiefs well, and on the other, you should wage this above-mentioned war. For this you should talk to the noblemen and tell them that now it is right for you and for us to be in their debt forever, and moreover, that I would do them much good and would grant them these same lands of these others who have left. By promising and telling them this, they would control themselves and serve you better, for by leaving them in castles and not telling them anything, they become angry about it and therefore resort to do the worst. The same you could have caused the councils whom you allowed to come so that you would keep them until others that are now coming with me arrived.

Don Fernando, concerning what they make you fear about funds, I want to tell you so much that you may know, whatever things I gave you as assistance for this, I did not take one coin from you. Moreover, I order all the other councils to leave as an army—from the small villages as well as the larger ones—so that I may have something very great with which I may assist you. And without this, I trust the collectors and the royal judges will help me very well now, and those from many other regions that I cannot mention to you by letter, but they do not have enough for all of this. But if you were to give it as you are giving it, and with me giving to the Orders of Uclés and Calatrava what I gave them, you are giving them monies and other excessive things there and are doing yourself harm; and I am dishonored, for they think that what I give them is nothing, when you give them what you cannot and should not give them. In such fashion, there is no fortune in the world that could pay it nor could I pay it. Moreover, you have there don Zulemán, from whom you can have great fortune; first, because he is in my service, and second, because you have need of him at this time; and besides, he will do you very great service. From this you can sustain yourself until I come to you with what I have here, for I immediately will come there as soon as I can; and I do not delay at all, but for the King of Aragón, because I do not know when he will come.

I beg you that you ponder on these things that these letters say and that you dedicate yourself vigorously to them, and you will immediately see that the news and rumors will change in a different manner. And when you read this letter, my son, may Alfonso Fernández be there with you; and don Jofré de Loaysa, Diego de Corral,[4] and none other be with you."

As soon as Prince Don Fernando saw this letter he understood that his father, the king, had become very angry and aggravated because of the treaty that was negotiated with the noblemen. But he did not cease to work as hard as he could, because of this, in bringing them back to serve his father, the king.

Henceforth, we will cease to relate this and will relate what King Alfonso did once he had sent the letter to Prince Don Fernando.

Notes

Paula K. Rodgers, "Alfonso X Writes to His Son: Reflections on the *Crónica de Alfonso X*," *Exemplaria Hispanica* 1 (1991–1992): 60–79, comparing the many versions of the *Chronicle*, edited the text of Alfonso X's letter to Infante Fernando. The letter probably was written in late May or early June 1273. O'Callaghan, *The Learned King*, 227.

1. Alfonso X commented that several Christian knights, including Pedro Fernández, *el Castellano;* Diego López de Haro; the Infante Pedro of Portugal; and King Sancho VI of Navarre (1150–1194) aided the Almohad caliph, Miramamolín, whose power was greater than that of the emir of the Benimerines.

2. Alfonso VIII of Castile was defeated by the Almohad caliph, Miramamolín, at Alarcos on July 19, 1195. His daughter Berenguela was married to Alfonso IX of León. The kings of Portugal and Aragón were respectively Sancho I (1185–1211) and Pedro II (1196–1213).

3. Diego López de Haro, grandfather of Lope Díaz de Haro, lord of Vizcaya, fled from the battlefield, thereby precipitating the defeat at Alarcos.

4. Diego del Corral was Infante Fernando's *mayordomo.*

Chapter 53

◙

How King Alfonso Sent the Queen to Córdoba
So That She Could Resolve the Affair
of the Noblemen Who Were in Granada

Prince Don Fernando had sent to tell King Alfonso that the noblemen, the masters, and the others who were there with him were
very angry about the long time they had been there. Some said
they did not have the funds to spend and that the king did not
send any to them. Others from the councils said they had fulfilled
the time they had to serve and that they wanted to leave, and that
for this reason the king could not have them at his service, as certain as it was necessary. Alfonso also received a letter from his son-
in-law, the marquis,[1] who sent word to him that he had received
much harm and great losses by supporting the empire, and that all
of this had befallen him because of the king's lateness, and that
because this journey was delayed so much, many had parted from
offering their support for the empire.

   The king, realizing how convenient it was for him to appease
the affairs of the noblemen in order to go to the empire—which
was something he coveted much—considered it good to send his
wife, Queen Violante,[2] to Córdoba so that she and Prince Don
Fernando could resolve the affairs of the noblemen and bring them
back to the king's service. Notwithstanding that the king gave her
in writing the things she had to resolve, he ordered her and pleaded
with her to resolve it to his honor. And for this reason the conditions that he ordered to place on the treaties were not placed here,
also because she resolved it better than what the king ordered her;
and the fashion of this resolution the *History* relates below. The
queen departed from Ávila and carried the king's letters for Prince

Don Fernando, and to the masters and the noblemen who were on the frontier, and for Prince Felipe, don Nuño, and don Lope Díaz. She also carried letters for the King of Granada and for the chiefs, and letters from the king in which he granted authority to the queen and Prince Don Fernando to accomplish all of these deeds. The king also departed from there and made his way to the city of Cuenca.

Henceforth, we cease to relate here the king's journey, and will relate how the queen and the prince resolved the treaties of the noblemen who were in Granada.

Notes

1. William, Marquis of Montferrat, married Alfonso X's daughter Beatriz in 1271.

2. Alfonso X and Queen Violante, before she was sent to Córdoba, were in Ávila in April–May 1273. He was in Cuenca on July 18–19, 1273. O'Callaghan, *The Learned King*, 228.

Chapter 54

◼

How the Queen and Prince Fernando
Sent Their Messengers to the Noblemen
Who Were in Granada

The queen arrived at Córdoba and had council with her son Prince
Don Fernando, the masters, and the noblemen who were with him.[1]
She found out from them the things that had happened until that
time. Also there was the Elect of Albarracín,[2] who had come with
letters and a message from King Don Jaime for don Felipe, don
Nuño, and the other noblemen who were in Granada. Prince
Fernando and the queen immediately begged and ordered the
Master of Calatrava and Gonzalo Ruiz de Atienza to go to Granada
with their letters to speak with the noblemen on behalf of the queen
and don Fernando. So the master and Gonzalo Ruiz went to
Porcuna, but the King of Granada refused to give them any assurance so that they could enter Granada. From there they sent word
to Prince Felipe, don Nuño, don Lope Díaz, don Esteban
Fernández, and the noblemen who were in Granada that the queen
had come to Córdoba to resolve their affairs, and that she begged
some of them to come with whom she and Prince Fernando could
discuss what she had come for, and they sent them letters from the
queen and the prince. Regarding this, don Felipe and those who
were with him spoke with the King of Granada, and they showed
him the letters that the queen, don Fernando, and the master had
sent them. They told him what they had found out concerning
why the queen had come. Concerning this, they agreed on how
don Nuño would go to Córdoba to see what the queen thought it
well to tell them, and don Nuño did just as he was instructed. As
soon as he arrived in Córdoba, the queen and Prince Fernando

discussed with him in whatever fashion might resolve the treaties and complaints they said they had against King Don Alfonso. The King of Granada, don Felipe, and those who were with him resolved what they were demanding in this fashion—the king was to forgive the complaints he had from the King of Granada and from his father, and observe the treaty of Alcalá de Benzaide.

The queen and Prince Don Fernando answered that the king would do it if the King of Granada gave him the four hundred and fifty thousand *maravedís* that he owed him for the last two years, and he had to give him from the rents of his land and the other debts they justly found he had to pay from past time. Also, the King of Granada had to give him as a gift two hundred and fifty thousand *maravedís,* which he had promised King Alfonso for the journey to the empire, and additionally to give him the rent of one year in advance. Also, because King Alfonso wanted to keep the treaty of Alcalá, the King of Granada was to grant a truce to the chiefs for two years; besides this, the King of Granada was to destroy and abrogate the treaties, contracts, and homages he had with don Felipe and the noblemen and they with him, and the King of Granada and they were to swear and promise that they had not made nor were making any other treaties between them. Concerning these things, don Nuño and don Esteban said that the King of Granada would give the rent from the last two years and the other debts that were found that he had to pay from past time— except that concerning the land held by the chiefs, the king's vassals. They also said that concerning the two hundred and fifty thousand *maravedís* they demanded that the King of Granada give for the journey to the empire, and also concerning the rent for one year in advance, and concerning the demand that the King of Granada come to Córdoba to the queen and Prince Don Fernando: this and more he would do for them, and that the aforementioned don Nuño and don Esteban would help so that it could be done. It was also decided that they would then destroy the contracts and undo the treaties and homages they held together, just as the queen and the prince wanted. Concerning the truce that they requested for the chiefs, don Nuño said that he advised the queen and don Fernando not to discuss it now but to grant the treaty of Alcalá de Benzaide, and when the King of Granada would come to the queen and the prince, he would do whatever they wanted and would grant it. Also, concerning what they demanded about what don Nuño and don Esteban requested—that they grant the statutes, uses, and customs to those of Castile and León, as well as those of the villages, and other things, and that they may have these statutes just as they had them during the time of King Alfonso [IX] of Castile and King Alfonso of León—the queen and don Fernando said that it was a good thing, and that they granted it on behalf of the king, and that the king would grant it, preserve it, and give his letter about it.

To what they demanded concerning the money [*moneda*]—that it be collected every seven years and not in any other fashion, according as it used to be collected during the time of the kings from whose lineage the king descended—the queen and don Fernando responded that the king had granted it and that they granted it on his behalf.[3]

To what they demanded concerning the tithes and the service tributes—that King Alfonso not collect them—the queen and don Fernando answered that the king had granted it to the other good men who were with him, and that they granted it on his behalf to those who went to Granada and to this don Nuño for him. Also, concerning this that they asked concerning the *maravedís* they wanted the king to augment in addition to what they held as land from him—that the king add this increasement and the *maravedís* from this year to the fortune that the King of Granada used to give—the queen and don Fernando answered this: that to those who would go with the king to the empire, and not to the others, the king would pay the monies that the King of Granada would give. And that what he would give them they should receive as credit for what Alfonso had to give them for the journey to the empire. Don Nuño was pleased with this answer and granted it to him. To what they requested concerning the territory of Álava and the inheritance for don Lope Díaz, the queen and don Fernando answered that what was in Álava, don Fernando held it, because those of the land received him as lord, and that he wanted to give it to don Lope Díaz so that he could hold it.

To what they asked concerning the inheritance that was in Urduña and Balmaseda, the queen and don Fernando granted on behalf of the king that he would give it to don Lope Díaz so that he could go to the empire with him. The queen and don Fernando also said that the king should give his lands to those noblemen so that they could hold them from then on, just like they used to hold them at the time they parted from him.

Concerning the crimes that the noblemen and those who went along with them committed at the time they left the kingdom, it was agreed by both parties that the king should order it investigated; and that once they knew those from whom they seized something, they should pay for it from what the king did to them as favor, and they would pay as much as they could, and what they could not pay, they would send to request of those from whom they seized it so that they act in such fashion that they may have their love.

Concerning the marriage of don Esteban Fernández, may the king do there that which he has granted on other occasions.

The treaties having been treated and discussed in these manners, they agreed that don Juan González, Master of Calatrava, and Martín Ruiz de Leyva would go to Granada with don Nuño to sign these treaties with the King of Granada, Prince Felipe, and the noblemen who were there. They carried the letters from the queen and Prince Fernando so that they be satisfied in it. But the queen and Prince Fernando charged and ordered the master and Martín Ruiz that they should not deliver these letters until they first receive letters and assurance from the King of Granada, Prince Felipe, and all of the noblemen who were with them—that they come to Córdoba immediately to sign these treaties and agreements that were discussed. The queen and Prince Fernando wanted Gonzalo Ruiz de Atienza to go with the Master of Calatrava concerning these treaties, but don Nuño refused to grant safe passage for Gonzalo Ruiz to go to Granada, for he was certain that if he were to go there, the King of Granada would order him killed because in each one of his trips in which he went there he took from him a great number of the knights who were with him and with the other noblemen in Granada.

As soon as don Nuño and the Master of Calatrava departed from Córdoba to go to Granada, the queen and Prince Fernando sent to tell the king about these treaties and in which fashion they had signed them.

Henceforth, the *History* will cease to relate about the queen and the prince who were in Córdoba, and of the noblemen also who were in Granada, and it will relate about King Alfonso, who had gone to the meetings of the King of Aragón, and of the answer he gave to these matters.

Notes

1. Violante's negotiations with nobles probably took place in July–August 1273. O'Callaghan, *The Learned King*, 228.

2. The bishop-elect of Albarracín was Pedro Jiménez de Segura (1272–1277).

3. *Moneda* was a tribute collected every seven years, originally in return for the king's promise not to alter the coinage during that time.

Chapter 55

❋

*How the King Being in Cuenca, the Queen's
Messengers Arrived to Discuss the Peace with
the King of Granada and His Noblemen*

We have related how King Alfonso departed from Ávila to go to
meet with King Jaime of Aragón.[1] He brought with him to the
meeting Prince Don Sancho, Archbishop of Toledo and the son of
King Jaime; Prince Manuel; Prince Sancho, son of this King Alfonso;
and his nephew don Alfonso, whom they called Molina; and other
companies of prelates, noblemen, knights, and citizens from the
cities. As soon as he had arrived in Cuenca, Alfonso found out how
King Jaime of Aragón was in great discord with his son and first
heir, Prince Pedro, and for this reason King Alfonso remained in
Cuenca for a few days, sending his messengers to the king and
Prince Pedro to work out peace and appeasement so that both of
them could come to the meeting. And the king being in Cuenca,
Gonzalo Ruiz came to him there with the letters from the queen
and Prince Fernando and told him how don Nuño had come to
Córdoba. He related to him in what fashion the treaties with the
King of Granada, don Felipe, and the noblemen who were with
him there had been signed. He also told him how the Master of
Calatrava, Martín Ruiz de Leyva, went to Granada to sign them.
The answers Gonzalo Ruiz told him concerning this having been
heard, Alfonso sent an answer to the queen and Prince Fernando,
speaking as follows:

To the queen he sent to report that he thanked her as much as
he could because he knew how well she worked in resolving these
matters, and notwithstanding that he trusted her much beforehand
as a wife and reared in place of a daughter, he trusted her even

more because she had resolved these matters so well and so much to his service, for he was very pleased and considered it to his greater honor than if he had resolved them, and he begged that they sign in the same fashion in which they were discussed. He was sending his letters so that they could act in such fashion that it be valid on his behalf. He also sent to tell his son Prince Fernando that he thanked him much because he had known so well how to settle the resolution of these matters, notwithstanding that he trusted him beforehand as his son, whom he loved with all of his heart, but that he trusted him more because he had served him and helped him so well, and because he knew how to set right the treaty, which without any motive they had made him authorize before the evil advisors. Notwithstanding that he was pleased because he had resolved it so well, he was even more pleased because these deeds were coming from the prince, for the king considered honor greater; and those with whom they agreed would always be obliged to the prince for what he had done in order to bring them to the king's service. And the answers of the queen and prince in this fashion having been made, the king gave his letters to Gonzalo Ruiz, which said as follows:

Because of the queen and Prince Fernando's request, and because don Felipe and the noblemen who were in Granada had made strong treaties with the Moors for which they could not serve him as they should, the king—in order to free them from those treaties and take them to his service—granted his pardon to the King of Granada so that he might observe the treaty that was made at Alcalá de Benzaide, as states the writ that was made concerning this; the King of Granada observing it for King Alfonso, Gonzalo Ruiz carried a letter sealed with the king's seal. He also carried another letter in which the king granted don Felipe and the noblemen and knights who were in Granada—on account of the queen and don Fernando—the statutes, uses, and customs they had during the time of the kings of Castile and León, they keeping for the king his lordship, statutes, and rights. Also, because the noblemen and knights who joined the king in Almagro asked him to remove the two tributes they had to give him for four years, stating that he may collect the tenth parts for six years and that henceforth he should not have them, he granted don Felipe and the noblemen who were with him in Granada this granting he had made to those who joined him in Almagro. He also granted them in this letter all the treaties and agreements that the queen and the prince made with them (which the *History* has related). He also told Gonzalo Ruiz to tell the queen the affairs of the meetings they had with the King of Aragón, and also to tell her how his sister the Queen of England and her sons sent to beg him to meet with them and to advise him on how he would act[2]; also, to tell them that the pope wanted to have a council concerning the election for the empire and other matters,[3] and that he needed to have these matters settled in order to go there, and that they should try to resolve them as fast as they could, and that the noblemen should agree that they would go to the empire with him, and that they should depart from Granada for Murcia, and that he would go there and take them with him. King Alfonso also ordered him to tell the queen and the prince that as soon as they had settled the affairs of the King of Granada and the noblemen, and having obtained the truce for the chiefs, they should go to the city of Jaén and should send their letters to the chiefs of Málaga, Guadix, and Tomarque, letting them know the manner in which the treaties were being resolved, particularly in order to remove the help the King of Granada had in those noblemen, but also so that they should know that the king would not forsake them.

Concerning all of these things, Gonzalo Ruiz carried the letters to the King of Granada, the noblemen who were with him, and to the chiefs; the king sent them to say that they should believe the queen and Prince Fernando in everything they said on his behalf. The king also sent a letter to don Nuño in which he thanked him and considered as service anything he had done in order to resolve these matters, and he begged and ordered don Nuño to serve him in this, promising to do him favor.

Henceforth, the *History* ceases to relate about this and returns to relate what the queen and the prince did in the resolution of these matters.

Notes

1. Alfonso X was in Cuenca in mid-July 1273.

2. The king's sister Leonor had married Edward I of England in the Cortes of Burgos in 1254. O'Callaghan, *The Learned King*, 34, 84, 151–52, 228, 267.

3. Pope Gregory X summoned the Second Council of Lyons, which met in 1274.

Chapter 56

◙

How the Noblemen Who Were in Granada
and the Master of Calatrava
Came to the Queen in Córdoba

After don Nuño and the Master of Calatrava left Córdoba concerning the discussion they had had with the queen and with Prince Fernando, they went to Granada, and with them went Martín Ruiz de Leyva. They showed the King of Granada, Prince Felipe, and the other noblemen from Castile and León who were there in what fashion the treaties were being discussed and signed, and they all considered it well and were pleased by it. They immediately sent their letters to the queen and to Prince Fernando in which they sent to tell them that don Nuño, don Lope Díaz, and don Esteban Fernández would immediately come to Córdoba with the obligations these treaties deserved.

A few days later, don Nuño, the Master of Calatrava, don Lope Díaz, and don Esteban Fernández came to Córdoba and brought letters from the King of Granada, don Felipe, and the other noblemen who were with them to the queen and Prince Fernando,[1] in which they sent to tell them that they had seen the discussion of the treaties that don Nuño was negotiating with the queen and don Fernando. They said that they were pleased with the discussion and agreement and that they were authorizing it and would be in favor of it. They also sent to tell them that all of them wanted to come to the king's grace and to place their treaties in the hands of the queen and Prince Fernando, for they considered that because of her they were assured of their heads and also assured of the treaties that they were making, and that through them they would resolve and do well for their affairs. They also said that the

King of Granada could not come to Córdoba but that he would come to Jaén. The queen and don Fernando considered it well to go there. Concerning this, don Nuño advised the queen and don Fernando to send don Lope Díaz and don Esteban Fernández with their letters to the King of Granada, saying that he would send his letter, and that he believed he would come to Córdoba; and the queen and the prince did the same. Don Nuño, don Lope Díaz, and don Esteban Fernández told the queen and don Fernando that Diego López de Salcedo was destroying the houses that the noblemen and knights who were in Granada owned in Castile, and that Payo Varela would do the same in Galicia; and they asked for his mercy to ask the king to order it stopped. Then the queen and don Fernando granted that they would do it, and they sent their letters to the king concerning this. They also asked the queen and don Fernando to grant that the king pay them for the lands that they held for him during these two years in which they had been in Granada, for they said that because during this time they did not do harm or damage in the land of their lord the king, and hence, they should not lose the *maravedís* they held as land from him. The queen said that this was an addition to what was discussed and placed in the agreements and that she could not grant it until she sent to tell the king.

Don Lope Díaz and don Esteban Fernández departed from Córdoba and went to Granada, and they spoke with the King of Granada and with don Felipe about their coming to Córdoba. They agreed that they would do it and that all of them would come there, but they told them that the queen, don Fernando, and don Nuño should send to tell King Alfonso to consider it good to come there or to another place on the frontier, and that the King of Granada would visit it and the others would come with him, and they would discuss their affairs with him.

While don Lope Díaz and don Esteban Fernández went to Granada, the queen and don Fernando told don Nuño that he had to go with the king to the empire. Don Nuño told them that he would do it gladly, but that he and his son don Juan Núñez would take a thousand knights and that the king should pay them, and that with less than such a company as this, they would not go there. But he said that if the king paid them for these thousand knights, both of them would go with him, for they considered it necessary for the king's service to take these thousand men and not less. In order to pay for these knights, the king should consider as good that don Nuño received the sums the King of Granada was now giving in this agreement, and whatever was required in addition to this for the salary of these knights, the king should pay it from another source. These matters being in this state, Gonzalo Ruiz de Atienza, who came from King Alfonso and who was bringing the king's letters so that those treaties could be signed, arrived in Córdoba so that they could sign these treaties. He discussed with the queen and Prince Fernando the matters the king ordered him to tell them, and he told them how the king, as soon as he had departed from those meetings with King Jaime of Aragón, wanted to go and meet with his sister, the Queen of England, and with his sons. He also said that the queen and don Fernando should speak with Prince Felipe and with the other noblemen so that they could go with him to the empire, and that from there they would depart afterward and go to the kingdom of Murcia; and because the King of Granada was to give him the sums, King Alfonso would go through there and they would go with him.

The queen and don Fernando, when they heard this answer, sent to suggest that he consider it good to avoid that meeting and that he should immediately come to Córdoba to settle matters, for the King of Granada and those noblemen were saying that as soon as they had seen the king and had made peace with him, the King of Granada would then go, if he wished it, as far as Logroño or any other place he wished and that the nobles would go to the emperor wherever he ordered. They asked his mercy to avoid the meetings with the Queen of England and not to delay his coming. If concerning this meeting he had sent to confide in the King of England and his sister, the queen, he should remember how at another time they asked him to trust them, and while he had been very weak, he went into the mountains during very harsh weather and great storms—during which he made a great effort to go to those meetings—and that the King of England and his sister, the queen, sent to tell him that they could not come there then because of some things they had to do there for their benefit. Just as everyone cares for what is to his benefit, he had a very good reason to avoid it, and even more so concerning such a matter as this in which he had benefit and great honor. Moreover, because the noblemen and knights who were there with Prince Fernando had lived eight and a half months on the frontier—and moreover, it had been three months and more since they had given them anything—for this reason they were asking each day if he would come there, and the queen and don Fernando said yes. And that they were certain that if the noblemen and knights knew the king was going to those meetings and that he would not come there, they would not be with them, but each one of them would go to his lands; and when she and don Fernando tried to detain them there, they could not since they did not have anything to give them. Moreover, the King of Granada and the noblemen would not come to the agreement, which was arranged and fixed, and therefore they were asking for his mercy to consider it good to come to Córdoba immediately and to postpone the meeting with the Queen of England, for he could see her at another time. If he was upset by having to cross mountain passes to go to the frontier, the queen and the prince would make them all go to Toledo, and hoped he would consider it well to go and wait for them there. They also sent to tell him of the discussion they had with don Nuño concerning the journey to the empire and of the answer he gave them. They also sent to tell him about what don Nuño, don Lope Díaz, and don Esteban Fernández asked them concerning the matter of the rents, and said he should consider it good to have sent what they had to say concerning this. Henceforth, the *History* ceases to relate this and will relate the meetings that King Alfonso had with King Jaime of Aragón.

Note

1. The meeting of the nobles and Violante in Córdoba probably should be dated in July–August 1273. O'Callaghan, *The Learned King*, 228.

Chapter 57

How King Alfonso and King Jaime of Aragón
Met at Requena, and of the Deeds
That Happened There

We have already told, and the *History* has already related it, that King Alfonso delayed his meeting with King Jaime of Aragón because his messengers, whom he had sent to negotiate an agreement and peace between this King Jaime and his first son and heir, Prince Pedro, concerning the disagreement and conflict that existed between them, were unsuccessful. Because this agreement could not be made, King Jaime came to the meeting and Prince Pedro sent to tell him that he should excuse him from those meetings because, since he could not have an agreement with his father, he desisted from coming to meet with King Alfonso in order not to anger his father. For this reason King Alfonso went to Requena, and King Jaime came to meet with him there. King Alfonso told him the wrong that Prince Felipe and the noblemen who were in Granada had done him. Notwithstanding that the queen was in Córdoba, in order to resolve the affair of the noblemen, they were telling him that Aben Yuzaf was crossing from overseas with great Moorish might, and that if he crossed, he could not avoid to fight with him; for this he had need of King Jaime's assistance. If Aben Yuzaf did not cross and the queen could not negotiate the treaty of Granada and of those noblemen, then he would want to invade the Moors' land and destroy the vineyards and the agricultural fields and not allow them to plant or harvest. Concerning this he was not only thinking of making one invasion or two during the year, but six or seven also—in winter as in summer. And he asked that King Jaime send his son and heir to invade through Almería and that he would do the same; for if they did this for two years, they would serve God and would make the King of Granada deliver the land to them, or it would become unprotected. King Jaime answered King Alfonso that if Aben Yuzaf were to cross hither, and that if King Alfonso had to do battle with him, he would come to the conflict in his succor. Concerning the noblemen who were in Granada, he told him that because the queen and his son had negotiated with them peace and accord on behalf of King Alfonso, he should consider it well to give the opportunity time so that they could settle their differences with the noblemen. King Jaime said this notwithstanding the fact that he had sent to them the Elect of Albarracín with his message in order to bring forth some agreement between the king and those noblemen, that he will send him there again to beg them to wish to resolve this treaty through the queen, since she had started to discuss it, that if there could be an agreement, he would help King Alfonso with men to wage war on the King of Granada. After this, King Alfonso departed from the meetings, and King Jaime went to Valencia. King Alfonso fell ill with tertian fever at Requena, and being so, the Count of Ventimilia and other Lombards came there to the king with a message from those who had elected him as emperor. The king then departed from Requena and went to Cuenca, and from there to Cañete, and there the letters that the queen and don Fernando had sent reached him. With the letters seen, he sent to tell them that due to the journey to the empire, and since don Nuño said that he wanted to take a thousand knights, King Alfonso understood well that he was not telling this agreement on his own, but he was telling it on behalf of himself and of the others who were in Granada; because neither don Nuño nor his son don Juan Núñez had a thousand knights. The king knew that don Felipe and the noblemen who were in Granada were all thinking about taking those funds and knights, and that don Nuño had negotiated afterward to take with him five hundred knights, and that don Nuño and his son don Juan Núñez should take these and some of the others who were in Granada who wanted to come with him. The sums that amounted to their pay should be taken from the money the King of Granada gave, and it should be agreed that the Order of Calatrava keep the sums under guard and in safekeeping to give them to don Nuño when they had to go with him. If don

Nuño said that he would not go with him to the empire with fewer than the thousand knights, it would seem very clearly to be a breaching of the treaty, since the Count of Ventimilia and the Lombards who were there with him had told him that five hundred knights were enough. With these and with those they could have had there, his authority could very well make his whole treaty valid. If they had the willingness to come to his service, they should not want things that seemed proper to them but rather as he saw that were advantageous to him. Those who refused this should abandon the journey to the empire and remain in Castile. To what don Felipe and the noblemen who were in Granada said—that because they were not stealing nor waging war in the king's land while they were with the Moors, they should have the *maravedís* they were getting from him— he responded to them that he was very surprised that the queen and don Fernando heard this agreement from them, for this was the greatest arrogance of the noblemen, and on the king's behalf, the greatest debatable treaty that ever was; for very great was the dishonor they did by robbing the land before they left it, for they robbed it while they were with his enemies; moreover, to rob it during the forty-two-day truce they had with him and that he gave them as a time limit to leave the land, and to commit such great robbery and so much harm as they did; and moreover, that being his vassals, having parted from him without justification, they should not demand the land during that time. And if they said that they did not do him any harm while they were with the Moors, they understood well that one of the great harms they could do him was what made him lose Granada and all that the king had in Granada. For if they had been with the king, he would have considered waging war on the King of Granada with the help he had from the chiefs, since in a very short time he would have taken Granada from the King of Granada and everything he had. Since they did not have anything for this service, he had to give them the sums of money. In addition to this, they did great harm to the chiefs, who were his vassals, about which they lamented much. Notwithstanding that they did all of this to him, he had protected the women and the inheritances and all they had; for this alone they ought to serve him instead of demanding such great insulting action as they were asking of him; moreover, none of these conditions were from those that the queen and the prince had granted them.

Concerning what they sent to say about coming to Córdoba or Toledo, he sent to say that his itinerary did not allow him to go to Córdoba, because if there were any changes in the affairs, it would not be to his honor to receive from them more insults than all those he had received, and that for this reason it seemed to him better that they should sign the treaties in Córdoba and that afterward they all might come to him at Toledo.

Before this answer reached the queen and don Fernando, they found out that the King of Granada refused to go from Granada to any other place but Córdoba or Seville. For this reason they immediately sent word to King Alfonso that because Alfonso refused to come to Córdoba, he should come to Seville and there would come to him the King of Granada, don Felipe, and the noblemen. So the King went to Toledo and from there to Seville.[1] Since the *History* has related the answer that the lord king sent to the queen and don Fernando, now we will relate what was resolved in the treaty of the King of Granada and the noblemen.

Note

1. The meeting of Alfonso X and Jaime I of Aragón at Requena took place between August 22–28, 1273. His journey to Cuenca, Cañete, and Toledo probably occupied most of September–November. He probably did not go to Seville until December. O'Callaghan, *The Learned King*, 228.

Chapter 58

◉

How King Alfonso Reconciled
with the Noblemen Who Were in Granada
and Made Peace with the King of Granada

In the twenty-second year of the reign of this King Alfonso, which was in the Era of 1312, and the year 1274 after the birth of Jesus Christ,[1] don Lope Díaz and don Esteban Fernández, having come to Córdoba with the answer for which they went to Granada, told the queen and don Fernando that the King of Granada and all of them were coming to Córdoba in honor of the queen and the prince, and that from there they would go to wherever the king might be. Don Nuño, don Lope Díaz, and don Esteban Fernández asked the queen and don Fernando to grant them what they had requested concerning the lands. So the queen and don Fernando gave them as an answer that which the king had sent to tell them. They also spoke with don Nuño and told him that the king could not provide the salary for the thousand knights don Nuño said he wanted to take with the king for the journey to the empire, nor did the king wish to take immediately more than five hundred knights. So they left with those answers for those requests they were making, and they signed the treaties under those conditions that had been negotiated before and that the queen and don Fernando had granted. They gave to the Master of Calatrava the king's letters that they had there concerning how the king granted and wanted to retain the agreements that were signed there, and stating that he should have these letters under his pledge until the King of Granada agreed to destroy the letter of agreement that was made between him, don Felipe, and the noblemen who were with him at Granada. The King of Granada, Prince Felipe, and all of the other noblemen who were in Granada came there to Córdoba, and the King of Granada ordered handed over to the Master of Calatrava the money he had to give to King Alfonso from past times, and also the sum he had to give him in service for the journey to the empire that he had brought to Córdoba. He gave it to the master in trust that with King Alfonso granting the treaties and agreements the queen and don Fernando had granted, the master could deliver the sum to the king. As to the treaty concerning the truce of the chiefs, they said nothing to the King of Granada, for they knew that if they told him, he would withdraw from the meeting for this reason.

While all these people were in Córdoba and the affairs were in this state, they found out how King Alfonso had arrived in Seville. They departed from Córdoba, and they all went with the queen and with Prince Fernando to King Alfonso, who had already come to Seville. With them came the King of Granada, don Felipe, don Nuño, and all the other noblemen who also were with them in Granada. The king was very pleased with those companies, and he welcomed them very well and did them much honor, particularly to the King of Granada. From this coming, he knighted him and gave him his treaty and his friendship as firm as the King of Granada could, according to what the queen and don Fernando had granted. The King of Granada also granted to King Alfonso to be always his vassal and to give him from his revenues three hundred thousand *maravedís* in the currency of Castile each year; and in all of this sojourn that they had in Seville, King Alfonso did much honor to the King of Granada. With the granting made and the treaties signed, the Master of Calatrava gave the king the fortune he had as trust, and he also ordered him to destroy the letter that had been delivered to him concerning the agreements that existed between the King of Granada, don Felipe, don Nuño, and the others who went to Granada.

As soon as these treaties were signed and resolved, the queen and don Fernando spoke with the King of Granada, giving him to understand that King Alfonso was not aware of it. They called don Felipe and don Nuño to this meeting, and they strongly pleaded with them to grant a truce to the chiefs for up to two years. The King of Granada was very grieved with this plea, for he realized that they wanted to protect them from him and that they had taken from him the sum that he had given so that they would forsake the chiefs, and he had not wished to do it willingly; but because of the great insistence of the queen and the prince, he had to grant this truce to the chiefs for a year. The queen and the prince immediately sent to tell it to them so that they should know they had a truce and would thus observe it. The King of Granada then departed from Seville, and King Alfonso and all who were there with him went out of the city to do him honor.

As soon as King Alfonso returned to the city, he spoke with don Felipe, don Nuño, don Lope Díaz, and with the others who came to his grace. He called them into his service and arranged that they could have their *maravedís* from him each year, according to how they used to have them; and he granted them and fulfilled all the conditions and matters that the queen and don Fernando had granted them in Córdoba.

Afterward, being in Seville, King Alfonso arranged with them which ones would go with him to the empire, and which knights and companies, and what each one of those who had to go there should bring. He wanted to send messengers to King Aben Yuzaf, because since the treaty with the King of Granada was settled there could be peace with the Moors overseas. He decided that it would be of great diminishment to ask him to commit to treaties, for after peace was made and signed with the King of Granada, King Aben Yuzaf had no reason to cross from there, nor did he have a town nor any territory to which to come, for all of the harbors belonged to the King of Granada; moreover, he thought Aben Yuzaf could not accomplish the invasion, wars having begun in his land, and hence, that the king was putting himself at a disadvantage by asking him to commit to an agreement he did not believe could be achieved. And that when he crossed over, Prince Fernando and those who remained with him could stand to forbid to him the land because of the peace and truce with the King of Granada. The king sent each one of those men who were there to their lands well pleased with many favors he bestowed on them. He then came to Toledo to order prepared the things he needed for the journey to the empire, for he wanted to start the journey from there. And during this year the historian did not find anything else that pertained to the *History*.[2]

Notes

1. The gathering of Violante, Muhammad II, and the nobles in Seville should be dated in December 1273, not 1274. O'Callaghan, *The Learned King,* 228–29.

2. The concluding phrase of this chapter, "*E deste año el historiador non fallo otra cosa que a la estoria pertenesca,*" seems to suggest that the text used by the compiler of the *Chronicle* ended at this point.

Chapter 59

◧

How King Alfonso Obtained the Things for Which
He Had Need in Order to Go to the Empire
Organized, and of How He Departed from Toledo

In the twenty-third year of the reign of this King Alfonso, which was in the Era of 1313, and the year 1275 after the birth of Jesus Christ, this King Alfonso, being in Toledo, and having collected the sum that the King of Granada had to give him, his brother Prince Manuel and the others who had to go with him to the empire were there with him. The king gave to these all the things for which they had need for that journey.[1] He also ordered loaded in Seville and in the harbors of Algeciras many ships with wheat, barley, wines, and other foods that he understood could go by sea, and he ordered them to be waiting for him at the harbor of Marbella. He also sent ahead over land many horses and mules loaded with all the things he thought would be needed during that journey. As soon as these things were prepared and readied, he ordered to come to Toledo don Fernando, his first heir son; the Archbishop Sancho, son of the King of Aragón; his brother Prince Felipe; and his sons Prince Sancho, Prince Juan, Prince Pedro, and Prince Jaime to come there to Toledo. He also ordered to come don Nuño; don Lope Díaz; don Fernán Ruiz de Castro; don Alfonso Téllez; the Masters of Uclés, of Calatrava, of Alcántara, and of the Temple; the Prior of San Juan[2]; don Esteban Fernández, Juan Núñez, and Nuño González, sons of don Nuño; Diego López de Haro, brother of don Lope Díaz; don Fernán Pérez Ponce; don Pero Álvarez de Asturias; don Gil Gómez de Roa; don Día Sánchez; don Diego López de Salcedo; don Rui Gil de Villalobos; don Rodrigo Rodríguez de Saldaña; and all of the high noblemen, *infanzones,* and knights of the Kingdoms of Castile and León. He spoke with them, telling them that they knew well that he had told them many times about the journey on which he had to go to the empire, for those from Lombardy had sent him their messengers many times concerning this, and that he would have gone there a year ago if the land had been calm. He told them that God had brought him to this situation, that there was peace with the Moors, and that the princes and noblemen of his kingdom were settled peaceably in his service. He said that he wanted to make the journey, and that with him were going his brother Prince Manuel and another knight whom he thought was necessary for this, and that in the kingdoms remained his first heir son, Prince Fernando, as natural lord of all in place of the king, and that they knew well how they had received him as king and lord after his own days. He said that if something happened to him on this journey, he ordered them to hold and preserve for don Fernando the treaty and homage they did him. He ordered don Fernando to honor and do much good to his brothers, the princes, and to do much honor and favor to all of his vassals, and to hold in justice the towns of the kingdoms. He ordered him even more to make great effort to have as help and in his service the leaders of Málaga, Guadix, and of Gomares and to protect them; and that with these he would conquer the land belonging to the Lord of Granada and would always have him under pressure so that he would never rebel nor leave his rule. He also told them that he was leaving don Nuño as governor on the frontier, since don Fernando would appoint as royal judges in Castile, León, and Galicia those he considered he needed, just as that one who had to preserve justice in the kingdoms; and he ordered that they obey and be under the authority of Prince Fernando and the officials he appointed in the land. And so that he could be able to appoint these officials, he left him a table of the seals and ordered him that with it he might appoint the officials, stating in letters that they belong to the king. He ordered that the letters should be given to the designated heir, Prince Fernando. The other letters that he had need to send throughout the kingdoms concerning the complaints that may come to him or concerning the other matters he might order to be done in the kingdoms, he ordered that don Fernando sent them sealed with his seal.

All of those who were there granted that they would obey what the king ordered them, and he left in all of his kingdoms his men so that in each one of their districts they could collect and gather the rents of all the land and distribute them—according to the order he had given—and preserve the rest so that they could do with it what he ordered. The king departed from Toledo in the month of March and went to the empire. And now the *History* will relate the things that happened in the Kingdoms of Castile and León while the king went on this journey, because what he did and how things transpired where he went the chronicler did not know nor did he place them here.[3]

Notes

According to Procter, Part III of the *Chronicle* begins here.

1. Arrangements for the journey to the empire were made in the Cortes of Burgos in March 1274, not in Toledo. O'Callaghan, *The Learned King,* 229–30.

2. Juan González, Master of Calatrava; Pelay Pérez Correa, Master of Uclés or Santiago; García Fernández, Master of Alcántara; García Fernández, Master of the Temple in Castile; Álvar Peláez, Prior of the Hospital of San Juan in Castile.

3. The author of this section of the *Chronicle* makes the point that he knows nothing of what happened on the journey to the empire, so he focuses on the internal affairs of the kingdom (*"ca lo que fizo el e las cosas commo pasaron do el fue, el escribidor non las supo nin las puso aquí"*).

Chapter 60

▦

Of How Prince Fernando Began
to Rule the Kingdom, and of How
All Were Very Pleased with Him

Prince Fernando departed from Toledo and went to Extremadura, and from there he went to the kingdom of León. He traveled through the cities and towns expounding and practicing justice in those places where it was required; and with the authority of the king's seal, he appointed royal judges in all of the king's land. He also appointed governors and officials in those cities, towns, and places where they requested it from him, and also in those he considered such to be necessary to resolve their conflicts. And he ruled and preserved all of the land in justice and in such fashion that all of those from the kingdom were very pleased with him. During the month of May he came to Castile, and he arrived in Burgos; and he was there listening and discussing with all of those who came to him and exercising justice for those with complaints. Of the things this prince did and went through after his father, the king, departed from the kingdom in order to go to the empire, we do not find any other matters to write here.[1] Hence, we will return to relate what the King of Granada did because of the truce they made him grant to the chiefs, and also of how Aben Yuzaf crossed over from abroad during this truce.

Note

1. The *Chronicle* fails to mention that Infante Fernando de la Cerda resolved a major dispute with the clergy at Peñafiel in April 1275. O'Callaghan, *The Learned King* 57–58.

Chapter 61

◼

*Of How the King of Granada Complained
to Aben Yuzaf Abroad*

The King of Granada was very aggrieved because of the truce he granted to the chiefs while he was in Seville, for he had given King Alfonso a great fortune and had destroyed the letter of the treaty that the noblemen had with him. All of this he had done thinking that the chiefs would remain in such fashion that he could conquer them and take from them the land they held. He realized that because they remained in a truce with him during that year, after that time the King of Castile would want to protect them again. Thus, he remained in harm on account of this treaty and the chiefs remained lords in the land. In order to seek vengeance for this, he immediately left Seville and sent his messengers to Aben Yuzaf, king from beyond the sea; he sent word of the harm he had received from those chiefs, who held the land forcefully that was his father's, and of how King Alfonso had forbidden it to him until then, and that his agreement with King Alfonso had required that he go to him in Seville and give him a great fortune from what was his. Also, he said that he had released the noblemen from the treaties and agreements they had with him and his father, the King of Granada, and that he had allowed them to destroy the letter that existed between them. Having done all of this so that they might weaken the chiefs, they made him give the chiefs a truce for a year; and he thought that as soon as the time limit of the year had elapsed, the King of Castile would want to protect them and that they would make him lose the kingdom. For this reason King Alfonso wanted to join the chiefs and leave them the land they held so that they serve him in it.

Afterward, he sent his messengers so that he and the chiefs could make an agreement. The chiefs—knowing how King Alfonso was going to the empire, fearing that if the King of Granada waged war against them they would not be succored—signed their friendship with the King of Granada. They were letting him know that the land of the Christians was now in such situation that if Aben Yuzaf crossed, he would be able to conquer a great portion of it with the help the King of Granada would give him—for King Alfonso was outside the kingdom, traveling to the empire. All the other people were guaranteed, and thus he could seize a great portion of the land of the Christians in a very short period of time. In order to facilitate Aben Yuzaf's crossing and in order to make him more willing, the King of Granada was giving him the harbors of Algeciras and of Tarifa, in which he could store food, weapons, and the other things he might bring from overseas and where he could live once he had crossed hither.

After Aben Yuzaf had heard the message from the King of Granada, he sent a very good answer to him, saying that he had heard what his messengers had told him, that it had pleased him much to understand his action, and that he wanted to cross there. Aben Yuzaf said he would have the King of Granada hand over the towns of Algeciras and Tarifa to the men whom he was sending, and he would immediately cross there with all the men he could have. As soon as the King of Granada had this answer, he sent to order that they deliver to Aben Yuzaf the towns of Algeciras and Tarifa. Aben Yuzaf immediately crossed to Algeciras with a few companies,[1] and he sent many other men who crossed after him; therefore, those who crossed were seventeen thousand knights. After these men had come to him, they departed from Algeciras and immediately came to the territory of Málaga, because the King of Granada sent to beg him that he go through there. He assured Aben Yuzaf that the chiefs would observe the treaties and agreements negotiated that were signed between them. The chiefs of Málaga and Guadix came to Aben Yuzaf, and they went along with him until the King of Granada came to meet Aben Yuzaf. They signed before Aben Yuzaf the treaties and agreements that were negotiated between the King of Granada and the chiefs in such fashion that the chiefs were in concord with the King of Granada and at his service. There they agreed how to wage the war, in this manner: Aben Yuzaf should go to attack the territory of the kingdom of Seville and he should start with Écija. The King of Granada should go to wage war through the Bishopric of Jaén. Aben Yuzaf sent to the King of Granada two of the most powerful Moors he had who had crossed with him, and they were brothers, the elder named Havojava Tali and the other named Uzmen. And because we have related how these Moors arranged to wage war, we will relate what don Nuño, the governor of the frontier, who was in Córdoba, did.

Note

1. The first contingent of Benimerines invaded in May 1275. Abû Yûsuf followed in August. O'Callaghan, *The Learned King,* 234–35.

Chapter 62

⊞

*How Aben Yuzaf of Morocco Fought with
Don Nuño and Defeated Him, and of How
Don Nuño Died in This Battle*

We have already related how King Alfonso, when he went to the
empire, left don Nuño as governor of the frontier. While don Nuño
was in Córdoba, he found out that Aben Yuzaf had crossed, and all
of those knights with him. So he immediately sent word to Prince
Fernando, who was in Burgos. Don Fernando immediately sent
letters to the princes, all noblemen, knights, and all of the others
of the kingdom to tell them how Aben Yuzaf had crossed hither
from overseas and that he was waging war and causing harm and
damage to the land. Also that he was ordering them to come to
him, and that later he would give them their salaries so that they
could prepare to go with him to the war against the Moors.

After don Nuño had sent these letters to don Fernando, he
sent to call all of those from the frontier to come to him at Écija,
for he knew that Aben Yuzaf was coming to attack the land of the
Christians through that region; and some men from the frontier
came to him, and also his vassals who were with him. While he was
there, Aben Yuzaf came with all of his army near Écija, and don
Nuño and all of those who were with him went outside the town
and placed their squadrons against the Moors. According to what
some say, don Nuño wanted to avoid the battle that day, for he
knew that Aben Yuzaf was bringing a very great force of men while
he had but a few. Some that were with him told him that because
the squadrons were so close and the foot soldiers could see each
other eye-to-eye, it would be a great loss for don Nuño to abandon
the battle and it would seem that he was fleeing.[1] Some say this was

the manner in which it was related, but it is not found written if the battle took place because of this or not. It is true that don Nuño and those who were with him fought with the Moors that came with Aben Yuzaf, and the Christians were defeated, and don Nuño and many of those that were going along with him died in the battle. More would have died, but they had the town of Écija close by where they could find refuge. It is also found written that don Nuño and those who were with him were such brave knights and they fought so much that Aben Yuzaf suspected his Moors would be defeated, for he was in a place from which he could see the battle. As soon as don Nuño was killed and the Christians had fled from the field, Aben Yuzaf went to see what men from the Christians died in that battle. They found don Nuño dead in the field, and around him laid many dead knights, four hundred squires who protected him, and many other Christians and Moors who died there. Aben Yuzaf showed that he was sorry about don Nuño's death, for he said that he wanted to take him alive, and he ordered to sever the head. He then sent it to the King of Granada and sent to tell him that he should take his share of that foray. The King of Granada replied to Aben Yuzaf that he was pleased with the portion he had sent him, but that he was very sorry about don Nuño's death, for he had done much so that he could become king; and this head he sent to Córdoba, with word that it should be buried with the body. The day on which don Nuño died was a Saturday, during the month of May,[2] in the year one thousand and three hundred and thirteen of the Era.

As soon as Aben Yuzaf had been victorious in this battle, he found out from some Christians whom they had captured that day that very few people had remained in the town of Écija. For this reason he stayed there that night near the town, thinking that he could capture it the next day. But during that night, don Gil Gómez de Villalobos, Abbot of Valladolid, arrived at Écija, and with his armies and other men who were coming to don Nuño, the abbot entered Écija with three hundred mounted men. As soon as he knew of the defeat of the Christians and don Nuño's death, and that Aben Yuzaf was so close from there with his army, don Gil Gómez suspected that he wanted to fight the town the next day. During that night, the abbot and those who entered with him watched and reinforced the gates. They divided in small troops the defense of the town, and they also requested the crossbows that they had and the supplies of arrows they had. The next day, Aben Yuzaf ordered the village fought, and because those who were inside defended it so well and wounded so many men, he ordered them to withdraw from there and went to dwell with his army farther off from the town. From there he sent part of his armies through the territory of the frontier to attack it and rob it; he ordered them to rejoin him between Écija and Palma and said he would be there until they rejoined him. This time his foraging party crossed the Guadalquivir River and stole all the cattle that the Christians had taken across the river out of fear for the Moors. Henceforth, we cease to relate about Aben Yuzaf, and we will relate how the Moors killed the Archbishop of Toledo.

Notes

1. This chapter refers to an oral tradition concerning Nuño González de Lara's choice to fight rather than flee, but notes that the written text used by the compiler does not make it clear—"*E esto dicen algunos que fue ansi dicho, mas non se falla en escripto si fue la pelea por esto o non.*"

2. Nuño González de Lara was killed at Écija on September 7, 1275, not in May. O'Callaghan, *The Learned King*, 235.

Chapter 63

❂

*Of How the Archbishop of Toledo Fought a Battle
with the Moors Who Brought a Cavalry
and Killed Him, and of How Don Lope Díaz
Fought a Battle Another Day with the Moors,
and What Happened There*

Throughout all of the kingdom of Castile and León spread the news of the multitude of the Moors who crossed with Aben Yuzaf and of the many harms they did in the land of the Christians. For this reason they prepared to go to the frontier. Prince Sancho, Archbishop of Toledo, son of King Jaime of Aragón, as soon as he knew about this had all the vassal knights of the king who lived in Toledo, Talavera, Guadalajara, and in Madrid summoned so that they could go with him. These knights, because of the order they had from don Fernando to go immediately to the frontier, and because of the summoning from the Archbishop of Toledo, they all went with him. With these and with all of the other men whom the archbishop could have from his own, he went to the Bishopric of Jaén. While he was waiting for some knights who had not arrived yet, a friar of Calatrava who was the Knight Commander of Martos, named Alfonso Garcí,[1] came to him and told him how the Moors had arrived at Martos, how they had led a great booty of cattle and of captive men and women, and how they came weary from the great territory they had traveled. If the archbishop were to go there with the men he had, he would seize the booty and would kill many of them, and he would do a very great service to God. These Moors were the ones the King of Granada had sent to ravage the land through parts of the Bishopric of Jaén, and there came those two brother knights who had crossed the seas, named Havojava Tali, and the other Uzmen. From the kingdom of Granada came the leader of Ascanvela, the leader Aben Macar,[2] and the chiefs of Málaga and Guadix, and they brought many great companies. The archbishop ordered that all of those who were there with him should ride and those of the town should do the same, and he immediately departed from there and that night went to Torre del Campo. Having arrived there, a knight who came with him whom they called Sandúcar came to him and told him how don Lope Díaz, Lord of Vizcaya, was coming that night, and that it would be good to wait for him. Alfonso Garcí, the friar, said to the archbishop: "The wicked enchanter draws out the snake from its dwelling with another's hand, and don Lope Díaz comes now with more armies, and they have not come to him yet. You have here all of this army, and if you wait for him and you and your men defeat the Moors, he shall have the fame, so take this honor for yourself." And Sandúcar told the archbishop: "Lord, you should not move because of what one man says." The knight commander told him so much that the archbishop refused to wait and departed from there the next day. Those who went with him in the vanguard met the might of the Moors who were traveling with the thefts they had made of many cattle and men and women whom they brought along as captives. The archbishop and those who went with him, thinking that they would be able to take away from them that booty, went to fight with them. But so much was the haste that the archbishop used in order to reach the Moors that all of his men did not arrive with him, and the Moors turned against the archbishop and fought with him. Because the Moors were many, the archbishop and those who went with him were defeated, and the archbishop was captured and many Christians were killed. Having removed his weapons and other vestments he was wearing, those Moors who were the leaders said that they would take him to the King of Granada. And Havojava Tali and Uzmen said that they would take him to Aben Yuzaf, for until they crossed from overseas, the King of Granada nor his men did not know which regions the Guadalquivir River passed; and concerning this, the Moors were about to have a great conflict among themselves. When the leader Aben Macar saw this, he spurred his horse and went to the archbishop where he was naked, and he struck him over his shoulder with a spear, which penetrated his body and killed him.[3] And Aben Macar said: "May the will of Allah not be that on account of one dog so many good men as are here kill each other," and they cut off his head and the hand on which he wore the ring, and they moved from there with their booty and left. On that day in which they captured and killed the archbishop, that Sandúcar who was his vassal, Juan Fernández de Veleña, Lorenzo Venegas de Talavera, Rui López de Hita, and other knights who had arrived with him died in that battle.

As soon as don Lope Díaz arrived at Jaén, he found out how the archbishop was in that attack and with the men he had there. He departed from Jaén the day after the archbishop left, and on the day that the Moors killed him, don Lope arrived at the area where they fought the battle; and many of those who escaped from the battle and were fleeing took refuge with him. The Moors who had been victorious in the battle, as soon as they saw don Lope Díaz coming, waited for him and were bringing the cross they had seized from the archbishop. Don Lope Díaz began to fight with the Moors, and in order to recover the cross they were carrying, the haste was so great in both parties that don Lope Díaz recovered the cross and the Moors killed the standard bearer and took from him the standard. Being in battle to recover the standard, night came, and the Moors pitched camp on top of a hill and the Christians on top of another. When morning came, each group was so far separated that they did not see each other, for during that night each of them was in their territory. As soon as the day broke, don Lope Díaz went to the place where they had killed the archbishop and brought his body without the head and the one hand, and the Moors took with them the booty they had seized. After this, don Gonzalo Romero, Knight Commander of the Order of Calatrava,[4] sent to demand from the Moors the archbishop's head and hand, and they gave them to him and the Christians took them with the body to Toledo to bury. Henceforth, we shall relate how Prince Fernando's death befell in Villa Real.

Notes

1. Alfonso García, commander of Martos, appears in documents of 1263 and 1269.

2. The governor or chief (*arraez*) of Málaga was Abû Muhammad ibn Ashkîlûlâ.

3. Archbishop Sancho II of Toledo (1266–1275), son of Jaime I of Aragón, was killed on October 20, 1275, near Jaén. O'Callaghan, *The Learned King*, 235.

4. Gonzalo Romero, Grand Commander of Calatrava, appears in documents in 1277–1280.

Chapter 64

Of How Prince Fernando Was Coming to the
Frontier of the War Against the Moors, and of
How He Died in Villa Real of Illness

After Prince Fernando had sent to summon all of those from the kingdoms, he departed from Burgos. He went on a short journey so that the princes, noblemen, and knights of the kingdom could catch up with him and so that as soon as they arrived at the frontier, some of his armies might arrive with him. On the way, he found out how the archbishop and don Nuño were dead. Notwithstanding that he realized his coming was much needed at the frontier, he also realized that it was not for his benefit or honor to arrive at the frontier with the few companies that were going with him. For this reason he went to Villa Real to wait for those of the kingdoms whom he had called. From there he immediately sent his letters to all of the councils of the frontier, in which he sent to tell them how he had arrived at that town and was waiting for the noblemen and knights of the kingdom he had summoned, and that he soon would be with them and would defend the land from the harms the Moors were doing in it. Don Juan Núñez, son of don Nuño, always attended him and never left him, and it befell that he was with him at the time Prince Fernando came to Villa Real.

Prince Fernando, being in that town, fell ill with a serious illness. Realizing that he was sickened unto death, he spoke with don Juan Núñez and begged him very insistently to help and act in such fashion that don Alfonso, son of this don Fernando, might inherit the kingdoms after the days of his father, King Alfonso. To make sure that he would take the greatest care in this matter, he charged don Juan Núñez with the rearing of his son don Alfonso, and he ordered that they should give him to him in order to be reared and that he should care for his training. Don Juan Núñez promised that he would carry it out according to what don Fernando ordered him, and soon after, this Prince Fernando passed away during the month of August.[1] All who had arrived there did not know what to do, and they waited there in order to have an agreement with the others who were coming to this war; and those from the frontier were greatly disconcerted by the death of this Prince Fernando. They took this prince to be buried in Huelgas de Burgos, for he had chosen his burial there, and don Juan Núñez traveled with the body of this prince in order to have it buried. Henceforth, we will relate the price that was paid in this war while King Alfonso was returning.

Note

1. Infante Fernando died at Villarreal on July 24, 1275, before the deaths of Nuño González de Lara and Archbishop Sancho II. O'Callaghan, *The Learned King*, 235.

Chapter 65

⬚

Of How Prince Sancho Came to the Frontier,
and How He Appointed Himself
Crown Prince of Castile

Prince Sancho, who had stayed in Burgos waiting for some of his vassals, departed from there in order to go to the frontier. Although he had learned about the archbishop's and don Nuño's death, he found out on the way about Prince Fernando's death, and he hastened his marches and traveled as much as he could and arrived at Villa Real. Before this, Prince Sancho had great friendship with don Lope Díaz de Haro, and this don Lope Díaz was coming to Prince Fernando, for he had found out that he was in Villa Real. On his way, don Lope Díaz found out how Prince Fernando was dead, and he increased the marches in order to look for Prince Sancho. Arriving in Villa Real, he found that Prince Sancho had come there and it pleased both of them much that they had found each other. Prince Sancho immediately spoke with don Lope Díaz and told him that because he remained as the oldest among his brothers, he should inherit the kingdoms after the days of his father. Prince Sancho begged don Lope Díaz to help him in this, and said that knowing it was certain, he would do him favor and good in such fashion that he would be the greatest and most honored man in the kingdom. And don Lope Díaz, for this reason, and because of the good relationship that existed between them, wanted to serve Prince Sancho. He also considered the charge that don Fernando had made to don Juan Núñez, in that he gave him the rearing of his son, don Alfonso, upon his death. He also feared that King Alfonso, as soon as he arrived, would want to give honors and advantages to don Juan Núñez, as his father used to do. If during this time he helped Prince Sancho well, then Sancho would be much in don Lope's debt, and that even though the king wanted to give advantage to don Nuño's sons, that don Sancho would compensate him well. For these reasons don Lope Díaz granted to Prince Sancho that he would do for him and for his service everything he had begged of him. Don Lope Díaz also promised Prince Sancho that he and all of those who should serve would make a treaty and do homage in order to have Prince Sancho as king after the days of his father, King Alfonso. Furthermore, he said he would talk with all of those of the councils of the towns of Castile and with many of those from the kingdom of León so that they do the same, but that he wanted him to promise that by doing what he had said, the prince would fulfill what he had promised. And Prince Sancho promised it to him. With the treaties signed by both in this fashion, don Lope Díaz advised Prince Sancho to speak with all of those who were there in Villa Real and to tell them that because his father, King Alfonso, was not in the kingdoms and his brother Prince Fernando was dead, that he wanted to go to defend the land, and that he ordered and begged them to go with him, and that they would serve him and help him in such fashion that the frontier could be protected while his father, the king, was returning or was sending to order what to do, and that with this, Prince Sancho would earn the love of his father, the king, for he would realize that Prince Sancho had the willingness to stand and defend the kingdom and that he deserved to inherit it after the king's days. He also would win the hearts of all of those of the kingdoms, and they would regard it as right to receive him as heir after the days of his father; and don Lope Díaz advised that Sancho immediately should call himself in his letters the oldest son and heir. Don Sancho immediately spoke with all of the noblemen and knights who had arrived there, and he told them that because he remained as the oldest son and heir after the days of his father, he wanted to go and defend the land. He begged and ordered them to go with him, and all of them granted that they would willingly do it, for many were dismayed by the death of don Fernando.[1]

Prince Sancho departed from Villa Real, and all of those men went with him to Córdoba. He sent his urgent letters to all of those who had not come there—noblemen, knights, and advisors—in which he sent to order that they should immediately come to him at Córdoba so that they could help him to defend the land. In this letter Prince Sancho immediately called himself the oldest heir, son of King Alfonso, and the very same from then on in all of the regions; and he was in this city of Córdoba until all of the rest of those for whom he had sent had come. Because the town of Écija was there very close to the Moorish border and those who were in that town were very dismayed by don Nuño's death and by the defeat they suffered, and because of what they had learned concerning Prince Fernando's death, in order to hearten them, Prince Sancho sent there don Lope Díaz de Haro. He also begged and ordered the Masters of Uclés and Calatrava to go to the Bishopric of Jaén; and he left don Fernán Ruiz de Castro and don Esteban de Galicia in Córdoba. He departed from there and went to Seville, because Aben Yuzaf had crossed to that region, and also in order to have the fleet armed and to make them go to guard the sea, for it was unprotected. He ordered that they move all of the cattle and that if Aben Yuzaf surrounded any place, those who were there should defend it; but if the Moors crossed again the Guadalquivir River, he would unite with all of those men and would go and fight with them. After Aben Yuzaf learned this—that Prince Sancho and all of the men from the kingdom were on the frontier, and that they had placed reinforcements in the towns and castles, and that they were prepared for war—and also because he had his food supplies in Algeciras and Tarifa, and because he could not have enough for so many men as he was bringing along, and also because he found out about the fleet that the Christians were arming, he went with all of his army to Algeciras, for he feared that the fleet would not allow him to bring the food supplies and that he would not be able to have them from overseas as he had been receiving them.

Now we will relate how King Alfonso learned of the deaths of Prince Fernando, the Archbishop of Toledo, and don Nuño.

Note

1. Infante Sancho rallied the Castilians in October–November 1275. O'Callaghan, *The Learned King*, 235–36.

Chapter 66

⬛

Of How King Alfonso Learned of the Deaths of
Prince Fernando and the Archbishop of Toledo

Of the things that befell to King Alfonso while he went to the empire, the *History* has avoided relating, for it was never found how they happened, although it was found that King Alfonso, being in Belcaire, a place near the Ruédano River, learned how Aben Yuzaf with great forces of men crossed from overseas and killed Archbishop Sancho and don Nuño.[1] He also learned how Prince Fernando was dead, and he thought it true that the land at the frontier was in such condition that it could all be lost—or at least a great portion of it—for he did not think that his son Prince Sancho would make an effort to defend it nor that he had there anyone to help him in it. For this reason, and also because he had learned that concerning the matter of the empire they were mocking him, and that he had wasted a very large fortune on this journey, he departed from Belcaire and set out for Castile. Because a very short period of time had elapsed since his father-in-law, King Jaime, had died, King Alfonso came through Catalonia and arrived at the monastery of Santas Cruces, where King Jaime laid buried,[2] and he made a commemoration. King Pedro came to him on the road and did him much honor, and he sent some of his men with him to the border of the kingdom.

Notes

1. Alfonso X visited Pope Gregory X at Beaucaire in southern France in May 1275. O'Callaghan, *The Learned King*, 231–33. The author of the *Chronicle* professes to know nothing of King Alfonso's journey to the empire— *"De las*

cosas que el rey don Alfonso paso en cuanto fue al Imperio, la estoria escusado se ha de las contar, por cuanto non se fallo en cual manera pasaron."

2. Jaime I of Aragón died on July 27, 1276, and was buried in the monastery of Poblet, not Santes Creus. He was succeeded by his son Pedro III (1276–1284). The story of Alfonso X's visit to Jaime I's tomb at Santes Creus is simply not true.

Chapter 67

※

Of How King Alfonso Came from the Empire, and of the Meeting He Held Concerning Prince Sancho's Demand

In the twenty-fourth year of the reign of this King Alfonso, which was in the Era of 1314, and the year 1276 after the birth of Jesus Christ, King Alfonso arrived at Requena. He came through the kingdom of Valencia, and from there he came to Cuenca, Huete, and then to Alcalá de Henares,[1] where he learned how his son Prince Sancho and the noblemen of the kingdom had reinforced the land so that it could be protected and not be lost. What Sancho had done pleased him greatly, and notwithstanding that before he loved him as his son, from then on he had better disposition toward him and he loved him and appreciated him much.

The king departed from there and came to Camarena, a place near Toledo, and he stayed there for a great part of the year. From this time, he refused to enter Toledo, and he sent to tell Prince Sancho how he had returned. Because King Alfonso was not prepared to make war, nor did he know anything about the state of the affairs of his kingdoms, he looked for a way to have a truce with Aben Yuzaf and the King of Granada. Aben Yuzaf was pleased with it, for the Christians' fleet that don Sancho had sent to safeguard the sea did not allow supplies to go through to him as fast as he needed, and the men he had with him had seen themselves many times starving. He also was pleased to have the agreement because he held the harbors of Algeciras and Tarifa, which he many times coveted so that he could cross hither whenever he wished, and it pleased him to have the agreement so that during that time he could go overseas. He sent to tell the King of Granada that even though he had not wished to have made war at that time, it pleased him to be in this truce and it was signed for two years.

Prince Sancho, the noblemen, knights, and advisors who were at the frontier immediately came to Toledo and went to see King Alfonso. With all being assembled there, don Lope Díaz spoke with them all in secrecy on behalf of Prince Sancho, so that they might request the king's grace that don Sancho might inherit the kingdoms after the days of King Alfonso, while all of them were pleased with what his son had done during his departure, and because he was the king's eldest son. Don Lope Díaz spoke with the king and told him what Prince Sancho had done for his honor and to protect the land from the Moors during the time in which Prince Fernando had died. He also told the king that since Prince Sancho was the oldest among his brothers, and while those men were all assembled there, it would be his grace to consider it well to order that they do him honor to have him as king after King Alfonso's days; and don Lope Díaz asked that the king send to order all the councils of all the cities and towns of his kingdom to send their solicitors with certain authority for this. Notwithstanding that in this he would do favor to don Sancho—for he would do much good to his service—the king would greatly please the hearts of all of those of his kingdom, for he learned from all of them that this would please them and that they would want this. By the king's wanting it, all of them would consider it his favor.

King Alfonso answered don Lope Díaz that he loved and cared for don Sancho a great deal and that he considered it good that he truly deserved to be king, but that he would have his agreement and he would give his answer concerning this. He ordered Prince Manuel called and others of his council, and he told them of the meeting don Lope Díaz had had with him concerning don Sancho's matter and asked them what they advised about it. All of those who were there had hesitated much in this advice, and don Manuel told him: "Lord, the tree of kings is not ruined by its planting, nor is the one who comes by nature disinherited, and if the greatest that comes from the tree dies, the branch that is the highest should remain. And there are three things that are not under question—law, nor king, nor kingdom. Anything that may be done against any of these is worthless nor should it be considered maintained."

In the writing that is found from that time it is stated that in that council only these words were spoken.[2]

The king, as soon as he learned how the truce with the Moors had been signed, departed from Camarena, and all the men who were assembled there went with him. He went to Segovia and sent letters to all of the cities and towns of his kingdoms so that they might immediately send their solicitors to him in Segovia with certain powers in order to make an agreement and fealty to Prince Sancho; to have him as king and as lord after his days.

Notes

1. The itinerary given for Alfonso X's return journey to Castile (Requena, through kingdom of Valencia to Cuenca, Huete and Alcalá de Henares) is false. He started home from Montpellier in late September or October; in November he was at Lérida in Aragón and at Alcalá on December 2, 1275. O'Callaghan, *The Learned King*, 236.

2. The author of the *Chronicle* had a written text before him as he remarks: "*E en el escripto que se falla desde aquel tiempo, non dicen que en aquel consejo fuesen dichas mas palabras que estas.*"

Chapter 68

*Of How King Alfonso Ordered That They Swear
Allegiance to Sancho as Crown Prince, and of
How He Killed His Brother Don Fadrique*

The king having arrived at the city of Segovia, the princes, masters,
all the high noblemen, *infanzones,* and knights of the cities and
towns of his kingdoms came to him. The king ordered that they
should make a pledge and do homage to Prince Sancho, his first
heir, so that after the days of King Alfonso they would have him as
king and lord; and all of them did what the king ordered them.[1]

As soon as these agreements and fealties were made, Queen
Violante, wife of this King Alfonso, sent letters to her brother don
Pedro of Aragón about the agreements that those of the kingdom
had made for Prince Sancho, and that concerning these she wanted
to go and speak with him, and that she would bring with her don
Alfonso and don Fernando [her grandsons]. The queen departed
from Segovia, and with her went doña Blanca [Prince Fernando's
widow], and they brought with them don Alfonso and don
Fernando. They went through the mountain pass and went to
Úbeda, and from there to Guadalajara, Hita, Atienza, and
Medinaceli. From there they went to Hariza, which is in the kingdom of Aragón, and King Pedro came there and took them with
him to Calatayud.[2] When King Alfonso found out how the queen
and doña Blanca were gone, it grieved him. He ordered the advisors to watch the roads and to not let them pass or go out of the
kingdom, and because of these letters and this order their journey
was hindered. The king departed from Segovia, and Prince Sancho
with him, and they went to Burgos; and because the king found
out some matters about his brother Prince Fadrique and about

don Simón Ruiz de los Cameros, he ordered Prince Sancho to go and seize don Simón Ruiz de los Cameros and to immediately have him killed.[3] Don Sancho immediately left Burgos and went to Logroño and found don Simón Ruiz there and arrested him; and this same day that they arrested him, Diego López de Salcedo arrested don Fadrique in Burgos by the king's order. Don Sancho went to Treviño and ordered don Simón Ruiz burned there, and the king ordered don Fadrique strangled. And of the other things that happened during this year, nothing else is found written.[4]

Notes

1. The king convened the Cortes to Burgos, not Segovia (in May 1276), to acknowledge Sancho as heir. Two years later he held the Cortes at Segovia to confirm Sancho's status and to give him additional authority as coruler but without the royal title. O'Callaghan, *The Learned King*, 236–40, 246–47.

2. The journey to Aragón of Queen Violante and Blanche, or Blanca (the mother of the Infantes de la Cerda, the children of Fernando de la Cerda), occurred in January 1278, not in 1276. O'Callaghan, *The Learned King*, 244–46.

3. The executions of Infante Fadrique and Simón Ruiz de los Cameros took place in March 1277. Diego López de Salcedo, who arrested Infante Fadrique, was *adelantado mayor* of Álava and Guipúzcoa. O'Callaghan, *The Learned King*, 241–43.

4. The concluding sentence of this chapter suggests that the compiler was using a written text as his source: "*E las otras cosas que acaescieron en este año non se falla mas en escripto.*"

Chapter 69

⧉

Of How King Alfonso Ordered Built a Very Large Fleet, Which He Sent Against Algeciras

In the twenty-fifth year of the reign of this King Alfonso, which was in the Era of 1315, and the year 1277 after the birth of Jesus Christ, King Alfonso, feeling great sorrow for the harm and damage that Aben Yuzaf had done him while he went to the empire—and also in order to prevent that he cross there by the harbor of Algeciras, just as he crossed the other time, and thus so that he could move quickly to have control over the King of Granada who had caused him to cross here—being in Burgos, King Alfonso spoke with those who were with him that it was his will to send to besiege the city of Algeciras so that he could capture it and prevent Aben Yuzaf from crossing through there again from overseas. He told them how much harm and damage could befall all of the multitude of people in the kingdoms if that king could cross hither from there the way it happened the other time.[1] Those who were there with King Alfonso told him that it was right, and for this they gave him two of the tributes from all of the kingdoms. The king left Burgos and went through the kingdom of León exacting justice and learning of the state of the land in each place he arrived. From there he went to Seville, and as soon as he arrived there he ordered built and prepared a very large fleet that consisted of eighty galleons and twenty-four ships—not counting the galleys and vessels with sails and oars and the other small ships. The king also ordered them to bring out many weapons and many crossbows and much unleavened bread, and all the other things necessary in order to send that fleet. He also ordered prepared and built many catapults in order to send them on the ships, and he ordered gathered bread and all the other things required so that as soon as the city was besieged, he could send to the army and the fleet the things that were necessary; and he ordered that in the fleet Pedro Martínez de Fe go as admiral. He also ordered that in it go a nobleman from Portugal whom they called don Melendo; Gonzalo Morante, brother of [the illegitimate] don Alfonso Fernández, the Child, from his mother's side; don Guillén de Savanaque²; and many other companies that were required to place them on board such a large fleet as this. Since the month of October had arrived, King Alfonso's fleet was outfitted with men, weapons, and all of the other things that were necessary. So that the Moors could not get ready to supply the city with food and men, the king ordered that they then move the fleet from Seville and go immediately to blockade Algeciras from the sea. They should not allow food or any other thing to come there by sea, for Granada could not supply them because they needed it for themselves; moreover, the leader of Málaga, who was King Alfonso's vassal, would not allow it to pass through his territory. Meanwhile, all of those men whom he ordered to go with it left Seville during this month of October, and they went to the strait and blockaded Algeciras from the sea; they blockaded it for a long time so that no ship from overseas could cross hither. As soon as King Alfonso had sent this fleet, he sent to summon all of the noblemen, masters, and advisors from the cities and towns of his kingdoms to come so that they all could go to that siege. And during this year, nothing else is found that pertains for the *History* to relate.

Notes

1. Plans for the siege of Algeciras were made during the Cortes of Burgos in 1277. The blockade by a Castilian fleet began in August 1278. O'Callaghan, *The Learned King*, 244, 247–48.

2. Pedro Martínez de Fe had participated in the raid on Salé in 1260 mentioned in chapter 19. He probably was dead by 1283. Gonzalo Morante had served as *merino mayor*, or governor of León; his half-brother, Alfonso Fernández, el Niño, was an illegitimate son of Alfonso X. Guillén de Savanaque was a Frenchman, Guillaume de Savaignac.

Chapter 70

Of How King Alfonso Sent Men from His Kingdoms to Besiege Algeciras and Gave Them as Captain His Son Prince Pedro

In the twenty-sixth year of the reign of this King Alfonso, which was in the Era of 1316, and the year 1278 after the birth of Jesus Christ, the men whom the king had summoned in order to send them to besiege the city of Algeciras were gathered in Seville. The month of March had arrived, and the king agreed with those who were with him there that because he had already sent the fleet, all of those who had to go to that siege by land might go with his son Prince Pedro, whom he gave them as their leader and captain of that army. He sent with Prince Pedro don Alfonso Fernández, the Child, the king's [illegitimate] son. Before those men departed from the city of Seville, the king spoke with them and told them how he was sending his son Prince Pedro as their leader and lord for the time in which that war might last and also for as long as the siege of Algeciras lasted. He ordered them to do for Prince Pedro just like they should do for the king himself if he were to go there; and all granted that they would do and fulfill what the king was ordering them.

Thus during this month of March, all of those companies departed from Seville, and all of those from that army went with Prince Pedro. Because don Alfonso Fernández, the Child, son of the king, was a man of great estate and the king loved him much, he took this army to the forefront. Prince Pedro led this army in proper order through all the roads through which they went, and as soon as they arrived in Algeciras at the start of the month of April,[1] Prince Pedro ordered the main body of the army to pitch camp around the city; and it was surrounded everywhere by sea and land. Those of the fleet who were at sea were very pleased with those of the army when they arrived there. The admiral and some of the knights who were in the fleet came to Prince Pedro and they all decided that as soon as the main body of the army was settled, and as soon as some foot soldiers who were coming by sea with the supplies had arrived, they should attack the city by land and sea—for the admiral and those who were in the fleet said that those of the city were very weak. They thought that if they were fought, the Christians would enter the city, and that meanwhile, the siege engines should go so as to shoot at the city. With this agreement made, they ordered the machines brought out, placed them in those places where they considered necessary, and ordered that they shoot with them at the city and the walls day and night as hard as they could. Since the time they considered appropriate for combat had arrived, they fought by sea and land, and because there were many wounded from those on the outside, they stopped the fighting and made an effort to prevent all food that they might bring from outside, either by sea or land, from entering the city. And because this city was besieged for many days, meanwhile, other things happened in the kingdom that are to be related, and the *History* will relate them here; and afterward, we will relate further on how this siege was resolved.[2]

Notes

1. The events of the siege of Algeciras occurred in February–April 1279. O'Callaghan, *The Learned King,* 247.

2. The final sentences in chapter 69 (*"E cuanto en este año non se falla otra cosa que a la estoria pertencezca contar"*) and chapter 70 (*"E de las otras cosas que acaescieron en este año, non se falla mas en escripto"*) suggest that the compiler of the *Chronicle* was working with a written text as his source.

Chapter 71

▣

*Of How Prince Sancho Conferred with
the King of Aragón So That His Mother,
the Queen, Might Return to Castile,
and That He Seize Prince Fernando's Sons*

While these men had this city of Algeciras besieged, King Alfonso
was in Seville, and Prince Sancho, his first heir, was in Castile. Because his mother, Queen Violante, left from Segovia for Aragón
and took with her her daughter-in-law doña Blanca, and the sons
of this doña Blanca, don Alfonso and don Fernando, Prince Sancho
made an effort during that time so that his mother, the queen,
might return to the kingdom.[1] He was not doing this without his
father's order, and he sent his very insistent letters to his mother,
the queen, and King Pedro of Aragón, his uncle and the queen's
brother, so that the queen might return to Castile. Concerning the
negotiation of the queen's return, Prince Sancho's messengers
spoke with King Pedro of Aragón saying that as soon as Queen
Violante had returned to Castile, the King of Aragón would order
don Alfonso and don Fernando held as prisoners so that they could
not be taken to France, nor could Prince Sancho face any obstacles
because of them. King Pedro loved much his nephew Prince
Sancho, and he sent to promise him that as soon as the queen
went to Castile, he would fulfill what Prince Sancho was begging
him to do. When the queen saw the messengers and the letters
that her son Prince Sancho was sending King Pedro and also the
assurances that her brother, King Pedro, was giving him concerning this, she said she could not leave Aragón nor go to Castile until
they paid a great amount of money that she owed in Aragón—this
she had spent during the two years that she had been there—and
also that they should give her something with which to go. So Prince
Sancho, in order to bring her to Castile, considered how that money

might be paid. In Castile and León there was a Jew, a collector of the king's rents, whose name was don Zag de la Malea. The sum that this Jew and the others who went with him collected was sent to the frontier for the maintenance of the army and fleet that were at Algeciras. When Prince Sancho learned how this don Zag had a great amount of *maravedís* to send, he sent for him and ordered him to give the money to him in order to give it to his mother, the queen, with which she might come from Aragón. So the Jew gave the *maravedís* to him, and Prince Sancho immediately sent them to his mother, the queen, and she then came to Castile. After she had come, King Pedro of Aragón ordered seized don Alfonso and don Fernando, sons of Prince Fernando and doña Blanca, and they put them in the Castle of Játiva, where they were imprisoned during the whole lifetime of this King Pedro. Doña Blanca, mother of don Alfonso and don Fernando, as soon as she saw them imprisoned, spent a short time in Aragón at a monastery for ladies; afterward she departed from there and went to France. The queen and Prince Sancho went through the cities of Castile carrying out justice. And the *History* ceases to relate this and will turn to tell about the things that befell during the siege of Algeciras.

Note

1. Queen Violante probably returned from Aragón to Castile in July 1279. O'Callaghan, *The Learned King*, 248–49.

Chapter 72

*Of How the Fleet of the King of Castile Was Lost,
and of How the Siege of Algeciras Came to an
End, and How the Moors Captured the Admiral*

We have already related how King Alfonso was in Seville while the city of Algeciras was besieged. Prince Pedro and those who were in that siege were pressing the Moors who were in that city as much as they could—on the one hand, by fighting many battles with them; and on the other, by shooting at them with the machines; and furthermore, by not allowing food to reach them by land or sea. Those of the army fulfilled the time for which they were paid in their contracts. Also, those at sea who were with the fleet safeguarding the sea during all of winter spent many days in which they went unpaid; and all of those at sea and on land sent to tell King Alfonso to send them something so that they could stay there. The king, who was thinking that he would send them succor from the fortune that don Zag de la Malea and those who were with him were collecting in Castile and León, learned how Prince Sancho had seized this money and had given it to Queen Violante. He was very angry with this, for he did not have anything from which to send payment to those who were in the army at Algeciras or to those in the fleet safeguarding the sea. But he searched in Seville for a loan that some merchants and others from the city would make him, and he sent the support that he could. Those of the fleet who had been safeguarding the sea all of winter had no renewal of clothes or food when they needed them, and the king sent to them very little assistance. For this reason these men of the fleet became seriously ill. For many of them, while they were in the galleys and not having food, it happened that their teeth fell out, and they suffered very great hardships, and they suffered many other illnesses that forced them to leave the sea and forsake the galleys. All of the men from the galleys were in cabins and huts they had built in that region where later on Algeciras la Nueva, was populated. Many of these ill men were also on the island in the sea near Algeciras, and all of these galleys and ships were abandoned, for there were no men in them except for a few in each one, and these were very ill and wounded. Notwithstanding that those of the army and the fleet were very stricken by disease and that they had a reduction of payment and of food, the Moors who were in the city of Algeciras had used up and eaten all of the bread they had, and they had reached such a state of hunger that they were falling dead in the streets of the city.

During this time, Aben Yuzaf was in the town of Tangiers.[1] With him were Garcí Martínez de Gallegos and other Christians who lived overseas and served Aben Yuzaf. Aben Yuzaf learned of the stress in which those of the city of Algeciras were in, and although they told him that the Christian fleet was ruined, he did not believe it; for he saw that there were many galleys and ships there and did not think that he, with the fourteen galleys that he had, could help those of the city. He had a council with the captains of his galleys, whom the Moors call chiefs, and with the others who were there with him as to which fashion they could assist Algeciras and how they might look for a way to take them some supplies. The chiefs told him that they did not know a manner as to how they could do it, for they saw there many galleys and they did not know in what condition they were. But they said that Aben Yuzaf should consider it good to send his messengers to the captain of that army with some agreement, and that these chiefs would go with the messengers as sailors so that they could not be recognized, and that they would examine the Christian fleet. From what they saw, they could tell what King Alfonso would be able to do. Aben Yuzaf considered that they were giving him good advice, and he immediately ordered a galley armed with men. On it went Abdalhaque el Rujamán and Garcí Martínez de Gallegos with a message from Aben Yuzaf,[2] and in this galley entered with them the chiefs, sons of Rudahe Abenpachón, and other knights dressed as sailors. As soon as they arrived near Algeciras, they made signs of peace and sent forward a small vessel. Prince Pedro ordered that they come safely, and the messengers came out of the vessel and went to speak with

Prince Pedro and the other noblemen who were with him in that army. They told him that Aben Yuzaf was sending to tell him that he would give to King Alfonso two hundred thousand gold coins to put an end to the siege of Algeciras, and that Aben Yuzaf would take this city and would deliver it to Aben Alhamar. After he had delivered it to Aben Alhamar, don Pedro might besiege it, but he would not help Aben Alhamar to defend it; hence, he would regain the city and the fortune. Prince Pedro answered him that he would not do any of this until his father, King Alfonso, knew it, and he would send word and they could come a certain day for the answer. While Aben Yuzaf's messengers were with Prince Pedro in this meeting, the chiefs, sons of Rudahe, went around examining the Christian fleet. They saw the galleys forsaken and the men in them ill, and they departed from there and went to Tangiers. As soon as the messengers had returned to Aben Yuzaf, they told him the answer that Prince Pedro had given them. Also, the sea captains told him to order armed those fourteen galleys with good men and well armed, and they would destroy all of that fleet. If the sea was cleared, they could then take whatever supplies they wished. King Aben Yuzaf then ordered that all of the seamen immediately board the galleys. He placed in them many of the best knights he had and very well armed with all of their weapons, and they hastened so much in this that during this day and the next, until the third hour, they were armed. They immediately departed from Tangiers and arrived at Algeciras. Of these fourteen galleys, four went to the galleys near the island, and ten went to the large area where the new town was occupied. Those of the four galleys who went to the island killed whomever they found, ill or healthy, and they burned all of the galleys there; the other ten Moorish galleys came against the other galleys of the Christians, and the men who were in them were so few and injured that not a single one of them thought to defend himself, nor could they move any of those galleys from where they were anchored. The Moors burned them all and killed those who were in them.

Furthermore, it is found written that the Moorish knights who went on the ten galleys came to land and arrived at that place where they later founded the new city and killed many of those who were sick. And even though it seems that the army should have defended those men, the history of what was found written about this feat is that when the Christians who were on the ships saw that the galleys were being destroyed and burned, and understanding that they were not so many that they could defend them, nor was the wind blowing in such a way that they could move them, the Christians sank and submerged them in the sea and fled in the small vessels to the main ship—all of this happened before the day was over. On those three ships Pedro Martínez de Fe, admiral, in one sought refuge; Gonzalo Morante in the other; and don Guillén de Savanaque in another.

Six Moorish galleys immediately crossed overseas during this night for supplies, and they came the next day and put them in Algeciras. The other galleys, which remained to fight another day with the three ships, went to battle in the morning, and those of the ships were on high seas in case the wind came to them so that they could flee or could fight. The Moors of the galleys approached the ships to fight them, and the Christians who were on the ships defended themselves very well. While they were engaged in this battle, the water current carried them until they reached Tangiers's territory. King Aben Yuzaf, who was in Tangiers, had learned how the Christian fleet was lost, and he saw that battle and sent to order two of his galleys to grant a truce to those of the ships. He also ordered that the captains of those ships come to him safely, for he wanted to speak with them. So the Moors did so, and Pedro Martínez de Fe, Gonzalo Morante, and don Guillén de Savanaque left the ships anchored. They came to King Aben Yuzaf, who was on the seashore. While they were talking with him, a wind and a great storm arose. The storm tore the anchors from the ships and those who were on them, in order not to lose them against the land in that storm, raised the sails and sailed to Cartagena, while Pedro Martínez, Gonzalo Morante, and don Guillén remained in that meeting with the king. As soon as Aben Yuzaf saw that the ships were gone, he ordered the three men seized. They remained in captivity for two years and later on escaped with some Moors who brought them to Seville.

Prince Pedro and those who were with him, as soon as they realized that the fleet was lost and the Moors were supplying food and all that they needed to the city, agreed on how they could leave from there. They left behind the siege machines, weapons, and many other things they could not carry, and the Moors came out and took away everything and put it inside the city. Aben Yuzaf immediately went from Tangiers to Algeciras and found many things made that the Christians left. Because he thought the place that is now known as the new city of Algeciras would be very dangerous if it were besieged again, and because Aben Yuzaf was told it could be lost, he ordered a town built there. They called it Algeciras la Nueva, and he populated it with houses the Christians had built on the settlements and lived in this Algeciras a number of days. Prince Pedro and those of the army went to Seville. As soon as King Alfonso learned of the destruction of his fleet and saw his men coming in that fashion, he was very grieved by it. Realizing that he could not obtain that city nor remove from this side of the sea Aben Yuzaf's might, he looked for a way to reconcile himself with this Aben Yuzaf so that he could wage war on the King of Granada. And King Alfonso and King Aben Yuzaf made their agreement together and remained in truce and peace for a while.

Notes

1. A Moroccan fleet commanded by the emir's son, Abû Ya'qûb, sailed from Tangiers for Gibraltar on July 19, 1279, to blockade Algeciras, which surrendered in August. O'Callaghan, *The Learned King*, 249.

2. 'Abd al-Haqq al-Tuyumân (Abdalhaque el Rujamán in the *Chronicle*) was an interpreter.

Chapter 73

◫

Of How King Alfonso Made a Truce with Aben Yuzaf, and Was Preparing Himself to Come to the Frontier for the War Against the King of Granada

After the army that King Alfonso had in Algeciras, of which his son don Pedro was the leader, was destroyed by Aben Yuzaf's might, and also his fleet—by which destruction King Alfonso, who was in Seville, was very dismayed—the king, thinking that he would not be able to conquer that city because of the might that Aben Yuzaf had across the sea, searched for a way to reconcile himself with this king so that he could wage war on the King of Granada. And King Alfonso and King Aben Yuzaf made their agreement in the year 1317 of the Era.[1]

King Alfonso left Seville and came to Badajoz, and with him came his brother Prince Manuel. He sent for Prince Sancho, his son, who was heir and who was in the land of Castile and León doing justice, and for his other sons, Prince Pedro, Prince Juan, and Prince Jaime; and they all came to him at Badajoz during the month of October. King Alfonso spoke with them and told them that because it had not been God's will that he regain the city of Algeciras, because of the loss and diminishment he received by the destruction of his fleet, and because of the men he lost, he had joined King Aben Yuzaf, for he wanted to return to the war with the King of Granada so that he could serve God and regain this land that the Moors held on this side of the sea.

King Alfonso immediately ordered called all of his armies so that they might go with him to Córdoba in order to enter the Vega of Granada. He also ordered Prince Sancho to return to Castile to draw out all of his armies, including those of noble descent as well as advisors, so that they might all arrive at the frontier in order to invade the Vega of Granada to cut the wheat. Because King Deonis of Portugal,[2] grandson of this King Alfonso, was in disagreement with Queen Beatriz, his mother, daughter of this King Alfonso, King Alfonso had to beg King Deonis of Portugal to come to Yélves, a town in the kingdom of Portugal that is three leagues from Badajoz. King Alfonso sent to King Deonis his son Prince Sancho, his brother Prince Manuel, and his sons Prince Pedro, Prince Juan, and Prince Jaime to beg King Deonis to come and meet with him there at Badajoz. King Deonis waited for three days, then answered that they should come and that he would then come to his grandfather, King Alfonso. As soon as they arrived at Badajoz, where their father, King Alfonso, was, they told him of the answer that his grandson the King of Portugal had told them. King Alfonso was pleased with it and remained waiting for King Deonis to come. The King of Portugal—suspecting that King Alfonso wanted to place him under the authority of his mother, Queen Beatriz, and by which he was not pleased—refused to come to Badajoz to meet his grandfather and instead went to Lisbon. When they told this to King Alfonso and he realized that his grandson the King of Portugal did not wish to prepare for him, he returned to Seville; and Prince Sancho and the other princes, his brothers, returned to Castile to prepare their men to go with the army to the frontier.

Notes

1. Alfonso X concluded a truce with the Benimerines in 1279. O'Callaghan, *The Learned King,* 249.

2. King Dinis of Portugal (1279–1325) was the son of Afonso III and Alfonso X's illegitimate daughter Beatriz. His meeting with Alfonso X at Badajoz did occur, in mid-October 1279. The *Chronicle* is mistaken on this point.

Chapter 74

❖

*Of How Prince Don Sancho Entered the Vega of
Granada, and of a Battle That the Master of
Santiago Fought and Lost, and of the Meeting
That King Alfonso Had with the King of France*

In the twenty-eighth year of the reign of this King Alfonso, which
was in the Era of 1318, and the year 1280 after the birth of Jesus
Christ, Prince Don Sancho strove to bring out all his noblemen
and counselors from the land so that they were all in Córdoba with
King Alfonso. Prince Don Sancho went to Toledo and took from
there all the knights and other men whom he could, and he set
out for Jaén. He arrived there in the month of June and sent his
message to King Alfonso, his father, in which he asked him when
he wished to move or what he wished to do.[1] King Alfonso had
agreed to enter the Vega through Rute and Prince Sancho through
Alcaudete so that he could join the armies in Alcalá de Benzaide.
It happened that King Alfonso had fallen ill with a pain in his eye,
and for this reason he was unable to go. So he sent all of his army
to his son Prince Sancho so that he could enter the Vega. Prince
Don Sancho moved immediately with all of his army and set out
for Alcalá de Benzaide. Waiting there four days for more men who
were to come, on a Saturday, which was the Vespers of St. John,
Prince Sancho sent don Gonzalo Ruiz Girón, Master of the Cavalry
of the Knights of Santiago,[2] and don Gil Gómez de Villalobos, who
was Abbot of Valladolid, and Fernand Anriquez. He gave them a
large company of counselors to go with them to protect the crops
and those who were gathering firewood for the encampment. They
arrived at a Moorish castle named Moclín, which is two leagues
from Alcalá, and the gatherers returned safely to the camp. As the
gatherers were returning, a hundred Moorish knights appeared

near the Castle of Moclín. As soon as Master Don Gonzalo Ruiz Girón saw this, since he was a man of great courage, he did not wait for any of the others, not even for his own men. And as soon as the Moors saw him, they started to flee. They led him to an ambuscade in which were two thousand Moorish knights. And at noon, as the ambuscade was discovered, they attacked him and wounded this Gonzalo Ruiz so that later he died. They also went after the other men and came close to the encampment's tents. They slew on that day one thousand eight hundred knights and foot soldiers, and most of the friars of the Order of Santiago; and they captured their knights and many others. Prince Don Sancho, when he learned of it, took in his hand a javelin and went out on a horse and passed through all the camp. He ordered all the men to be calm and stayed there until the Sabbath day. On Monday, which was St. John's Day, Prince Sancho ordered Master Gonzalo Ruiz, who was very badly wounded, to return to Alcaudete; and so great was the alarm most of the men felt due to the deaths of these men whom the Moors had killed that they left with a number of men from the camp. When Prince Don Sancho learned of it, he ordered them to return, since he did not wish that through Gonzalo Ruiz's situation the encampment be vacated and that the entry he had to make into the Vega be hindered. And just then the master died.

The next day, Thursday, Prince Don Sancho went out from there with all his people and set out for Moclín, that castle. From there he set out for the Vega, and he came close to Granada, burning wheat and laying waste, and tearing down all that he found. As soon as the entire Vega had been devastated, Prince Don Sancho went back with all of his army to Jaén, and from there to his father, the king, in Córdoba. The way Prince Don Sancho had managed the army so well pleased the king greatly. The king and his sons with him moved from Córdoba and went to Seville, and Prince Sancho lodged in San Francisco. The king had the Jews, who were collectors of rents, arrested, including the greatest of them, don Zag de la Malea—who had been ordered to bring succor at the siege of Algeciras and had not done so. The misappropriation of the funds don Zag de la Malea collected that he had given to Prince Don Sancho—who was here in the land—to give to Queen Doña Violante, his mother, when he brought her from Aragón to Castile, did not please the king, his father. In order to punish Prince Don

Sancho for this annoyance he had done him, the king commanded this don Zag de la Malea be taken to San Francisco, where Prince Don Sancho was residing with all of his brothers, and that they drag don Zag up to the outskirts.[3] As soon as Prince Don Sancho found this out, he wanted to go forth and take him, but those who were with him did not agree to it. But Prince Sancho remained in great belligerence against the king because of the death of this Jew, and he believed that the king had done it all on account of the service don Zag had rendered him.

King Philip of France, son of Saint Louis, sent many times to bring King Alfonso to find some way that don Alfonso, son of Prince Don Fernando might live; and because King Don Alfonso loved him very much and desired that he, the King of France, and the King of England might cross the sea to the land of Africa against Morocco, he believed that his passage might be prepared that they would be able to do the greatest service to God and that from there they would then conquer the Holy Land. Concerning this, the king sent his reply to the King of France—on the one hand, to settle peaceably the matter of don Alfonso, son of Prince Don Fernando; and on the other, in order to speak during this time, because there was need that both the kings meet together. And they agreed to meetings in Bayonne in the month of December.[4] As to the matter of don Alfonso, King Alfonso concealed it from Prince Don Sancho, his son, fearing he would not play a part in it, and he moved from Seville and came to Valladolid and left the royal seal of his family there with his officials. They sent throughout the kingdom in great secrecy letters in which he ordered that all the synagogues of the Jews be seized on a Sabbath day. When they were all seized, King Alfonso made a pact with them for twelve thousand *maravedís* of that current coinage each day, until repayment had been made. King Alfonso was in Bayonne with all his sons, and the King of France came and reached Salvatierra in Gascony and sent the Prince of Morea,[5] son of King Charles of Sicily, to treaty with King Don Alfonso about the pact of agreement concerning Prince Don Fernando. He had come to certify that King Alfonso would give him the kingdom of Jaén and that he would be his vassal and the vassal of Prince Don Sancho. When Prince Don Sancho learned of this treaty that his father, King Alfonso, was making, it grieved him. The king wanted to satisfy him and he never could. And the king responded and told him that he, during his lifetime was king and lord of everything, and that he had no cause to give anything he owned, and that after his life, Sancho would keep it all and he would not lack anything. Prince Sancho advised him to make an agreement with King Don Pedro of Aragón, who was his neighbor and who held this don Alfonso prisoner, and he assured King Alfonso that the King of France should not be against him in any way. King Don Alfonso had to agree to this advice; and after the King of France saw that King Don Alfonso was not replying to the agreement, he returned to his country.

Notes

1. Infante Sancho was in Córdoba on June 11, 1280.

2. The defeat of the Castilians at Moclín took place on the eve of the Feast of St. John, June 23. Gonzalo Ruiz Girón was Master of Santiago from 1275 to 1277. O'Callaghan, *The Learned King*, 249–50.

3. Zag de la Maleha, a royal tax collector, was executed in September 1280.

4. The interview with Philip III, the uncle of the Infantes de la Cerda, at Bayonne took place just before Christmas 1280. O'Callaghan, *The Learned King*, 250–51.

5. The Prince of the Morea was Charles, son of Charles of Anjou, King of Sicily, who in turn was the uncle of Philip III of France.

Chapter 75

◧

*Of How King Alfonso Entered the Vega of
Granada and Wasted It, and What Happened
Afterward, and of Other Deeds in the Kingdom*

In the twenty-ninth year of the reign of this King Alfonso, which
was in the Era of 1319, and the year 1281 after the birth of Jesus
Christ, King Alfonso came to Burgos and held the marriages of his
sons Prince Pedro and Prince Juan. Prince Pedro wed the daughter of the Lord of Narbonne, and Prince Juan married the daughter of the Marquis of Monferrat, who was wed to Princess Beatriz,
his daughter.[1] And the Marquis of Monferrat asked King Alfonso
to give him something for the land he had in Normandy. So the
king gave him in pay two tallies in coin, which amounted to fifteen
coins per *maravedí*, and he also gave him many horses and many
gifts. When Prince Sancho and his brother saw this, that he gave to
the Marquis, they took it to heart and considered it bad. It was one
of the matters King Alfonso had in his actions that later were to be
against him. Likewise, there in Burgos he knighted his son Prince
Jaime, who was the Lord of Los Cameros. Then King Alfonso sent
to promise King Pedro of Aragón that they would meet, and King
Pedro came to Tarazona and King Alfonso came to Agreda, and
they met together and made their covenants in such a way that
through it they remained friends.[2] King Pedro took from King
Alfonso the castles of Val de Ayora, which belonged to Alfonso's
brother Prince Manuel, and gave in exchange for them the town
of Escalona on the condition that in all the time that his heirs held
those castles, they would leave Escalona to the king or to those
who might reign after him. King Alfonso demanded all of his armies
to be summoned to go to enter the Vega of Granada again,[3] and all

of the armies were assembled in the month of June. He moved with all of his armies. Prince Sancho led the vanguard, while Prince Pedro led another part, and Prince Juan another, and a son of King Alfonso who was illegitimate and who was named Alfonso, the Child, led the rear, and he was the Lord of Molina; King Alfonso went in the middle. So they entered the Vega, waging fierce war and laying siege to the city of Granada.

Prince Don Sancho left the encampment one day to lay waste to the vineyards, and after he had cut down a large part of them, he went to a hill close to the city. The King of Granada and all those Moors considered it an insult and a grievance; therefore, fifty thousand bearing leather shields, and twice as many archers, and all the people in the city, well-mounted Andalusians, came out to drive them from there. The men who were with Prince Don Sancho all abandoned him, except for a few who stayed there with him. But he showed himself to be so strong and so ardent that through his strength alone he protected everyone, and after this danger he made evident his honor and great prowess.

The King of Granada sent his messengers to King Don Alfonso to ask that Alfonso send someone with whom to speak. Then King Alfonso sent Gómez Garcí de Toledo,[4] who later was Abbot of Valladolid and who was a confidant of Prince Don Sancho, and the King of Granada began many parleys with him. The treaty was arrived at in such a fashion that the King of Granada gave King Don Alfonso one-third of all the rents he had from treaties, and King Don Alfonso said that he would give the King of Granada the castles and fortresses, which he was already giving, and nothing more. With this he departed, and King Don Alfonso came to Córdoba with all his host, and he and the entire cavalry departed for the frontier castles to fulfill the time they were to serve. Likewise, a large company of rogues had been going about in the mountains, killing and stealing all they found, since King Alfonso had pardoned them so that they could accompany him to the Vega; and as soon as they were out of it, they demanded of the king many things with which to support themselves. Because he did not give those things to them, they went about threatening that they would go to the mountains and commit every evil they could in the land. When King Alfonso learned of this, he ordered all of them seized and slain.

Also he agreed there in Córdoba to hold court in Seville,[5] and he sent to his entire realm and every city and every town to send his procurators there, with individuals trained to represent all that came to his attention. They came there quickly, and when all were assembled, he spoke to them and told them about the war with the Moors and how he had them in a good place for conquering the land. He also told them that it was necessary to look for a way to get funds to do so and to finish with it. And he told them he had learned that all the rents were diminished—on one hand, because of the debasement of coinage during the time of King Don Fernando, his father, due to the great need he had for the conquest of the Moors, which he carried out in the kingdom of Murcia; and also due to the great war he waged with King Aben Yuzaf of Morocco, which took place there. For what was taking place here, King Alfonso found that the best way he could keep himself and ensure himself from losing anyone in the realm was to mint two coins— one of silver and another copper—so that they could be distributed through all the markets great and small, and the people could take care of themselves, and all would live according to precept and law and have sufficient money to have the things they needed. They replied to King Alfonso more through fear than with affection that he should do what he considered good and what he pleased. As soon as they had agreed in this way, the king believed that he had settled it with them. He looked for a way to make the treaty with the King of France for this grandson, Prince Don Fernando's son Alfonso, who was in prison in Játiva under the power of the King of Aragón. But he hid the treaty from his son Prince Don Sancho so that Prince Sancho was unaware of it.

The king told Prince Don Sancho that he would send Bishop Don Frédolo of Oviedo to the pope to petition his blessing for the war on the Moors.[6] And the king sent him to the pope so that the pope would confirm the treaty with the King of France as to the case of don Alfonso. This Bishop Don Frédulo was a Tuscan and Prince Don Sancho immediately suspected the message concerning this treaty, since don Frédulo was not his subject. And don Sancho suspected that the king, his father, was sending him contrary to his interests with the treaty he had begun concerning don Alfonso, Prince Don Fernando's son—and Prince Don Sancho brought it up to King Don Alfonso. The king answered Prince Sancho that he was only sending the bishop because he was in favor with the pope and was the right one for collecting those blessings for the war with the Moors. But no matter that he said this, Prince Don Sancho kept his suspicion of the king, his father, concerning this treaty. And when King Don Alfonso asked his counselors if there was anybody there who wanted to share this treaty with Prince Don Sancho concerning don Alfonso, none of his counselors wanted to commit themselves to it, nor did they dare to tell him so.

A friar named Aimar,[7] an appointee of Ávila, told the king that he desired to speak for him, and the king said he agreed. This Friar Aimar went to Prince Don Sancho and talked with him in secret. Prince Don Sancho told the friar he was crazy and brash and that if it were not for the habit he wore, he would make an example of him so that no one else would dare to say such a thing. As soon as King Don Alfonso learned about this reply that Prince Don Sancho had given, he said that he would tell it all to him even though he did not want to. The king came to speak with Prince Don Sancho, and Prince Sancho replied that he beseeched King Alfonso not to speak about this treaty nor to order him to accept it, because there was nothing in the world in it to which he would agree. King Don Alfonso was enraged at this reply and told him that even though he did not want the agreement, he would have it and that he would not desist from having it, neither because of Sancho nor because of the homage the people of the realm had paid him, and that he, Prince Sancho, should agree to it or be disinherited.

When Prince Don Sancho heard this reply, he turned against King Alfonso and spoke these words: "Sire, you did not make me, rather, God made me, and He did much in creating me. But He killed my brother, who was older than I and who was to inherit the kingdom from you, if he had lived longer than you. God did not kill him so that I could inherit from you after your days are ended. I could well excuse the word that you used [disinherited]. There will come a time when you will regret having uttered it."

With all this, the two departed from one another very angry. King Alfonso kept his plan to finish what he had begun with the pope and with the King of France; and he again had the council who were there summoned to give him advice, and he asked that they agree to mint those coins as has been said. But they, who felt very aggravated, dared not tell King Alfonso, and they went to speak with Prince Don Sancho, begging him for mercy's sake to take pity on them, because if they returned to their lands with this reply, they would be very badly received and everybody would be very angry at them. They said that he, Prince Don Sancho, knew very well how many deaths, how many outrages, and how many cruelties and sufferings the king, his father, had brought about in the kingdom, for which all of them were angry at him. They begged Prince Sancho to protect and defend them and that he cleave to them so that they would not be as endangered as they were; moreover, they could not get along without finding some other way to avoid enduring all the harm they were experiencing with the king. Understanding what they were telling him, which was true, and distrusting the king, his father, concerning the treaty he had agreed to—because perchance the people of the realm might act in such a way that he might lose his inheritance of the realms—Prince Sancho had to say that he desired that they go back and be with his father, the king, in Seville. He wanted them to grant King Alfonso whatever he wished and said that he would go back to Córdoba and would tell them what to do. Prince Don Sancho told the king, his father, that he wanted to go to Córdoba, and that if he considered it a good thing, he would send to the King of Granada and recognize the treaty he had recognized when he was in the Vega; and King Alfonso said it pleased him.

So Prince Don Sancho came to Córdoba and sent the plea on his behalf to the King of Granada by Garcí Gómez de Toledo, who later was the Abbot of Valladolid, so that he signed the pact with him. Then Prince Don Pedro and Prince Don Juan, his brothers, came there to him, and they signed their pact with him that they would stand with him against King Don Alfonso, their father. And then he, don Sancho, spoke with the Cordovans and they made this treaty.

Notes

1. The marriages of the king's third son, Infante Pedro, with Marguerite, the sister of Aimeric, Viscount of Narbonne, and of his fourth son, Infante Juan, with Joanna, daughter of William, Marquis of Montferrat, took place at Burgos in February 1281. O'Callaghan, *The Learned King*, 252–53.

2. Alfonso X and Pedro III concluded a pact at Campillo between Agreda and Tarazona on March 27, 1281. O'Callaghan, *The Learned King*, 253–55.

3. The invasion of the plain of Granada took place in June 1281. Sancho defeated the Moors on June 25. O'Callaghan, *The Learned King*, 255–56.

4. Gómez García de Toledo, Abbot of Valladolid and one of Infante Sancho's intimates, served as notary in the kingdom of León in 1283. He was elected Bishop of Mondoñedo in 1286 but died that same year.

5. The Cortes of Seville was summoned for Martinmas, November 11, 1281. O'Callaghan, *The Learned King*, 256–58.

6. Bishop Frédolo of Oviedo (1275–1284).

7. Bishop Aimar of Ávila (1281–1284).

Chapter 76

❖

*How Prince Don Sancho Spoke Against
King Don Alfonso, His Father, and of
the Happenings That Took Place in the Kingdom*

In the thirtieth year of the reign of this King Don Alfonso, which was in the Era of 1320, and the year 1282 after the birth of Jesus Christ, Prince Don Sancho then sent Prince Don Juan, his brother, with letters and with empowerment to all the cities and towns of the kingdom of León to speak with them so that they might support this way and this authority to supplicate the grace of his father so that he not encroach upon their rights, arrest them, nor be angry at them. Prince Don Juan went everywhere urging that they support Prince Don Sancho; and they all, every town and council, made a pact and covenant by letters and fealty to support Prince Don Sancho. As soon as Prince Don Juan arrived in Zamora, he went to seize the Alcázar of Zamora from a lady—the wife of Garcí Pérez, King Alfonso's high judge in Galicia—who was there. This lady was the sister of Pay Gómez Cherino.[1] She sent him the reply that she would not release the *alcázar* to him, because her husband held it for King Don Alfonso. Prince Don Juan knew that this lady had given birth to a son not more than eight days previously and that they were rearing him in a village outside of the town. He ordered the child seized and took him to the gate of the castle and sent to tell the lady that if she did not yield him the *alcázar* immediately, he would kill him. The lady, due to the great love which she had for her son, feared that Prince Don Juan would kill him, and she surrendered the *alcázar* quickly. Then Prince Don Juan sent to tell Prince Don Sancho how he was holding the entire kingdom in peace and how he had taken the *alcázar*. Prince Don Sancho went to Andújar and to Úbeda and they made the same treaty. Then he sent to Jaén and they yielded him the *alcázar,* and they all made this same treaty. The Master of Santiago, and don Pedro Muñiz, and don Juan González, Master of Calatrava, came to him there, and they made the same treaty as the others. To all the counselors, all the prelates, and all the others of the realm of the king he sent his letters to tell them that he wanted to speak for them with the king, his father: to ask him not to kill them, not to dispossess them, nor encroach upon them, as he had done up until then. All of them should go to Valladolid in the month of April, for he wanted to meet with them all. Prince Don Sancho then sent his messengers to the noblemen who had been banished from the kingdom, and they were the following: don Lope, Lord of Vizcaya, and don Diego, his brother; Diego López; Lope Díaz and his minions, sons of don Lope, the Younger; don Fernán Pérez Ponce; don Ramir Díaz; don Pedro Páez de Asturias; don Ferrand Rodríguez de Cabrera; and other noblemen and many knights who were cast out of the realm. Prince Sancho sent the messengers to say that they should all come to him in Valladolid and he would hand over to them all their inheritances that the king, his father, had taken from them. He also said he would restore their lands and soldiers very well and would act with much goodness and grace.

Then the King of Portugal, who was in disfavor with his grandfather, King Don Alfonso, because the latter was holding his mother, made a treaty with Prince Don Sancho to support him against King Don Alfonso. Likewise, Prince Don Sancho quickly sent his messengers to King Don Pedro of Aragón, telling him the stance he was taking and begging him to let them love each other so that he would help him if there were need. This greatly pleased King Don Pedro, and he immediately signed the treaties with him since this King of Aragón had a very great fleet prepared, which for a very long time had been outfitted to go to the kingdom of Sicily. As soon as this message came to King Don Pedro of Aragón, he moved with his entire fleet to the kingdom of Sicily and took it from King Carlos,[2] who was holding it. As soon as he had taken it, he left Queen Doña Constanza, his wife, and Prince Don Jaime and Prince Don Fadrique, his children, there and set out for Aragón. As soon as Prince Don Sancho was certain about all those treaties, he took the road to Toledo and spoke with the Toledoans about all this,[3] and they made their treaties with him. From there he went to Ávila and Segovia, and they all made treaties with him.

He learned that King Don Alfonso had killed his uncle Prince Don Fadrique, who lay buried in a foul place where King Don Alfonso had ordered him buried.[4] Prince Sancho removed him from there and buried him in a very honorable sepulcher that he built in the monastery of the Monks of the Trinity in Burgos. Then he went to Valladolid and found there Queen Doña Violante, his mother, who was awaiting him there. She was very pleased with this position that he had taken against King Don Alfonso, her husband. When Prince Sancho arrived there, all of the realm and the nobles who were outside were united. They all agreed that they would give him the kingdom's power. Prince Sancho did not wish to agree that he be called king of his realm during his father's lifetime. About this they reached an agreement, and they agreed that they would require that King Don Alfonso yield all the fortresses and that they gave Prince Don Sancho the rule and the wealth of the kingdom. And Prince Don Manuel, King Don Alfonso's brother, declared this decree in the *Cortes* of Valladolid; and then Prince Don Sancho gave Prince Don Manuel as an inheritance Chinchilla, Porquera, Almansa, Aspe, and Beas. Prince Don Sancho granted to the people of the land the petitions they made for whatever they wanted, in which he gave them his letters with leaded royal seals. He divided the rents; he divided parcels of land among all the princes and nobles, just as they used to have them; and besides, he gave them what was for the maintenance of the king, to wit, the rents from the Jewish quarters, the *diezmo* tax, and the ancient duties on exports of Toledo, Talavera, and Murcia, and the rents of all the Moorish quarters. He did not keep for himself anything, so as to be sure that they were paid.

As soon as Prince Don Sancho had dismissed the *cortes,* he went to Toledo; and when he arrived, he married doña María,[5] daughter of the Prince of Molina. He also wed his sister Princess Doña Violante to don Diego, don Lope's brother. To Prince Don Manuel, his uncle, a son was born in Escalona to his wife, the Countess of Savoy.[6] Prince Don Sancho had to go and baptize him, and they named him Juan. Prince Don Manuel asked him to give him Peñafiel, and Prince Don Sancho gave it to him on the conditions that the royal privilege states. After this he went to Córdoba, and the news reached him there that the town of Badajoz had revolted. He left the princess, his wife, in Córdoba, and immediately went there; and he left with her the Master of Calatrava, the Master of Alcántara, the Prior of the Hospital, and don Ramir Díaz with many companies of knights. Prince Sancho took with him don Diego, don Álvaro, and all the other nobles. But when they arrived at Badajoz, the people of Badajoz did not wish to receive them and he returned to Mérida. A message reached him there from Prince Don Juan, his brother, concerning how he was speaking with the councils of Toro, Zamora, Benavente, Villalpando, and Mallorca so that Prince Sancho might talk with them; likewise, that his brother Prince Don Pedro was speaking with the councils of Salamanca, Ciudad Rodrigo, and with all the people of the kingdom. A message also reached Prince Sancho as to how don Lope had spoken with the councils of Castile and was obtaining their treaty against the king. Also there came to him a message about how King Alfonso, his father, and King Aben Yuzaf of Morocco had arrived at Écija and were coming against Córdoba.[7] All their messengers took counsel so as to advise Prince Sancho what to do: some advised him to go to the kingdom of León lest he lose it; and others advised him to go to the kingdom of Castile lest he should lose it; others counselled him to go to Córdoba, where he had left his wife, and said if he did not go, he would lose the city and his wife would be in great danger.

Since Prince Don Sancho saw what advice each gave him—and he was certain as to the coming of Aben Yuzaf from overseas, who was coming to aid King Alfonso, his father—he decided to go to Córdoba so that he might prevent the greatest danger, which was the advance of the king, his father, with the might of Moors from across the seas. He went immediately to Córdoba, traveling in one day and one night the twenty-two leagues. He arrived there by night and entered the city. On the next day, the armies of King Don Alfonso and King Aben Yuzaf arrived at Guadajoz, one league from the city. Believing that Prince Don Sancho was in the territory of Guadajoz, they sent four thousand Moorish knights to march. The next day, when they learned that Prince Sancho was in Córdoba, King Don Alfonso and King Aben Yuzaf came to lay siege to the city. Aben Yuzaf stopped with all of his knights above Los Visos, and King Don Alfonso descended to a place down below, closer to the city. He took his banner with seven knights and sent it toward the grange at La Puente.

The knights asked if Ferrand Muñiz was there and said they were speaking on King Don Alfonso's behalf so that Muñiz remember how he had raised him and had wed him; and how he had knighted him and had appointed him high governor of the city of Córdoba; and how he had given it to him, and had given him its keys. Now King Alfonso was demanding refuge in it and that Ferrand Muñiz turn over its keys, warning that if not he would call him a traitor. After they had spoken these words to don Diego, don Álvaro, and the sons of don Juan Núñez, who were in the grange, they announced to the knights in these words: "Tell the king, our lord, that we, Diego López and don Álvaro, who are here with Prince Don Sancho, due to the many deaths and outrages that he caused—especially in that he killed both Prince Don Fadrique, his brother, and likewise killed don Simón de los Cameros, our uncle, who reared us and did us a great deal of good, and for the many other deaths he caused with violence to the nobles, and for the many encroachments he made upon our vassals in the entire realm—for these reasons, we had to appeal to the grace of Prince Don Sancho, who is his son and heir, to speak with us, and he did so. If King Alfonso should come as a king and lord should come, we and Prince Don Sancho would open the gates of the city and would receive him as king and lord. But since we see you in the armies of our enemies, of our law, our faith, and especially with King Aben Yuzaf, who is coming there, who slew don Nuño González, grandson of don Álvaro who was there, and who had killed don Ferrand Ruiz, son of don Rodrigo Álvarez and other noblemen and knights; and who also killed Prince Don Sancho of Aragón, Archbishop of Toledo. Because of the way he approached, they will not receive him in the city."

With all this as a reply, they went to him and told it all to him. Immediately King Don Alfonso sent to inform King Aben Yuzaf, who was above Los Visos; and when the message reached King Aben Yuzaf, he ordered the war drums beaten and ordered all of his cavalry to go to war. He descended from Los Visos, and the host went through the fields and laid siege to the city. Then, since night was coming, they returned to the encampment, where they rested; they stayed there twenty-one days making war against the city. Then they left there and went to Andújar, and then to Jaén, and later to Úbeda. The foraging parties of the army went up to Terrinchez, making war and burning and wasting all they found; but they were unable to seize any of the towns, so they retreated. King Aben Yuzaf went across the sea with his army and King Don Alfonso remained in Seville. When Prince Don Sancho found out that King Aben Yuzaf had gone, he then sent to tell the King of Granada to meet with him, and the King of Granada met with him in Priego. They signed their treaties, and the King of Granada asked Prince Sancho for the Castle of Areras, which was his and which King Alfonso, his father, had taken, and Prince Don Sancho gave it to him. They parted as friends, and Prince Don Sancho came to Córdoba and went from there to Medellín, and from Medellín he planned to go to Talavera because he thought to capture the master there. And then he went to wage war against the castles, because he had the might of his father, King Don Alfonso, against him.

Notes

1. Garcí Pérez was *merino mayor,* or governor, of Galicia in 1282. Pay Gómez Cherino was a knight and a poet whom Sancho IV later appointed as admiral.

2. After the revolt of the Sicilian Vespers on March 31, 1282, Pedro III of Aragón sailed for Sicily on June 6 and seized the island from Charles of Anjou.

3. Infante Sancho made his journey northward to Castile early in 1282. He was in Toledo in February and passed through Ávila, Arévalo, Palencia, Castrogeriz, and Burgos (where he gave honorable burial to Infante Fadrique) in March. By April 15 he was in Valladolid. O'Callaghan, *The Learned King,* 258–64.

4. The account of Fadrique's execution had been narrated previously in chapter 68.

5. Sancho married his cousin María de Molina (the daughter of Fernando III's brother Alfonso de Molina) at Toledo in early June 1282. O'Callaghan, *The Learned King,* 261–62.

6. Juan Manuel, the son of Infante Manuel and the Countess of Savoy, was born at Escalona in May 1283. He became a distinguished author and politician.

7. Abû Yûsuf invaded Spain again in the late summer of 1282 and concluded an alliance with Alfonso X on October 24. After a brief siege of Córdoba, they separated. In his will of November 8, 1282, Alfonso X disinherited Sancho, and he denounced him as a traitor on the next day. O'Callaghan, *The Learned King,* 264–65.

Chapter 77

◈

About the Things That Happened in the Kingdom
Concerning the Meeting Prince Don Sancho Had
Against His Father, King Don Alfonso, and
About the Death of the Above-Mentioned King

In the thirty-first year of the reign of this King Don Alfonso, which
was in the Era of 1321, and the year 1283 after the birth of Jesus
Christ, Prince Don Sancho came to Cáceres and then to Puente de
Alcántara. And to him came a message as to how Prince Don Pedro,
his brother, who was in Ledesma, was on his way to desert Prince
Sancho and to meet with King Alfonso, his father, because the king
would give Prince Don Pedro the realm of Murcia of which they
would name him king. As soon as Prince Don Sancho found this
out, he planned to travel fast so that dawn would come without any
suspicion in Ledesma. When he arrived there, he spoke with his
brother don Pedro and told him that he knew very well how through
his advice he had had this meeting with those of the realm and
that now that he knew about the treaty he had with their father; he
beseeched him not to wish to keep it, and that he ask him for whatever he wanted and he would give it to him. Prince Pedro then
asked Prince Sancho to give him the rents of his chancellory, that
he name him chancellor, that he grant it to him, and also he asked
that Prince Sancho give him Tordesillas as an inheritance; and
Prince Sancho gave it to Prince Don Pedro. Then Prince Don
Sancho left there and Prince Don Pedro with him, and they arrived in Palencia. A message came to him there concerning how
Fernán Pérez Ponce had gone to King Don Alfonso in Seville.[1]
During this time, Nuño Fernández de Valdenebro; don Juan
Fernández, son of the Dean of Santiago; don Fernand Pérez de
Limia; and other knights of Castile met, and they talked with King

Don Alfonso. Prince Don Sancho was against them. Seeing that they could not endure it, they said they wanted to depart their land and said Prince Sancho should give them someone to take them safely to Portugal. So Prince Don Sancho begged Prince Don Manuel, his uncle, to go with them, and he got them safely to Portugal. As soon as they were ready, they went to Portugal by way of Seville to King Alfonso. Prince Don Juan went in the realm of León in order to watch those towns, and Prince Don Sancho sent to Prince Don Juan to make peace with him, and he came to him in Palencia and was welcomed by him. Then Prince Don Juan took his wife and his people from Palencia. He took the road to Portugal and thence to King Don Alfonso, his father, in Seville. A message came to Prince Don Sancho from Córdoba about how Aben Yuzaf was coming over the sea with a great host of knights and in that message they begged Prince Sancho through his grace to send some people with whom they could defend themselves. So Prince Don Sancho sent them the councils of León, and he sent Sancho Martínez de Leyva with a great host of knights to Córdoba.

When King Aben Yuzaf came close to Seville, he and King Don Alfonso agreed that King Aben Yuzaf would go to war against the King of Granada because he had the support of Prince Don Sancho. King Aben Yuzaf asked King Alfonso to give him a thousand Christians, and they went with him and he gave him don Fernán Pérez Ponce, who was there with six hundred knights whom he had in his retinue. King Aben Yuzaf gave him wages for all who were with him, and they moved with their entire army and entered the land of the King of Granada.[2] Because don Fernán Pérez Ponce did not wish to camp with the Moorish army, unless separately, this made King Aben Yuzaf suspicious that don Fernán Pérez was untrustworthy. Therefore, they had to separate the Christian soldiers from the soldiers of King Aben Yuzaf. When Aben Yuzaf saw this, he sent to demand of them the wages he had given them, and they gave them to him rather than stay with him. They departed discordant from him and made their way to Córdoba and camped on the banks of the River of Guadajoz. When Prince Don Sancho and don Fernand Anriquez, and those who were in Córdoba with Prince Don Sancho learned of it, they went out and fought them so that don Fernán Pérez Ponce and the others who came with him conquered the Cordovans and they slew on that day: Fernand Muñiz, Lord Mayor of Córdoba, and they cut off his head and took it to King Don Alfonso, who ordered it hung up on the scaffold of Seville on hooks. Likewise on that day they killed Rodrigo Esteban, Lord Mayor of Seville, and it greatly grieved King Don Alfonso. Then King Alfonso gave the mayorship of Seville to Diego Alfonso. A message came to Prince Don Sancho as to how Prince Don Jaime, his brother, who was Lord of Los Cameros de Haro; and don Juan Alfonso, who had come to meet with King Don Alfonso against him; and the castles that don Juan Alfonso held all rose up against him. Then Prince Don Sancho went to Soria, and thence he went to Agreda and found the alcázar and the Moorish Quarter all in uprising against him.[3] He besieged it and made war on it with siege machines and took it. In this siege, don Lope, Lord of Vizcaya, and don Diego, his brother, were with him there. A message came to him that a knight named Martín de Aymar, who held the Castle of Treviño, had revolted in the castle on King Don Alfonso's order and don Juan Núñez had taken shelter in the city. Then Martín de Aymar went out with a large company and came to aid Burgos, and he returned with much booty to Treviño.

When the news reached Prince Don Sancho, he was grieved by it. He sent don Lope there immediately in order to aid him against don Juan Núñez, and don Lope did so. Don Lope then went there one day with six hundred knights to camp near the gates of Treviño against don Juan Núñez, and he sent to tell him that never had don Juan Núñez been in such a precarious spot before. Don Juan Núñez sent to tell don Lope that if he had as many and as good men as he had, he would not be coming to the gate as he had come, since he did not find the battle to his advantage. When don Lope saw this, he returned to Miranda and remained there with all his army. And so never did Prince Don Jaime, nor don Juan Núñez, nor don Alfonso, nor the others who were there in Treviño dare to come out to pillage nor to seize anything in the land.

Because the King of France was grieved about the conquest that King Don Pedro of Aragón made against King Carlos, his uncle, he sent a challenge to King Don Pedro of Aragón,[4] and he then went back to war against him and sent seven thousand knights to Navarre with the constable. King Don Pedro sent his message to King Carlos, in which he sent to tell him that if he wished, let him depart from this contest over the kingdom of Sicily. King Don Pedro said that he considered the kingdom was his because he inherited it from the queen, his wife, and that he—because King Carlos held it wrongfully—would fight with him, one by one, or five by five, or a thousand by a thousand; and that they should choose a place that could be safe, and he would go there on the day they set. King Carlos sent to tell King Don Pedro that it pleased him and the place would be Bordeaux, and he agreed that both would be there on the chosen days. As soon as the pact was decided upon and signed, King Carlos came there with a large company of knights, and he ordered all the roads guarded so as to see if King Don Pedro would come to seize him. When King Don Pedro learned this, he left Aragón and took with him a merchant of his from Calatayud named Domingo de la Figuera. He, unrecognized with this merchant, for he went as his servant, went to Logroño and Vitoria and by Guipúzcoa to Bayonne and thence to Bordeaux, and he lodged in Bordeaux in the house of a knight who was his vassal.[5] He armed himself and insisted that he would enter the jousting field that day, which was the day of the agreement, and that King Carlos was not coming as he had agreed. As soon as King Don Pedro had signed with the scribes, he left the field and went with that merchant, Domingo de la Figuera, along that road on which he had gone before, and he came as the merchant's servant. He arrived in Fuenterrabia, which was of the kingdom of Castile, and from there he came to Vitoria and sent for his men, and three hundred knights came from Aragón. Then he came to Logroño. Because they tried to invade Castile, King Don Pedro was there on the frontier for a good three months and a half, and they never dared to invade. When the Navarrese saw that King Don Pedro was in Logroño, they went to Tudela, and with them went Prince Don Jaime, don Juan Núñez, and don Juan Alfonso. From there they decided to go to Tarazona to lay waste whatever they found. As soon as King Don Pedro learned of it, he sent to tell Prince Don Sancho how he wanted to invade the land of the Navarrese and that he should go to help him. So Prince Don Sancho went to him in Logroño and took a good two thousand knights, and they both left Logroño and went to Tarazona. King Don Pedro sent for the nobles and knights, and they all came there. He asked them to go with him, because he wished to fight with the French. They replied that they would not do it, since they considered the French all well-supplied, but that if he would supply them, they would go with him. Don Pedro said he did not have time to do so, but that they should go with him and that if he lived through it, he would supply them. They told him that they would not go without supplies, and they left him and went to their lands, so only a small company was with King Don Pedro. Prince Don Sancho did not want his people to go fight the French. And Prince Don Jaime, don Juan Núñez, don Juan Alfonso, and the nobles and knights of Castile who were with the French—who numbered a good thousand knights under King Don Alfonso's command—told them that if they came to fight for King Don Pedro, since Prince Don Sancho was with him, they would not go with them, and that they would stay with Prince Don Sancho, who was their lord. No matter how much they might lay waste the land, they would not go against his person. When the French understood what the Castilians said, they abandoned the invasion and returned to Pamplona.

This King Don Pedro was very grateful to Prince Don Sancho for what he had done, since but for him the French would have invaded his land. King Don Pedro went to Catalonia, and Prince Don Sancho came to Burgos and from there to Valladolid and thence to Olmedo, and he carried out justice in all of Extremadura. Prince Don Sancho, being in Olmedo, a message came from Talavera concerning how a robber named Romero, with a group of knights and men from the hinterland, rebelled under King Don Alfonso's command. Immediately Prince Don Sancho went there between day and night as fast as he could; he reached there at dawn. That Romero, who was a robber, as soon as he saw that Prince Don Sancho had arrived in the hinterland, came out on horseback and fled. Prince Don Sancho went after him until he came to Puente de Pinos, which is on the Tajo River. When the robber passed over, he tore down the beams of the bridge, which was wooden, so that one could not come across it. The robber took refuge in a castle named Cabañas that he had seized, which is in the territory of Trujillo. And when Prince Don Sancho found no way to go over, he went back through the hinterland and slew all the men and women he found there who had given Romero and his knights shelter—and more than three hundred people were slain there. When Prince Sancho had committed this cruel and pitiless exemplary punishment, he came to Toledo and found there some knights who were going about stirring people up at the order of King Alfonso, his father.[6] Prince Sancho tried to calm them down, and then he came to Segovia. A message came to him there concerning how Prince Don Pedro, his brother, had died in Ledesma; and it pleased him greatly, because he knew that don Pedro went about telling lies and that he wanted to go with the king, his father.[7] From the land that this Prince Don Pedro owned, he gave part of it to the prince, his son. There also came a message concerning how doña Urraca Díaz,[8] wife of don Fernán Ruiz de Castro, and sister of don Diego and don Lope, was dead; and because this doña Urraca had adopted this Prince Don Sancho and had made him her heir, and because she had died, he inherited from her these towns: Santa Olalla, Iscar, Paredes, and that of Cuellar. Then he left from Segovia and came to Palencia,[9] and there were united with him Prince Don Manuel, his uncle, don Lope, and don Diego. He urged them to strongly consider finding some way to reconcile with the king, his father, and they considered it a good thing. They told him it was very good, each one of them swearing it. And even though they said that it pleased them, it was not so, rather it grieved them because they feared that the agreement would be against them.

Then Prince Don Sancho made don Diego López de Salcedo go with a message to a nephew who lived with Prince Don Manuel whose name was Gómez Fernández de Maqueda, and then to King Don Alfonso to see if he wished a treaty, saying that the lordship and treaty with Prince Don Sancho should be protected, and also the lands and inheritances of these good men. Prince Sancho also ordered that because Pope Martin,[10] a Frenchman, had given letters in which he excommunicated and interdicted all the kingdom of Castile and León if they did not obey King Don Alfonso, that anyone who carried these letters be killed with them; and he ordered that no interdict that the pope proclaimed would be carried out. Then Prince Don Sancho, on behalf of himself and of those of the land, sought an appeal of this interdict either from a new pope, or from a council, or from God Himself.

They told Prince Sancho that the town of Toro was forming bands of knights and a council, and on account of the many deaths that had befallen, they told him he should go there. A knight of the town named Lope García came out to receive him with a good three hundred mounted men—and this was one of the rabble-rousers who went about in the town. Prince Sancho seized and killed two brothers then, and he killed a number of people who had lodged in Villa Vieja, close to Tordesillas. Then he came to Toro and killed this Lope García, and he killed other knights and many other people so that he left the town quiet. He arrived there and ordered Prince Don Juan, his brother; don Álvaro; don Fernán Pérez Ponce; Nuño Fernández de Valdenebro; don Pedro Páez de Asturias; don Ferrand Fernández de Limia; and don Juan Fernández, son of the Dean of Santiago, who had come from Seville to Mérida, which belonged to the Master of Santiago, to come there to fight and to take the town by force. Then Prince Sancho sent for don Alfonso, son of the Prince of Molina; don Esteban Fernández; don Juan Fernández de Limia; don Ramiro Díaz; don Ferrand Rodríguez de Cabrera; don Pedro Álvarez; don Pedro Díaz; Nuño Díaz de Castañeda; and other nobles and knights so that he had a very great host for going there. And Prince Sancho being in Toro, a message came to him concerning how don Juan Núñez, who was in Navarre and who had gone forth with four hundred knights and had invaded the land of Alfaro, had overrun the Bishopric of Calahorra and later the Bishopric of Osma, and had taken up a position in the salt marshes of the Bishopric of Sigüenza. He had also taken much booty at Albarracín. Prince Don Sancho sent to order don Lope and don Diego, his brother, to set out for that war against don Juan Núñez. Also a message came to Prince Sancho concerning how Prince Don Manuel,[11] his uncle, had died; and of the land he had owned, he gave a part of it to don Juan, his son. Prince Sancho left Princess Doña María, his wife, who was pregnant in Toro. And then Princess Doña Isabel was born there. After this, Prince Don Sancho left Toro and went to Cáceres, and from there he went to Mérida and found Prince Don Juan with those noblemen whom King Don Alfonso had sent there, and he considered going to him. But they did not think it was prudent to do so. Because he knew that the king, his father, was in Constantina, he went to Guadalcanal and tried to be with the king; but the noblemen did not consent to it nor did they want them to meet. When each of them understood this, they found another way to make a treaty so that they might meet. King Don Alfonso took his daughter Queen Doña Beatriz of Portugal, and Prince Don Sancho took

Princess Doña María, his wife, and both of these ladies secretly began the bargaining between King Don Alfonso and Prince Don Sancho. They dealt with one another concerning the agreement of each of the lords. King Don Alfonso betook himself to Seville and Prince Don Sancho went to Salamanca.[12] Prince Don Sancho was in very great pain and had no faith in the physicians. So don Gómez García, who was Abbot of Valladolid and the king's confidant, seeing how the prince had reached the point of death and was distrustful of physicians, sent a letter to his friend don Álvaro, who was with King Don Alfonso, to tell him how Prince Don Sancho was dead and should have King Don Alfonso's grace; and that he would have him given Toledo and many other towns. When the letter reached don Álvaro, he went to King Don Alfonso and showed it to him. When King Don Alfonso saw that it said in the letter that Prince Don Sancho, his son, was dead, he grieved greatly; and so as not to reveal it before those who were with him there, he withdrew to a private room so that no one dared to go to him in it. King Alfonso began to weep hard for Prince Don Sancho, and so great was the grief he experienced from it that he spoke very dolorous words, saying many times that the best man he had in his family was dead. When those of King Alfonso's house saw that he was so withdrawn, they realized that he was demonstrating much great sorrow on account of the death of his son; so one of his confidants named Master Nicolás dared to go to him in the chamber,[13] and he spoke these words to the king: "Sire, why are you showing such grief for Prince Don Sancho, your son, who has dispossessed you? For if Prince Don Juan and these other nobles who are here with you realize it, you will lose them all and they will make some movement against you." And so as not to reveal that he was weeping or grieving for Prince Don Sancho, King Alfonso concealed it so that he could keep them from realizing that he was grieving for him; and he spoke these words: "Master Nicolás, I am not weeping for Prince Don Sancho, but I weep for myself, a miserable old man; because since he died, I shall never recover my realms, because the people of my towns and all the nobles feared me so much for the orders I gave for the harm they did me that they will not want to give them back to me; and more quickly would I have recovered them from Prince Don Sancho, only one man, if he had lived, than from so many others." And with this reason he hid the grief for his son.

Prince Don Sancho, being in Salamanca and not cured by his physicians, God wished to restore his health. And when King Don Alfonso realized how Sancho loved him, he was pleased by it, although he did not dare to let it be known.

When Prince Don Sancho recovered, he went to Ávila. During this time, King Don Alfonso grew so ill that he was near death. Realizing that he would not be able to recover, Prince Don Juan asked King Alfonso to give to him the kingdoms of Seville and Badajoz, with all their towns. Even though the king gave Prince Don Juan a favorable answer, he did not want to. And when he was stricken by his illness, he said before them all that he forgave Prince Don Sancho, his son and heir, because he acted so due to his youthfulness. King Alfonso also said that he forgave all of the subjects of the kingdoms who had worked against him; and he quickly ordered documents written concerning this, sealed with his golden seals so that all the people of this kingdom would know that he had given up complaints against them and that he forgave them so that they would be safe from any vituperation whatsoever. After King Alfonso had finished and stated all this, he received very devoutly the Corpus Christi, and after part of an hour he gave his soul to God.[14]

Prince Don Juan and all the nobles, the Queen of Portugal, his daughter, and the other princes, his sons, wept greatly for King Alfonso; and afterward they buried him in Saint Mary's of Seville, close to King Don Fernando, his father, and his mother, Queen Doña Beatriz.

Notes

1. Fernán Pérez Ponce was the royal *mayordomo* in 1284.

2. The Benimerines forced the King of Granada to submit to them on July 9, 1283. They raided as far north as Talavera in October. O'Callaghan, *The Learned King,* 266.

3. Sancho was at Agreda from May 20 to June 2 and at Soria on June 6, 1283.

4. Pedro III's proposed duel at Bordeaux with Charles of Anjou, his rival in Sicily and Naples, and the uncle of Philip III of France, was scheduled for June 1, 1283.

5. Pedro III and Sancho met at Logroño-Tarazona in June–July 1283.

6. Sancho was in Toledo on October 24, 1283.

7. Infante Pedro died at Ledesma on October 19, 1283.

8. Urraca Díaz, widow of Fernán Ruiz de Castro, sister of Diego López and Lope Díaz de Haro, adopted Sancho as her heir.

9. Sancho summoned an assembly to Palencia for All Saints' Day, November 1, 1283; he was there on November 27.

10. Pope Martin IV excommunicated Infante Sancho and imposed an interdict on the kingdom on August 9, 1283.

11. Infante Manuel died in December 1283.

12. Sancho was in Salamanca on March 8, 1284, where he fell ill.

13. Master Nicolas, one of the king's physicians, later served Sancho IV in the same capacity.

14. Alfonso X died at Seville on April 4, 1284, and was buried in the cathedral in the sumptuous tomb he had erected for his parents and himself. O'Callaghan, *The Learned King*, 266–69.

Selected Bibliography

Ackerlind, Sheila R. *King Dinis of Portugal and the Alfonsine Heritage.* New York: P. Lang, 1990.

Alfonso X el Sabio Institute. *Estudios Alfonsinos y Otros Escritos: En Homenaje a John Esten Keller y a Aníbal A. Biglieri.* New York: National Endowment for the Humanities, 1991.

Ballesteros y Beretta, Antonio. *Alfonso X.* Barcelona, 1963. Reprint, Barcelona: El Albir, 1984.

Bibliography of Old Spanish Texts, 3d. ed. Madison: Hispanic Seminary, 1984.

Burke, James F. "Alfonso X and the Structuring of Spanish History." *Revista Canadiense de Estudios Hispánicos* 9, no. 3 (spring 1985): 464–71.

Burns, Robert I. "Alfonso X of Castile, The Learned: 'Stupor Mundi.'" *Thought* 60 (1985): 375–87.

———. *Emperor of Culture: Alfonso X the Learned of Castile and His Thirteenth-Century Renaissance.* Philadelphia: Univ. of Pennsylvania Press, 1990.

———. *The Worlds of Alfonso the Learned and James the Conqueror: Intellect and Force in the Middle Ages.* Princeton, N.J.: Princeton Univ. Press, 1985.

———. "Warrior Neighbors: Alfonso el Sabio and Crusader Valencia, An Archival Case Study in His International Relations." *Medieval and Renaissance Studies* 21 (1990): 142–202.

Casto, María del Rivero, "Indice de las personas, lugares y cosas notables que se mencionan en las tres Crónicas de los Reyes de Castilla: Alfonso X, Sancho IV y Fernando IV." *Hispania* 2 (1942): 163–235, 323–406, 557–618.

Catalán, Diego. *La Estoria de España de Alfonso X: Creación y Evolución.* Madrid: Universidad Autónoma de Madrid, 1992.

———. "La historiografía en verso y en prosa de Alfonso XI a la luz de nuevos textos." *Anuario de Estudios Medievales* 2 (1965): 291.

———. *Un prosista anónima del siglo XIV* (La Laguna, 1955), 124.

Crónica de Alfonso X, ed. Cayetano Rosell, in *BAE* 66. 1875. Reprint, 1953.

Crónica de Alfonso XI, in *BAE* 66. 1875. Reprint, 1953.

Crónica latina de los reyes de Castilla, ed. Luis Charlo Brea. Cádiz, Spain: Universidad de Cádiz, 1984.

Craddock, Jerry R. "Dynasty in Dispute: Alfonso X el Sabio and the Succession to the Throne of Castile and León in History and Legend." *Medieval and Renaissance Studies* 17 (1986): 197–219.

Dyer, Nancy Joe. "Alfonsine Historiography: The Literary Narrative." *Emperor of Culture: Alfonso X the Learned of Castile and His Thirteenth-Century Renaissance.* Robert I. Burns, ed. Philadelphia: Univ. of Pennsylvania Press, 1990, 141–58

———. "Gender and Manuscript Culture in Alfonsine Historiography." *La Corónica* 26, no. 2 (1998): 161–71

Eisenberg, Daniel. "Alfonsine Prose: Ten Years of Research." *La Corónica* 11 (1983), 220–30.

Estudios Alfonsinos y Otros Escritos: En Homenaje a John Esten Keller y a Aníbal A. Biglieri. New York: National Endowment for the Humanities, 1991.

Fernández-Ordóñez, Inés. *Las Estorias de Alfonso el Sabio.* Madrid: Istmo, 1992.

Fita, Fidel. "Biografías de San Fernando y de Alfonso el Sabio por Gil de Zamora." *Boletín de la Real Academia de la Historia* 5 (1885): 308–28.

Fraker, Charles F. "Alfonso X, the Empire and the *Primera crónica.*" *Bulletin of Hispanic Studies* 55 (1978): 95–102.

———. *The Scope of History: Studies in the Historiography of Alfonso el Sabio.* Ann Arbor: Univ. of Michigan, 1996.

General Estoria. Primera Parte, ed. Antonio G. Solalinde. Madrid: Molina, 1930; *General Estoria. Segunda Parte.* 2 vols., ed. Lloyd Kasten and Victor Oelschlager. Madrid: Consejo Superior de Investigaciones Científicas, 1957–1961.

Gingras, Gerald L. "Sánchez's *Tres Crónicas:* An Alfonsine Legacy?" *Romance Quarterly* 33 (1986): 289–94.

———. "The Medieval Castilian Historiographical Tradition: From Alfonso X to López de Ayala." *Romance Languages Annual* 2 (1990): 419–25.

González, Cristina. "Alfonso X el Sabio y *La Gran Conquista de Ultramar.*" *Hispanic Review* 54 (1986): 67–82.

———. *La tercera crónica de Alfonso X, La Gran Conquista de Ultramar.* London: Tamesis Books, 1992.

González Crespo, Esther. *Colección documental de Alfonso XI: Diplomas reales conservados en el Archivo Histórico Nacional, Sección de Clero. Pergaminos.* Madrid: Universidad Complutense, 1985.

González Jiménez, Manuel. *Alfonso X, 1252–1284.* Palencia, Spain: Diputación Provincial de Palencia, 1993.

———. *Diplomatario Andaluz de Alfonso X.* Seville: El Monte. Caja de Huelva y Sevilla, 1991.

González, Julio. *Reinado y Diplomas de Fernando III.* 3 vols. Córdoba, Spain: Monte de Piedad y Caja de Ahorros de Córdoba, 1980–1986, 1:278–394.

———. *Repartimiento de Sevilla.* 2 vols. Madrid: Consejo Superior de Investigaciones Científicas, 1951.

Gran Crónica de Alfonso XI, 2 vols. Madrid: Editorial Gredos, 1977, 1:15.

Herrera, Miguel de. *Chronica del muy esclarecido principe y rey don Alfonso: el qual fue par de Emperador e hizo el libro delas siete partidas y ansimismo al fin deste libro va encorporada la Chronica del rey Don Sancho el Brauo, hijo de este rey don Alfonso el Sabio.* Valladolid, Spain: Sebastián Martínez, 1554.

Jiménez de Rada, Rodrigo. *De rebus Hispaniae,* in *Opera,* ed. Francisco de Lorenzana. Madrid, 1793. Reprint, Valencia: Anubar, 1968.

Kagay, Donald and Joseph Snow. *Medieval Iberia: Essays on the History and Literature of Medieval Spain.* New York: Peter Lang, 1997.

Kasten, Lloyd. "Alfonso el Sabio and Thirteenth-Century Spanish." *Thought* 60 (1985): 407–16.

Katz, Israel J., and John E. Keller. *Studies on the* Cantigas de Santa María*: Art, Music, and Poetry. Proceedings of the International Symposium of the* Cantigas de Santa María *of Alfonso X el Sabio (1221–1284) in Commemoration of Its 700th Anniversary Year—1981.* Madison, Wis.: Hispanic Seminary of Medieval Studies, 1987.

Keller, John E. *Alfonso X, el Sabio.* New York: Twayne, 1967.

———. "The Art of Illumination in the Books of Alfonso X (Primarily in the *Canticles of Holy Mary*)." *Thought* 60 (1985): 388–406.

——— and Annette Cash. *Daily Life Depicted in the* Cantigas de Santa María. Studies in Romance Languages 44. Lexington: Univ. Press of Kentucky, 1998.

——— and Richard P. Kinkade. *Iconography in Medieval Spanish Literature.* Lexington: Univ. Press of Kentucky, 1984.

Kinkade, Richard P. "Alfonso X, Cantiga 235, and the Events of 1269–1278." *Speculum* 67 (1992): 284–323.

———. *Ordenamientos Dados a la Villa de Peñafiel, 10 de Abril de 1345. Reconstruction of the Manuscript Text with an Introduction and Annotated English Translation.* Madison: Hispanic Seminary of Medieval Studies, Ltd. Spanish series no. 112.

Linehan, Peter. "From Chronicle to History: Concerning the *Estoria de España* and its Principal Sources." In Alan Deyermond, *Historical Literature in Medieval Iberia.* London: Queen Mary and Westfield College, Department of Hispanic Studies, 1996.

———. *History and the Historians of Medieval Spain.* Oxford: Clarendon, 1993.

———. "The Politics of Piety: Aspects of the Castilian Monarchy from Alfonso X to Alfonso XI." *Revista Canadiense de Estudios Hispánicos* 9, no. 3 (spring 1985): 385–404.

Lomax, Derek W. "The Authorship of the *Chronique latine des rois de Castille.*" *Bulletin of Hispanic Studies* 40 (1963): 205–11.

Márquez Villanueva, Francisco. *El Concepto cultural alfonsí.* Madrid: Mapfre, 1995.

Mas Latrie, Louis. *Traités de paix et de commerce et documents divers concernant les relations des chrétiens avec les arabes de l'Afrique septentrionale au moyen âge*, 2 vols. Paris, 1866. Reprint, Philadelphia: Burt Franklin, 1963.

Montoya Martínez, Jesús. "La 'gran vingança' de Dios y de Alfonso X." *Bulletin of the Cantigueiros de Santa María* 3 (1990): 53–59.

———. *O Cancioneiro Marial de Afonso X, o Sabio.* Santiago de Compostela, Spain: Universidad de Santiago de Compostela, 1991.

Moxó, Salvador de. "El patrimonio dominical de un consejero de Alfonso XI: Los señoríos de Fernán Sánchez de Valladolid." *Revista de la Universidad Complutense de Madrid* 22 (1973): 123–62.

———. "La promoción política y social de los 'letrados' en la corte de Alfonso XI." *Hispania* 35 (1975): 13–18.

O'Callaghan, Joseph F. *A History of Medieval Spain.* Ithaca: Cornell Univ. Press, 1975.

———. *Alfonso X and the* Cantigas de Santa María*: A Poetic Biography.* Leiden, The Netherlands: E.J. Brill, 1998.

———. "Alfonso X and the Castilian Church." *Thought* 60 (1985): 417–29.

———*Alfonso X, the Cortes, and Government in Medieval Spain.* Aldershot, Great Britain: Ashgate, 1998.

———. "The Ideology of Government in the Reign of Alfonso X of Castile." *Exemplaria Hispánica* 1 (1991–1992): 1–17.

———. *The Learned King: The Reign of Alfonso X of Castile.* Philadelphia: Univ. of Pennsylvania Press, 1993.

Ordenamiento de la Banda, El Escorial, Y.II.13, fols. 11–12.

Paredes, Núñez, Juan. *La Guerra de Granada en las* Cantigas de Alfonso X, el Sabio. Granada, Spain: Universidad de Granada, 1991.

Primera Crónica General, ed. Ramón Menéndez Pidal, 2 vols. Madrid: Gredos, 1955.

Procter, Evelyn. *Alfonso X of Castile, Patron of Literature and Learning.* Oxford: Clarendon, 1951.

———. *Curia and Cortes in León and Castile, 1072–1295.* Cambridge: Cambridge Univ. Press, 1980.

———. "Materials for the Reign of Alfonso X of Castile, 1252–1284." *Transactions of the Royal Historical Society, 4th Series,* 14 (1931): 52.

———. "The Castilian Chancery During the Reign of Alfonso X, 1252–1284." *Oxford Essays in Medieval History presented to Herbert E. Salter.* Oxford: Clarendon, 1934.

Puyol, Julio. "El presunto cronista Fernán Sánchez de Valladolid." *Boletín de la Real Academia de la Historia* 77 (1920): 507–33.

Reilly, Bernard F. *The Medieval Spains.* Cambridge: Cambridge Univ. Press, 1993.

Rico, Francisco. *Alfonso el Sabio y la* General Estoria. Madrid: Ariel, 1984.

Rodgers, Paula K. "Alfonso X Writes to His Son: Reflections on the *Crónica de Alfonso X.*" *Exemplaria Hispánica* 1 (1991–1992): 58–79.

————. *Prolegomena to a Critical Edition of the Crónica de Alfonso X.* 2 vols. Ph.D. dissertation, Davis: Univ. of California, 1983.

Rodríguez-Puertolas, Julio. "A Comprehensive View of Medieval Spain." *Americo Castro and the Meaning of Spanish Civilization.* Berkeley: Univ. of California Press, 1976

Rosell, Cayetano. *Crónicas de los Reyes de Castilla desde don Alfonso el Sabio hasta los Católicos Don Fernando y Doña Isabel.* 3 vols. In *Biblioteca de Autores Españoles* (abbr. *BAE*), vol. 66 (Madrid, 1875. Reprint, Madrid: Real Academia Española, 1953).

Roth, Norman. "Two Jewish Courtiers of Alfonso X Called Zag (Isaac)." *Sefarad: Revista de Estudios Hebraicos, Sefardíes y de Oriente Próximo* 43, no. 1 (1983): 75–85.

Rymer, Thomas. *Foedera, conventiones, litterae et cuiuscunque acta publica inter reges Angliae et alios quovis imperatores, reges, pontifices, principes,* 3rd ed. 10 vols. The Hague: Joannes Neaulme, 1739–1745.

Scarborough, Connie. *Women in Thirteenth-Century Spain as Portrayed in Alfonso X's* Cantigas de Santa María. Lewiston, N.Y.: Edward Mellen Press, 1993.

Sánchez Alonso, Benito. *Historia de la historiografía española.* Madrid: Consejo Superior de Investigaciones Científicas, 1947.

Scott, Samuel Parsons. *Las Siete Partidas.* New York: 1931.

Siete Partidas del Rey Don Alfonso el Sabio, Las. Real Academia de la Historia, 1807. 3 vols.

Tuy, Lucas of. *Chronicon Mundi,* ed. Andreas Schott, *Hispania Illustrata.* 4 vols. Frankfort: Claudius Marnius et Heredes Joannis Aubrii, 1603–1608.

Zurita, Gerónimo. *Anales de la Corona de Aragón.* 9 vols. Ed. Ángel Canellas López. Zaragoza, Spain: Consejo Superior de Investigaciones Científicas, 1970–1985.

Index

www.ingramcontent.com/pod-product-compliance
Lightning Source LLC
Chambersburg PA
CBHW020403100426
42812CB00001B/181